INFINITE
WELL-BEING

INFINITE WELL-BEING

By
Barbara B. Brown, Ph.D.

NEW HORIZON PRESS   IRVINGTON PUBLISHERS, INC.
NEW JERSEY   NEW YORK

7-86

Library of Congress Cataloging in Publication Data

Brown, Barbara B.
  Infinite well-being.

  Bibliography: p.
  1. Biofeedback training.   I. Title.
RC489.B53B76   1985   615.8'51   84-28846
ISBN 0-88282-006-0 (New Horizon)
ISBN 0-8290-1158-7

Typography by Dimensional Graphics, Roselle, New Jersey

Printed in the United States of America

Table of Contents

Introduction

PART I
Biofeedback—Birth, History, and Visions   1

Section 1—Concepts, Techniques, and Mechanisms   3

On the Nature of Biofeedback: Exercises in Concept Generation ... 3/ All About Biofeedback ... Briefly ... 17/ The Basics of Biofeedback ... 31/ Perspectives on Biofeedback ... 43/ Relaxation and Dealing with Stress ... 55

Section 2—Brain Wave Biofeedback   69

EEG Biofeedback: Techniques and Applications ... 69/ Recognition of Aspects of Consciousness through Association with EEG Alpha Activity Represented by a Light Signal ... 93/ Identifying One's Own Brain Waves: A Trial Run to the Subconscious ... 107/ Exploration of EEG Alpha Biofeedback As a Technique to Enhance Rapport ... 125/ Learned Control of EEG Theta Activity ... 131

PART II

Mind and Dis-ease. The Origins
of Stress Ills   139

A Conceptual Analysis of "The Stress of Life"
Phenomenon... 141/ Understanding Stress: Mus-
cle Tension. The Habits of Stress... 167/ Muscle
Tension and Relaxation... 177/ The Second Ill-
ness... 205/ The Dis-ease Immune System, A
Creation of the Psyche... 211

PART III

The Hidden Intellect and Beyond   217

Section 1—Evidence for a Powerful Intellect
Within

Biofeedback and the Deeper Levels of the
Mind... 219/ Biofeedback: Implications for Concepts of Mind and Consciousness... 239/
Biological Awareness as a State of Consciousness... 259

Section 2—Toward Knowing the Infinite Mind

Quintessential Consciousness... 279/ On the Nature of the Human Mind... 295/ The Group Mind:
Consensual Consciousness and the Group Subconscious... 307

Permissions

Introduction

From the time my experiments revealed the extraordinary phenomenon of biofeedback,* I have argued that biofeedback represents an entirely different kind of learning mechanism from any ever previously described. Briefly, I have presented, in many papers, the concept that biofeedback learning is implemented by an innate, biological information processing mechanism possessing an extraordinary "intellect," (see *Biological awareness as a state of consciousness*). The bottom line of this concept is that neural tissue possesses the ability to detect how sequences of certain biological activities *will* occur.** I have called this ability the "sense of order," the innate biological ability to anticipate orderly sequences of events.

The evidence to support my notions about biofeedback is readily developed from an analytic procedure long proved to produce remarkably accurate conclusions: reasoning syllogistically from universally accepted observations. The technique is widely ap-

*Few are aware that I conceptualized the biofeedback phenomenon a full year before the phenomenon became recognized (at the first meeting of the biofeedback society (later the American . . .) when I named the phenomenon "biofeedback." I had delayed announcing my data because, as I said then, repeatedly, "My God, I'm sitting on an atom bomb."

**This is *not* a supraphysical ability. It is more reasonable to assume first that there exists a parallel (and faster) neural system that modulates ("corrects") primary biological responses much like certain circuits of the reticular system relay impulses to the cortex to modulate incoming and slower impulses of the primary sensory pathways, such that *interpretation* is modulated by higher level influences.

plied in research but is applied almost exclusively within a narrow window that deals with a single aspect of a phenomenon. This is, of course, the familiar "hypothesis testing" technique in which we construct a syllogism such as the following example:

Premise 1: Virus 92xyz is a new and unique virus; premise 2: Virus 92xyz is found only in A.I.D.s patients and is found in 87 percent of all A.I.D.s patients; conclusion: Virus 92xyz causes A.I.D.s. Next step = test hypothesis (conclusion).

Despite the popularity of the hypothesis testing technique in scientific research, it is rarely used to develop *new* hypotheses about the essential nature of a phenomenon *as a whole*. The reasons for such lack of use are many, but lack of time for such a tedious mode of thought and its relative poverty of rewards are two principle reasons.

Although I have frequently used the syllogistic approach for concept generation, the introductory chapter of this book is the first time a full exposition of its application to the biofeedback phenomenon has been published. I have chosen to initiate this volume with several versions, using 4 different sets of circumstances, to illustrate the extraordinary power of the deductive process in the analysis and synthesis of concepts. I believe the technique not only provides an avenue to always startling new insights about human nature but also defines precisely both the mechanisms and valid applications of biofeedback.

I have been championing this concept generating technique for a dozen or more years as it has yielded more and more important, useful insights. Applications of it are found in my four books as well as in a number of scientific papers. The process consists of:

1. Assembling the most significant and universally accepted observations about a phenomenon yet to be satisfactorily explained and understood. I call these the consensual observations.

This step includes the sorting out, selection, and confirmation of observations with the principle criterion being the universality of the observations.

2. Conducting a logical analysis, using deductive reasoning (syllogistic argument), of the observations and drawing valid conclusions.

This step includes (logical) tests for continuity and congruity among the observations and for the universality of application of the resulting conclusions.

Since the observations are literally universal, conclusions reached from a logical analysis of related observations are likely to qualify as universal abstractions, i.e., as universal principles or laws.*

The procedure for analyzing conceptualized information rather than analyzing physical or numeric evidence is surprisingly unused these days in science. Yet, strangely, we use the technique daily (and couldn't survive without it) in such "intuitive" logic as: "I must have left my wallet in the car," or "His work is suffering because he's upset about the divorce." These kinds of conceptual analyses are, in fact, the way in which virtually all new discoveries are made. It is the idea first, then the supporting evidence.

Some short, abbreviated and very simplified examples:

1. *Observation:* A few decades ago long-time morphine addicts became ill only when their morphine supply was exhausted.

Logical conclusion: For such people, morphine probably substitutes for some natural brain neurohormone critical to feelings along the depression-euphoria axis (the despair-joy dimension).**

2. *Observation:* Racial characteristics appear to be maintained by selective, within-race breeding.

Conclusion: Mixed racial characteristics are caused by mixed breeding.

Law: Like genes produce like genes.

3. *Observation:* Death of a loved one causes deep grief.

Conclusions: Extreme grief is caused by a severe personal loss, especially of a loved one.

---

*Also as in proverbs, "A rolling stone gathers no moss," or allegories (the fox and the grapes). (For other illustration of the technique, see also my pieces: "On the Nature of Man," "Quintessential Consciousness," and "The Creation of Mind."

**It is only with the discovery of the endorphins (the "brain opiates," although I prefer "brain euphoriates") that it has become acceptable to consider such concepts as reasonable. Yet this idea was submitted nearly half a century ago.

This technique of analytic thought is most applicable when there is a need to understand the more fundamental and obscure characteristics of phenomena. Such circumstances, however, also require two other important elements; one, a broad spectrum of knowledge, and two, the time to speculate broadly, across the different fields of information. In the modern day of specialization, production urgency, and competition, few people have the luxury of intensely focused analytic thought. Sustained intellectual conceptualizing really requires minds that gravitate toward a "Renaissance Mode."

In my case, there was an unusual juxtaposition of events at the very time I stumbled across the biofeedback phenomenon. First, I found it while exploring neurophysiological correlates of natural behaviors and thus lacked (or avoided) the bias of experimental psychology explanations; second, I had accumulated intimate knowledge of nearly every branch of study and research that could relate to the phenomenon, including biochemistry, cellular neurophysiology, etc.; third, I have a powerful drive to solve challenging, unanswered problems; and fourth, I felt that I had spent a lifetime in all varieties of medical research and it was time to work on the problem of integrating the vast stores of information about the real nature of man.

Barbara B. Brown
Rancho Santa Fe, California

Part I
Biofeedback—Birth, History, and Visions

On the Nature of Biofeedback: Exercises in Concept Generation

It was Selye's "childish" observation that people who are sick, regardless of cause, all show the same look of sickness he called "just being sick" that led him to his remarkable biochemical and neurohormonal research on physical stress. I hope this essay further illustrates the way major insights about the nature of man can chain and crescendo toward a climax of knowing.

And, although I have conceptualized and written bits and pieces of a conceptual analysis of biofeedback, I had never been able to reduce its complexity to a mentally digestible set of statements. With the advent of this volume, I decided it was time to get my complete concept of biofeedback into print. After all, I *was* one of the discoverers, and the first to offer a theory about its mechanism (the only non-Skinnerian concept) and I *did* name the phenomenon biofeedback.

So, the following is my penultimate word on biofeedback.

Because the syllogistic analytic technique is used so infrequently for developing new formulations about and concepts of natural phenomena, and because the experimental and clinical methods and analyses of biofeedback are so diverse, I am providing 4 very different examples to illustrate how such conceptual analytic techniques of very different sets of observations can show remarkable coherence and congruity and develop identical conclusions.

Analysis of the biofeedback phenomenon using 4 different sets of circumstances

A. and B. *Two applications of conceptual analysis to the biofeed-back phenomenon*

> One, based on observations using a popular clinical procedure (biofeedback learning to control vascular activity in Raynaud's syndrome)

> Two, based on observations using a sophisticated neurophysiological technique (biofeedback learning to control a single motoneurone in the spinal cord)

Objective: To deduce the nature of the biofeedback learning phenomenon.

Learning, as a concept, is poorly defined. Strictly speaking, learning is simply the acquisition of information, with the implication that somehow the information is used for some purpose and thus alters the way the individual responds to change.

Experimental psychology typically measures the amount of learning in terms of amount or quantity of input information. There is virtually no information available about (a) the *efficiency* of learning or (b) the use of already acquired information to generate new kinds of information.

What I have done in the following two specific example analyses, a general analysis and the summary analysis, is to qualify (define) as precisely as possible the factors involved in biofeedback learning and deduce from these the essential nature of the biofeedback phenomenon.

Since the internal information processing cannot be measured, there are only two components of the biofeedback learning process that can be characterized and evaluated:

1. the information. In the case of most biofeedback procedures this is of 2 kinds:
   a) biological (the signal containing the biological information)

b) conceptual (reinforcements, verbal support, etc.)
2. the learned performance

We are thus limited to defining and measuring these two elements.

Example one. A conceptual analysis of biofeedback based on use of the biofeedback technique to develop control over peripheral (hand) vascular activity in Raynaud's syndrome.

(For a brief description of the technique, see *Biofeedback and the deeper levels of the mind.*

Characteristics of the available information (Consensual observations)

1. the biological information can be characterized as:
abstract
symbolic
requires interpretation
represents events occuring in the time and space of the brain
is substitute information i.e., it is information that is
communicated via a different route than is used for
homeostatic regulation

2. the conceptual information can be characterized as:
a) explicit (optional)
instructions, explanations, suggestions and reinforcements, all of which require both intelligent interpretation and association with biological events
b) implicit
surrounding attitudes, set and setting, potential success or failure and implying temporal limits

Characteristics of the performance (Consensual observations)

1. Development of control over previously unsensed components of physiological activity
2. The learned control overrides both the spontaneous activity and innate homeostatic regulatory activity

3. The control is exerted selectively
4. Control is compatible with intention
5. Learning is rapid
6. The mode of control is unknown to conscious awareness
7. The control over biological functions is accompanied by mental fatigue

Deductions

Biofeedback learning:

1. involves interpreting both abstract biological and conceptual information in terms of selected, directed physiological activity
2. involves an *ordered* alteration of biological activities
3. involves establishing a predetermined goal, unrecognized until accomplished
4. involves anticipating orderly sequences of integrated mind-body activities
5. generates internally identifiable internal states

Example two. A conceptual analysis of the phenomenon of learned voluntary control of motor units.

A description of Dr. Basmajian's many experiments on motor unit biofeedback is given in detail in *New Mind, New Body.*

A. *Conditions of the learning situation*

1. Visual/auditory information about the activity of many individual motor units, each motor unit firing 3 to 300 muscle fibers and originating from a single motoneurone in the spinal cord.
2. Conceptual information
   a) explicit information (optional) of instructions or command to perform
   b) implicit information
      1. Task is possible
      2. Person is capable of performing the task

3. Person can learn the task in a reasonable time

B. *Observations of the learned performance*

1. Rapid learning (2 to 5 minutes)
2. Complex manipulations of motor unit activity can be learned
3. Intense mental fatigue occurs as performance is sustained
4. Subjective reports indicate no conscious awareness of how performance is achieved
5. The learned performance is compatible with both the instructions and with the maximal capabilities of the biological systems involved

Characteristics of the information used in the learning process

1. Abstract, representational
2. Substitutes for internally derived, proprioceptive information
3. Requires complex processing
4. Is remote from experience

Inferences

1. Human beings possess a capability to use representational, substitute information very precisely toward achieving a specific, functional biological objective.
2. Human beings possess a biological awareness of physiological activities inaccessible to conscious awareness.
3. Human beings possess a sense of order, a function that anticipates and effects the ordering of physiological processes to meet intended actions.
4. Intention is an independent function that makes decisions to perform based on evaluations of goals and projected consequences.
5. Acts of intent require still an additional mechanism to execute them: a directing mechanism that selects the correct channels of neural networks to effect an action.

A generic analysis of the biofeedback phenomenon
(using the syllogistic technique)

Consensual observations

1. When human beings are: (a) provided with signals containing information about the activity of physiological systems of which they have little or no prior conscious awareness, and are *also* (b) given other, temporally related signals designated as request to alter the selected physiological activity in a specific direction, they frequently respond with the changes requested by the signal.

   The modern, Skinnerian conditioning paradym (a response to a biofeedback signal is rewarded)

2. When human beings are provided with signals about a selected physiological activity of which they have little or no prior awareness or information, and are given *no* other related information, they either (a) respond appropriately to suggestions to change that activity or (b) initiate changes of the physiologic activity. In both cases, the changes produced can be sustained, repeated, or both.

   The bare-bones biofeedback paradym, i.e. biological information only is given

3. When human beings focus attention on either specific or general physiological functions, they develop an ability to affect the physiological functions selectively.

   By means of concentration, exercises, yoga postures, imagery, mental rehearsal, etc.

4. Repetition of any of the above situations usually results in learning to alter the selected physiological activity voluntarily and selectively.

   Biofeedback learning and self-regulation.

Conclusion

The term biofeedback has come to mean the learning situation in which biological information about a specific or general physiological function is sensed or detected by the generator of that information and used to alter the physiologic activity intentionally in a predetermined direction.

Supporting consensual clinical observations

1. When human beings practice any of the biofeedback conditions described in *Consensual Observations* 1, 2, or 3, the following additional consequences are observed:
   a) fewer subsequent disturbances of those physiological functions
   b) improved subjective and physical states
   c) altered awareness of the involved physiologic activity to levels lower than those usually perceived.
2. Varieties of biofeedback procedures result in reduction of the two principle signs and symptoms of stress:
   a) relief of mental and emotional concern (subjective anxiety)
   b) physical tensions and homeostatic imbalances
3. Varieties of biofeedback neuromuscular techniques assist the repair of disturbed neuromuscular systems.
4. Varieties of biofeedback techniques can foster general states of well-being, contribute to increased self-awareness, and benefit an individual's social behavior.

Observations on the nature of the biofeedback therapeutic process

1. Reliable information about a selected physiological activity is provided dynamically to the individual generating that activity.
2. The physiologic information is provided in the form of signals that are easily perceived and interpreted.
3. The physiological information is continuous or almost continuously available.
4. Conceptual information useful to the learning process is also available and facilitates learning.
5. These factors allow the individual to interact with and experience internal states.

6. Complex mental events are evoked that influence the physiological activities.
7. The individual learns voluntary control over a physiological activity.
8. Once learned, the identity and control of the self is shifted from external to internal dependance.
9. Performing control over a physiological function communicates information about internal states and internal events that are otherwise inexpressible.

Identification of all common characteristics of the observations

Factors common to all of the above situations are:

1. the availability of specific information about a selected physiological activity
   (e.g., re pulse feedback, the information inherently contains information about rate, regularity, cyclic and rhythmic activity, variability, and strength of signal)
2. the detection and appreciation (perception) of biological information by the generator of that information
   (Mainly nonverbally understood and expressed, i.e., expressed by performance)
3. the acquisition of a selected or general skill affecting that physiological function specifically
   (psychobiological self-regulation, as in controlling sweaty palms, muscle tensions, etc.)
4. the selective and intentional application of the acquired skill in a predetermined direction
   (e.g., all athletic performances operate via learning biofeedback; control of tension headaches)

Deductions

These observations identify a phenomenon with 3 distinctive characteristics:

1. Learning. i.e., the acquisition of a skill
2. Intention. i.e., intentional alteration of a physiological function

3. Regulatory control over physiological activities

Conclusions

Based on these observations, biofeedback can be defined as: the phenomenon of learning to exert voluntary control over selected physiologic activities by using information about those activities.

Summary

Summary of a descriptive analysis of the essential features of the biofeedback phenomenon (where phenomenon = an observable event)

Definition

The biofeedback phenomenon is the learning to exert voluntary control over selected physiological activities using information about those activities.

Qualifiers of the biofeedback phenomenon set

1. Learning
2. Regulatory control of physiological activities
3. Uses information about the physiological activities involved
4. The exerting of voluntary control

Definitions of the qualifiers

1. Learning in biofeedback is the change from little or no influence to a quantifiable influence over a selected physiological activity.
2. Physiologic activities are the biological activities of the organism.
3. Biofeedback information is any information about the physiologic activity involved available to the organism that is relevant to the learning process.
4. Voluntary control is the application of biofeedback learning at the intention of the organism.

Set designation of the biofeedback process

The biofeedback process consists of the use of information about the selected physiologic activities available for communication to the generator of the physiologic activities.

Subsets of the biofeedback process qualified as to the information involved

1. Information about the physiologic activities
   a) biological (biofeedback) information
   b) cognizable, nonbiological information
2. Information about the learning process
   a) strategy information
   b) Information having conceptually reinforcing value
   c) Implicit psychologically supporting and consolidating information

Subsets qualified as to procedures:

1. Instrumental—the use of devices
2. Noninstrumental—external devices not used

Inferences from set designations

1. Process techniques
   Noninstrumental techniques qualify as biofeedback process facilitators when they meet the conditions of the definition (e.g., yoga, progressive relaxation, autogenic training, structural integration, etc.) but not when they neither provide information about the physiologic activities involved in the learning or when they are not used to learn voluntary control over physiologic activities (e.g., hypnosis, self-suggestion, imagery, etc.)
2. Process operations
   a) Cognizable nonbiological information is that information that provides organizing information about the physiologic dynamics involved in the process (e.g., explanations, instructions).

b) Strategy information is information contributing to the learning process itself (e.g., relaxation exercises, mental discipline techniques, record keeping).

c) Reinforcing information consists of both the biological signal changing in the desired direction and all the explicit reinforcement signals.

d) Implicit psychologically supporting and consolidating information consists of all nonverbal liminal or subliminal influences (set and setting, attitudes).

Applications

Set designations for conditions amenable to biofeedback learning

1. *Stress problems:* all psychological or physiological problems that are:
    a) specifically incited or aggravated by psychosocial factors
    b) evidenced by subjective, muscular, or visceral tension

2. *Neuromuscular problems:* any neuromuscular problem caused by:
    a) increased neural activity
    b) decreased neural activity
    c) irregular neural activity

3. *Personal growth:* any human condition considered to be benefitted by:
    a) facilitating subjective or physiological recognition (awareness) of internal states, or,
    b) facilitating "mental discipline" related to either the psychological or physiological components of psychosocial behavior

Epilogue

As I moved more and more deeply into the intangible elements that appeared to underlie the biofeedback phenomenon, the questions increasingly became: is biofeedback a universal phenomenon i.e., is it integral to all activities of living things? And if it is, what is the universal function it serves?

Few, if any, of the life sciences recognize, let alone are concerned with, the absolutely vital role of the feedback phenomenon in every aspect of life. Once the phenomenon was exposed as an important (or THE) mechanism in the self-regulation of the body, expanding the principle to its fullest should have been a natural consequence. Instead, the phenomenon was/is exploited pragmatically. I seem to be the only theorist available who is interested in (or who could successfully buck the Skinnerian argument) pursuing the implications of biofeedback for its role in the more arcane chambers of the human mind and psyche. Fortunately these pursuits have been gratifyingly productive.

First, it became obvious that a highly sophisticated mechanism existed that could translate biofeedback signals which could not be processed as sensory signals (see "interpretations" under Raynaud's syndrome example above). Moreover, a similar, highly elegant mechanism is required for learning control of single motor units. Most convincingly also, studies demonstrate how the restraints of situations using the conditioning paradym actually inhibit the learning of self-regulation.

Such conclusions and inferences strongly suggest a complex data processing system characterized by (a) operating while wholly inaccessible to conscious awareness and (b) capable of anticipating action sequences to effect physiological activity intended by a conceptual formulation either consciously or unconsciously.

These conclusions raised the question: if living organisms possess such exquisite self-regulating capacities, why does the process of just living the ordinary life so often interfere with well-being and lead to ailments we say are caused by the stress of life? The conceptual analyses I used to answer this question are partly in this volume and in my book *Between Health and Illness*.

Although my conceptual analysis of the biofeedback and stress of life phenomena are self-contained, there are, however, still other and more complex and more arcane issues to be explored in the search to understand the nature of man. I have covered these briefly in other writings, but deal with these new challenges in a Trilogy (to be published in 1985-6). The 3 volumes are: *W-4, The Wonderfully Wise Wizard Within* (an account of the subliminal intellect), *Slipping into Another Consciousness* (an analysis of 15 states of nonpathological, nondrug, nonordinary ordinary states of consciousness), and *Searching for Psyche* (updating and greatly expanding the Jungian concept of the psyche). The major way stations along the ideational journey culminating in the Trilogy are contained in the present volume.

All About
Biofeedback ... Briefly

One of the most fascinating discoveries of the 20th century has been the discovery of the biofeedback phenomenon. Biofeedback simply means learning how to exert voluntary control over the body's internal, vital functions such as heart rate, blood pressure, skin temperature, muscle tension, or brain waves. Any body function that can be measured fairly precisely and fairly continuously can be trained to come under voluntary control. Biofeedback is a popular new technique for treating stress problems such as headache or insomnia, where learning how to control muscle tension causing the headache or insomnia can provide considerable if not complete relief. But biofeedback has many other uses, such as learning how to lower blood pressure in essential hypertension. I'll describe most of the uses a little later. In a way, biofeedback is similar to certain types of yoga, but biofeedback has the considerable advantage of using instruments to let the learner know his moment-to-moment progress in learning. In yoga there is no direct index of how well a person is learning how to control a body part or physiologic function, and because of this lack of important information, learning to control body functions with yoga, particularly internal functions, is much slower and not as exact. Thus, while yoga is a valuable health aid, biofeedback learning is more efficient, particularly in dealing with specific medical and psychologic disorders.

Biofeedback learning is not difficult, but it does require instruments that can detect and display information about the selected body activity so that the learner has a good indication of how the physiology he is trying to learn how to control is behaving. There are many different kinds of biofeedback, called modalities, that use different kinds of instruments to learn how to control different body functions. To learn to control certain brain waves, special instruments are used that have been designed to detect the desired, specific brain wave. Other instruments have been specially designed to detect and feedback information about heart rate, blood pressure, gastric acid, gastric motility, and nearly every body activity that is accessible for measurement.

Biofeedback has attracted so much attention from all kinds of people, such as professional therapists, biomedical engineers, psychology researchers, etc., that the word biofeedback has come to have many meanings. To many people it is simply a technique using an instrument that feeds back information about selected internal functions of the person hooked up to the machine. To other people biofeedback means a special kind of learning process, and to still other people it means an entirely new approach to the treatment of many different kinds of illnesses.

The Learning Process in Muscle Biofeedback

The most widely used kind of biofeedback is EMG or muscle biofeedback. Muscle biofeedback training is now widely used to relieve the effects of muscle tension that result from anxiety or tensions about daily social problems. The most common tension state is the tension headache. When a person receives biofeedback training for recurring tension headaches, a very interesting and pleasant treatment procedure is used.

The treatment consists of a number of training sessions, generally 7 to 10 for most problems, although more learning sessions may be needed for more serious disorders. Each training session is about 30 to 45 minutes in length. The instrument used is called an EMG biofeedback instrument from the word electromyograph, meaning a record of muscle electrical activity. To work with the instrument, it is attached to the patient by means of small metal sensors placed on the skin over the muscles causing the tension. The sensors detect the resting muscle activity, called muscle tension, and transmit information about the muscle tension to the biofeedback device, which amplifies the small muscle electrical currents, electronically processes the information, and then displays the muscle tension levels in forms that are easy to understand. Sometimes the information is displayed by a meter something like an old gasoline gauge with the needle reading high or low tension. Often tones are used which vary in pitch, with low muscle tension being signalled by low tones and higher tensions as higher pitched tones. Sometimes light signals are used, with changing intensity of the light indicating changes in muscle tension levels. Thus the patient can see or hear, or sometimes both see and hear, signals of exact muscle tension and hear or watch it change.

The objective of the training is, of course, to learn how to lower muscle tension since it is the excessive tension that is causing aches and pains in the muscles. In the case of tension headache, the sensors are usually placed over the small muscles above each eye in the forehead, known as the frontalis muscles.

This is the preparation part of the treatment. Now comes the learning process.

Learning how to control internal physiologic activities, even muscle tension, is quite a new experience for most people, and so they need all the learning aids they can get, learning aids that will help them to learn how to control the tensions as quickly and as efficiently as possible and so to relieve their symptoms.

One of the first things the patient has to understand is that vigorous effort actually can interfere with the learning. After all, effort means tension, and if you are trying to relieve muscle tension, you are trying to achieve relaxation. The problem here is, if you are trying to learn how to relax and reduce muscle tension, how do you do it without using some effort and conscious direction? The answer is that you have to allow the relaxation to happen, you have to forget trying to make an effort, and achieve a passive state so that the muscles can relax. A part of the learning process is also becoming aware of the sensation of relaxation. There are now many learning aids to help you do this. These aids are mainly either relaxation exercises or self-suggestion exercises, the use of imagery, or meditation exercises. All of these relaxation and awareness exercises are designed to focus awareness on internal states and learning how to appreciate internal events.

During the training sessions, the therapist or technician usually tells the patient that he can use some mental means to change the muscle tension. This is where the relaxation and awareness exercises come in.

In addition to the learning aids, learning how to control internal states can also be made more efficient by having the patient informed about what he is working with. This means that the patient can learn better if he is given some information about how the biofeedback instrument works, some information about the body's physiology for the particular body system the patient is working with, such as information about muscles, along with the information about how to learn, that is, the relaxation and awareness exercises. Once the patient knows the idea about how he and his muscle relate to the machine, something about what has caused his muscles to be tensed, he can practice the exercises more effectively.

To sum up, in order to learn well, the patient needs a variety of information about what he is to learn and how he can go about learning. He has the physiologic information provided by the biofeedback instrument, and this keeps him informed about his muscle tension level and whether he is being effective in reducing the tension. He has also been given some information and understands something about how muscles get their tensions, and how muscles operate during relaxation, and he has been told how the muscle tensions cause pain. On top of all of this new information, the patient is given all the learning aids, all the clues about how he can use his mind so that he can learn how to change muscle tension or any other body function.

This is still not quite the end of the learning process. Like all learning, biofeedback learning needs psychological support. That is, all of us need to know that what we think we are doing right really is right. This is the function of the therapist, to encourage the patient in his learning efforts, and to reinforce his efforts that are successful. It is this encouragement and reinforcement that consolidates the learning.

The Importance of Auxiliary Learning Aids

There are some other interesting learning aids for relieving tensions and learning relaxation that the patient can use that also help the biofeedback learning. These are mainly common sense techniques, but they had not been used much in medicine until the biofeedback discovery. The first is record keeping. If, for example, you are doing biofeedback training to relieve tension headache, it is helpful to keep a record for some time before beginning training, a record about the severity and frequency of occurrence of the headaches. This is useful for two reasons. First of all, it is important to know whether the way you are learning is producing a good result, and if so, just how good the result is. You can know this only if you know exactly how many headaches you had before training and in general how bad they were, how long they lasted, etc.

The second reason for keeping records is a very interesting effect of the record keeping itself. If you keep records faithfully, say records for every hour or every few hours of the day, what happens is that the subconscious mind begins to develop an awareness of situations that cause the tensions, and the subconscious mind influences consciousness to begin to avoid such situations. For example, unexpected visits by your mother-in-law may irritate you and make you tense. After some record keeping about your tensions and headaches, along with some awareness and biofeedback relaxation training, you may find that you have discussed the situation with your spouse and have made arrangements for visits at fixed times, but exactly why you began to assert yourself this way may still escape recognition by your conscious mind. But the effect is that the occasions for tensions have been reduced, and so are the headaches. In other words, the record keeping makes part of your mind attend to situations involved in your tensions, and you almost automatically begin to avoid these, or, if and when they do eventually come to consciousness, you recognize the problem and deal with it.

Another important part of biofeedback learning is how to use the effects learned with the instrument at times when you develop tensions but don't have the instrument handy. This is the process of transferring the learning from the biofeedback training sessions into daily life. The first part of this transfer process is consistent practice away from the instrument. One can practice by using the prescribed relaxation exercises, or by using cassette tapes of relaxation or imagery or meditation exercises. The more home practice, the stronger the learned control ability becomes. The second very important part of the transfer process is practicing to become aware of developing tensions during various social activities. The biofeedback training has given you an increased awareness of both tension and relaxation feelings, and during social activities all that is necessary is to remember to direct the attention to the state of the muscles. It is not too difficult to remember to relax because the biofeedback training has become part of everyday life and comes to mind easily. So when you begin to feel yourself developing tension during social activities, you remember the relaxation, take a little time to relax, and this prevents the tension build-up.

The Muscle Tensions of Worry

Most of what we have been discussing has been about muscle tensions and tension headache, but the general principles apply to all kinds of biofeedback learning, that is, learning how to control any physiologic function of the body. Before we discuss other types of biofeedback, I want to point out the extreme importance of tension in all kinds of physical and emotional disorders. Most people know by now that just the stress of modern living is responsible for an enormous number of human illnesses and problems. These are now being called stress-related disorders because they all have in common the way in which the body reacts to psychological stress. A wide variety of illnesses result from what I call the "worry syndrome." That is, when we are worried, either consciously or subconsciously, we are worried about our social and financial security, about social relationships, or worried about our ability to perform at work, at school or at home, or worried about sex, or any disturbance in our social lives. And with the worry we become anxious and insecure.

The kinds of emotional and physical disorders that can result from the worry syndrome are much more numerous and of many more different types than most people realize. There are at least 4 major categories of stress problems; emotional problems, psychosomatic illnesses, physical disorders that are activated by stress, and general problems in social achieving. The worry syndrome also aggravates all illnesses regardless of origin, illnesses such as severe infections or injuries or after surgery, and stress and worry also slow the recovery from any kind of illness.

The emotional problems that can result from excessive worry are anything from tension headache and insomnia to sexual dysfunction, from learning problems in children to anxiety, neuroses, phobias, and even anginal pain.

The psychosomatic disorders are such things as asthma, ulcers, colitis, certain cardiac arrhythmias, peripheral vascular problems, certain types of rheumatoid arthritis, and the very harmful essential hypertension.

Epilepsy and migraine headache are organic disorders that are often triggered by stressful occasions.

There are many other ailments that stem from worry and anxiety, and all of those ailments have one thing in common. That is, there is increased tension in the body. The muscles can be tense or the viscera, that is, the internal organs of the cardiovascular, pulmonary and the other vital systems, can be tense. Even the activity of the brain can develop what is called subjective tension, that is, the real sensation of tension in the mind.

Because muscle tension occurs most frequently in all of these tension states, EMG, or muscle biofeedback is the most useful biofeedback modality. Learning how to reduce muscle tension in the body goes a long way in relieving many of the illnesses I have just listed.

Vascular Tensions

Sometimes, however, tensions can be mainly visceral, and in these cases it can be appropriate to work with biofeedback instruments designed to detect the activity of the visceral organs or systems more specifically. For example, a heart rate biofeedback device can be used to learn how to control certain kinds of cardiac irregularities, or a blood pressure device to learn how to lower blood pressure. One common device is the temperature biofeedback instrument with which the patient learns how to regulate the temperature of a certain body part. The importance of this is because skin and body temperature is related to blood flow, and for disturbances such as general body tension or increased blood pressure or for peripheral vascular problems, learning how to control skin temperature really changes blood flow, and relieves the vascular tensions.

Let's take the example of peripheral vascular disease and show how it can be treated by biofeedback. The most common disorder of the peripheral vascular system is called Raynaud's syndrome. The symptoms are very cold hands, and sometimes feet, because the blood vessels of the hands, or feet, become intensely constricted from time to time, and the hands not only become cold, but blue and quite painful. The reason the blood supply becomes constricted and the blood flow impaired apparently is because of some peculiar and very local reaction to stress, that is, local in the sense that the dysfunction is confined to the hands or to the hands and feet. For a long time this ailment was confused with what is now being called Raynaud's disease to distinguish it from Raynaud's syndrome. Both have identical signs and symptoms, the cold, blue, painful hands, but Raynaud's syndrome is apparently due to psychological stress while Raynaud's disease is of some as yet unknown organic cause.

Basically, in Raynaud's syndrome, the person's tensions are manifest as localized tension in the blood supply to the hands, and the blood vessels constrict. In a way this reaction to tension is similar to the tension headache, but in Raynaud's syndrome the tension is in the blood vessels of the hand.

The treatment principle is essentially the same as that for tension headache I described earlier. That is, the idea is to learn how to reduce the blood vessel tension. And as in the case of tension headache, since the cause of the tension is a reaction to stress and not an organic cause, it is possible for patients to learn how to prevent the blood vessels from constricting and causing pain.

The biofeedback treatment procedure is also very similar to that for tension headache except that in the case of Raynaud's syndrome the biofeedback instrument is one that can detect changes in the blood flow of the hands. The most frequently used instrument for this is the temperature biofeedback instrument, because the hand temperature reflects the amount of blood flowing through the hand, and the amount of blood flowing through the hand depends upon how constricted or dilated the blood vessels are. There are more complicated instruments that measure actual blood flow, but they are not generally available at this time, and the temperature device has been quite successful.

It is, moreover, relatively easy to learn how to control the temperature of the hand, and there are many kinds of temperature biofeedback instruments now available, ranging from inexpensive ones to expensive electronic thermometers. The devices use thermal sensors pasted on the hands or fingers, and the temperature can be read from a display like an ordinary thermometer or a meter.

The learning process during the training is then just like that I've outlined for learning to control muscle tension. That is, the patient is given information about the instrument, about how his condition happened, and the various learning aids and mental exercises.

Brain Wave Biofeedback

Brain wave biofeedback is also becoming an important aid in the treatment of anxiety as well as in the treatment of quite different kinds of illnesses such as epilepsy. Different brain waves are usually used for each different condition treated, although alpha biofeedback is the most popular and generally most useful form of brain wave biofeedback.

What we call brain waves are really only an approximation of the electrical activity of the brain. Since the brain is encased in the skull, and the brain's electrical signals are extremely small, it is quite difficult to detect the brain's electrical activity. This causes considerable difficulty in detecting and recording brain waves very faithfully, and it requires considerable electronic sophistication to record brain waves properly. What can be recorded from sensors placed on the scalp are very small electrical potentials of very mixed frequencies. Like household electrical current that is 60 cycle alternating current, many brain waves also occur rhythmically but are of slower frequencies. Alpha brain waves tend to be the most dominant brain waves under relaxed conditions, and, in fact, are said to be associated with feelings of tranquillity and an aware kind of relaxed state. Alpha waves vary in frequency between 9 and 12 cycles per second. A second rhythmic wave is called the theta wave or theta activity, and this is usually about 4 to 7 cycles per second in frequency. Theta waves are associated with a variety of behaviors, such as kinds of alert behavior, in dreams, but also are found in drowsy states just before the onset of sleep.

Obviously, since alpha and theta brain waves are associated with behavioral states that are desirable, especially to relieve tension states, alpha and theta biofeedback can have important clinical uses. Generally speaking, people who are anxious and apprehensive tend to have very few alpha waves, thus learning how to produce more alpha activity often leads to a reduction of their anxiety feelings. Similarly, some kinds of insomnia can be treated by training people to produce theta wave activity and then intentionally practicing this learning at times when they want to sleep.

The potential of brain wave biofeedback for the treatment of epilepsy has been a remarkable advance in medicine. Epilepsy has always been difficult to treat, and most epileptics must depend upon drugs for their entire lifetimes. It has long been known that epilepsy originates from certain excitable brain structures, and it is now known that epileptics can learn how to control brain states in several ways to reduce the excitable nature of the brain tissue, and this results in preventing epileptic seizures. One of the brain waves used in the biofeedback treatment of epilepsy is a special wave that has a frequency of 12 to 16 cycles per second, and when epileptics learn how to increase the production of this particular wave, their seizure activity decreases remarkably. Some researchers claim that learning how to control alpha activity is also successful in treating epilepsy.

There are many special applications of the biofeedback learning principle that cannot be described in this brief discussion, and I refer you to the several books written about biofeedback for further detail and information.

Biofeedback and Muscle Rehabilitation

One special application, however, that deserves discussion here is the use of a special kind of biofeedback in the area called muscle rehabilitation. This is a field that treats those kinds of problems in the brain and nerves that cause problems in muscle activity. There are two main kinds of muscle problems in addition to the muscle tension of anxiety. First is paralysis such as that following cerebral stroke, and second is overactivity, such as uncoordinated or inappropriate or erratic muscle activity, as in muscle tics or spastic conditions. In the latter cases EMG biofeedback is used to achieve relaxation much as in tension headache.

The use of biofeedback in the treatment of the paralysis of stroke, however, is a quite different use of biofeedback. This condition demands that muscle activity be activated and restored, not reduced. The treatment is difficult because often the paralysis is so extensive that a particular muscle has no obvious activity left. It is here that simple electronics takes advantage of the peculiar nature of muscle tissue.

Muscles are made up of families of muscle fibers that are related as families because they all receive their nerve impulses from the same last nerve fibril dividing off from the main motor nerves. Without nerve impulses, muscles have no activity at all. The families of muscle fibers are called motor units, motor simply meaning muscle in medical lingo. When the motor unit receives an impulse from its nerve, all the related muscle fibers of the family become active together, and when they are activated, they release an electrical potential. Some motor units have as few as 3 muscle fibers while others may have as many as 300, and so when different motor units become active, they each give off a different amount of voltage and for different times, so that each motor unit gives off a distinctively different electrical potential. Rather simple devices can sense the activity of these motor units, and when amplified, the electrical activity can be displayed on a simple oscilloscope. This means that patients can see the activity of muscle fibers that don't produce any muscle movement because not enough motor units are working together to produce movement.

In the stroke patient, some motor unit activity can usually be found by these sensitive techniques, and although the patient has no muscle sensation at all, he can see some muscle activity on the oscilloscope screen, and this gives him the information he needs to learn how to make the motor units become more active. Then an astounding thing happens. When these unfelt, small fragments of muscles are goaded into more activity, through some obscure, local nerve-hormone influence, the nerve begins to send off new fibers, and these new fibers grow out and attach to the motor units that have lost their nerve supply through the damage caused by the stroke. In this way more and more muscle activity can be recruited until finally enough motor units become active to produce movement, and the patient recovers at least some, occasionally all, muscle activity.

The many different uses of biofeedback dramatically illustrate the revolutionary nature of the biofeedback discovery. It should be obvious by now that the effects of biofeedback training hinge upon the ability of human beings to learn how to control all kinds of internal functions that they cannot feel and cannot experience, and that the way they learn this control is by using rather abstract information about the internal functions, information supplied by the biofeedback instruments, along with some learning aids that the mind uses to accomplish the learning. What this means is that some fairly sophisticated mental activities go on in the sub-conscious mind—remember, conscious effort usually prevents this learning—and that these subconscious mental activities come to control the physical events of the body whenever the conscious mind decides. This is quite a new concept for medicine, yet we now know that virtually every human being has this ability. It has been found that children as young as 5 learn such control easily, and moreover, that mental retardates do just as well as normal people. We can infer then that the ability to learn how to control internal but unfelt and vital physiologic activities of the body is an inherent mental ability of human beings.

Thus biofeedback gives us evidence that the action of the mind can and does control the physical activities of the body. Under normal circumstances, when the body is not under stress or injured or otherwise adversely affected, most of the body's activities are carried out by the automatic regulating systems of the brain and central nervous system. But the mind often intervenes in normal functioning, such as when the mind feels there are social problems, and causes the body to react by tension. But now we have learned that we can use the mind also to intervene to restore the body to normal functioning.

The question is often asked, do I need a therapist for biofeedback training? The answer is that certainly for disturbances or disorders that interfere with normal body and emotional functions, a therapist is needed, both to give the right kind of guidance and to ensure that the problem is what it was thought to be. But the use of biofeedback training for preventive reasons still poses a problem for the biofeedback specialists. No bad side effects of biofeedback have yet been found for well persons, but professional people always worry about the misuse or overuse of certain biofeedback techniques, and the consensus appears to be that even when biofeedback is practiced for preventive reasons, it is wise to consult with an expert from time to time.

The one potentially harmful reaction to biofeedback use has occurred during the treatment of certain kinds of endocrine disorders as diabetes and thyrotoxicosis. Since the endocrine system is involved in reactions to stress, one should always be alerted to the possibility of untoward reactions.

Another frequently asked question is, where can I get more

information about biofeedback? There are two generally reliable sources in addition to the books. First, one can write to the Biofeedback Society at the University of Colorado Medical Center, 4200 East Ninth Avenue, Denver, Colorado, 80262. The second source is the psychology department of any university or college. Either source can generally supply special information or refer you to a person or clinic.

The Basics of Biofeedback

While there is as yet no standard definition of biofeedback, it is generally considered to be the process of learning control over a selected physiologic activity by making representative information about the physiologic function available to the organism generating that physiologic activity. As the definition stands, it could easily encompass biological control induced by yogic practices, hypnosis or autosuggestion, or, in fact, by all homeostatic regulating mechanisms.

Because biofeedback has many origins and many variations in procedure, it is difficult to develop definitions and concepts acceptable to researchers and practitioners alike. The problems can be seen most clearly through an example. Suppose we record an EKG from an individual, but in place of the conventional EKG machine, we use a device that averages three consecutive interbeat intervals and displays this average on a meter calibrated in beats per minute. In a biofeedback context, the subject watches the meter and tries either to increase or decrease heart rate "by some mental means." Within a matter of minutes, certainly less than thirty, the average individual executes the instructions significantly and reliably.

The relationship between the individual and his biological information is, obviously, a feedback one; given this unembellished situation and its prompt result, definition should be a simple matter. Problems arise, however, when we try to reconcile our knowledge of learning processes with the peculiar features of biofeedback that involve three exceptional elements: the experience of perceiving the dynamics of unfelt physiologic activity; a manipulation of automatic regulating mechanisms; and a requirement to use mental activity to affect physiologic activity.

To the biomedic scientists, these new elements conflict with the traditional belief that activity in the autonomic nervous system is largely automatic and beyond voluntary control, that is, beyond direction by higher mental processes. To the psychologic theorist, on the other hand, the difficulties in characterizing biofeedback lie in reconciling traditional learning concepts, such as reinforcement and the shaping of responses, with the effects of continuously available information and the difficulty of the apparent duplicity of stimulus and response. In other words, does the change in meter reading reinforce a spontaneous change in heart rate and so shape the direction and degree of change, or does the meter reading confirm the result of a mental effort, or both? Further, if virtually every physiologic system can be brought under control by appropriate techniques analogous to the heart rate example, then what can be generalized under the rubric of biofeedback?

Biofeedback is first, of course, a new procedural tool, in which "private," internal physiologic activity is not only revealed to the patient, but, essentially, becomes the patient's responsibility. The consequences of this break with the custom of withholding interval information from patients has far-reaching implications. It is a new experience, tinged with uncertain emotions about a changing doctor-patient relationship in which the patient is an active participant in treatment, and the therapist shifts to a new role resembling that of a coach. During actual biofeedback training, the patient has little option but to direct attention to subjective states, both definitive and non-specific—a limiting circumstance that fosters changing awareness. These are only a few of the subjective events that exert greater or lesser influences during biofeedback learning.

So although biofeedback is a medical technique, the many elements involved suggest that it also can be characterized as a distinctive therapeutic approach. And, since learning is essential to its effectiveness, biofeedback is a learning process too. And finally, biofeedback appears to be a fundamental psychophysiologic phenomenon in which complex cerebral (mental) events override, by intentional self-direction, the automatic regulating mechanisms of the body, including those of the brain.

The Roots of Biofeedback

It has taken some time to put biofeedback into perspective. The reasons are as diverse, and as fascinating, as the phenomenon itself. Biofeedback grew from psychology, from neurophysiology, from muscle rehabilitation procedures, and from the application of cybernetics theory in physiology. Each in turn has claimed the "discovery," yet probably the most striking observation abut the evolution of biofeedback is that it *did* arise from several quite different disciplines at roughly the same time.

The most proprietary voice claiming biofeedback belongs to experimental psychology, and particularly to the researchers of conditioned learning theory. Operant conditioning employs a methodology in which changes of behavior in a desired direction are reinforced (rewarded). When researchers began using information about changes in physiologic activity (or some signal indicating that physiologic activity had changed) as the reinforcement, it was concluded that the resultant learning met the criteria of operant conditioning. I believe that the biofeedback process is quite different.

The work of L.V. DiCara and N.E. Miller (1968, 1969) has been publicized as the biofeedback break-through. Historically, however, their research was more a prelude to the operant conditioning form of biofeedback since information about changes in the physiologic system selected for learning were neither a reinforcement nor a biofeedback signal for their subjects. Rather, when the rats changed heart rate (or other autonomic functions) in the desired direction, they were rewarded with electrical brain stimulation that had been determined to be an effective incentive for lever-pressing rats. The important departure from operant theory here was the demonstration that physiologic systems innervated by the autonomic system could be so conditioned, a process popularly interpreted as "learning." Miller (1969) interpreted this and similar research as indicating the inherent susceptibility of involuntary systems to voluntary control.

A significant number of research reports more directly relevant to biofeedback appeared about the same time as the DiCara and Miller reports, beginning with G.D. Shearn (1961), and including J. Kamiya (1962), J. Brener and D. Hothersall (1966), T.W. Frazier (1966), M. Hnatiow and P.J. Lang (1965), M.J. Fuhrer (1964), B.T. Engle and R.A. Chisin (1966), P.J. Lang et al. (1967), and M.W. Headrick, B.W. Feather and D.T. Wells, (1970). Each of these investigations used operant techniques to demonstrate the conditionability of autonomically innervated systems. Yet more significantly, all these studies, except that of Kamiya, used some index of cardiovascular activity as the reinforcement signal, and used human beings as subjects. The general result of these studies was to establish the operant conditioning form of biofeedback.

The biofeedback principle, as it ultimately evolved for use in clinical practice, was approximated most closely by the research of E.E. Green, A.M. Green, and E.D. Walters (1970), who used biofeedback of muscle activity as a relaxation technique, by the work of T. Budzynski, J. Stoyva and C. Adler (1970), who used a combination of muscle biofeedback information and operant conditioning reinforcement for learning to reduce muscle tension, and by my research (B. Brown, 1970) using continuous monitors of EEG alpha activity for learning voluntary alpha control. My experiments differed most clearly from other methodologies in that the selected physiologic activity (EEG alpha) was displayed continuously to the subjects and no external constraints were placed upon the participants.

The contribution of clinical neurophysiology has been surprisingly unnoticed in the genesis of biofeedback. Muscle rehabilitation specialists have long used biofeedback techniques. To restore function to paralyzed muscles, for example, residual muscle potentials are displayed on an oscilloscope while the voltage of each potential activates an auditory signal. So, the patient receives both visual and auditory biofeedback information about muscle activity—activity that he can neither feel nor recruit for movement. Induced activity within a paralyzed muscle (such as that produced when a therapist manipulates the damaged components) easily establishes the goals for muscle re-education. This technique has been employed since the mid-1950s, but the underlying biofeedback principle was not recognized until the extensive work of J.V. Basmajian and colleagues (1963, 1967, 1972) and others was published. Their research firmly established the neurophysiologic validity of the inherent ability for learning to control not only isolated motor units, but groups of motor units selected on either a spatial or temporal basis. The experimental technique is identical to the muscle rehabilitation technique, requiring only some form of feedback information about motor unit activity, some instructions, and some encouragement.

Although the impact of the experimental cybernetics approach to applied biofeedback has been small, the systems attack of T.B. Mulholland, who relates biofeedback to internal control systems, has supplied important insights into the underlying mechanisms of biofeedback. Mulholland (1962, 1968) was an early enthusiast of biofeedback technology. He used lights activated and inactivated by the presence and disappearance of alpha activity in the EEG pattern to explore relationships between alpha activity and visual accommodation.

Methodologies of Biofeedback

The diverse origins of biofeedback, along with its fundamental capability to affect all physiologic systems, have produced many methodologic approaches in the different modalities for each system. The profusion of scientific reports has made it difficult to standardize biofeedback procedures. Consequently, any scientist interested in developing an understanding of biofeedback is confronted with a flood of confusing literature. For the purpose of understanding the majority of biofeedback, most research and clinical data can be divided into two major types of methods. The two methods are operant conditioning and augmented biofeedback.

The conditioning method uses biological (biofeedback) information chiefly as reinforcement for the desired physiologic change, although it often employs additional verbal encouragement as a secondary reinforcement. This technique is employed most frequently in research studies designed to isolate influential variables, but it has also been incorporated into behavior modification programs by adding biofeedback information about selected physiologic activities to the existing reinforcement program.

When the principal purpose of operant conditioning biofeedback is to influence the functioning of physiologic activity, the effects are limited. The results of most research studies require rather elegant statistics to demonstrate changes. In fact, few of these studies have been controlled for biological variation, adaptation, or reliability. More often than not, research studies are conducted during short periods of time, like 15 minutes, and so these results can scarcely be considered comparable to those from clinical biofeedback training that spans a much longer period. Nonetheless, because of the great numbers of psychological reports, concepts stemming from such inadequate studies have been widely popularized and accepted; when the operant technique has been used with biofeedback in clinical applications, the results have been generally disappointing.

The second technique, augmented biofeedback, is widely used in clinical work and is significantly different from the conditioning technique in a number of ways. First, in augmented biofeedback, the biological information is provided as continuously and quickly as is feasible—given a convenient integration time for electrical muscle activity, for heart rate, or for specific EEG waveforms. Some physiologic studies, such as blood pressure feedback, are limited by the mechanics of measurement. Second, the desired changes in physiologic activity are communicated to the patient, because the responsibility for change is given to the patient rather than retained by the therapist. Third, many additional facilitating procedures, like verbal encouragement, are employed. Clinical research confirms the markedly superior effectiveness of augmented biofeedback. In fact, the technique is successful when only two types of augmentation (biofeedback information and instructions) are included. The additional procedures used most frequently in the general clinical practice of biofeedback include the following: Progressive Relaxation (PR), Autogenic Training (AT), guided imagery, home practice with instruments, home relaxation exercises, record keeping by the patient, psychotherapy or counselling, and desensitization procedures.

The biofeedback modalities used most frequently are: (1) voltage integrated EMG activity and skin temperature, used chiefly for relaxation and stress reduction effects; (2) skin temperature and specific cardiovascular parameters, such as blood flow, pulse volume, heart rate and blood pressure, used for cardiovascular effects; (3) motor unit activity used for muscle rehabilitation; and (4) EEG components (alpha, theta, 12–16 Hz rhythm) used to reverse clinical conditions, including anxiety, insomnia, chronic pain, epilepsy and learning dysfunctions, which are accompanied by excesses or deficiencies in specific EEG components.

There are two important differences between operant conditioning and augmented biofeedback procedures. These differences are of both theoretical and practical importance. The first is the difference in efficiency of learning. In conditioning when the biofeedback information is used as a reinforcement, the changes in physiologic activity are usually accumulated and averaged over a short period of time, like two minutes. This means that the exact time of acceptable performance, of changing the physiologic activity in the desired direction, is unknown. And, a significant time interval may elapse before information about successful performance is actually presented to the patient. When dealing with dynamic physiologic behavior, this delay can amount to a time interval exceeding that necessary to allow percept formation. Then associations between the unfelt physiologic activity and the meaning of the reinforcement become difficult. In heart rate or EEG alpha biofeedback, for example, signalling the patient that he has successfully changed the activity at some unidentified time during the previous two minutes means that the patient is apprised of appropriate performance only *after* that performance has been completed. If perceptual appreciation of association is necessary to the learning process, then giving the crucial biofeedback information after performance is complete suggests that additional cerebral mechanisms are required to consolidate the associations between the goal directed performance and the reinforcement. Also the instrumentation used often contributes to distorting both the temporal and informational elements of the biofeedback signal, since many biofeedback instruments, particularly EMG instruments, simply add muscle potential voltages.

On the other hand, when biofeedback information is provided continuously, and particularly when other relevant information is available to facilitate the disposition of the biological information, then the patient can integrate the information and the subjective associations on a continuous basis. While this type of biofeedback also reinforces performance, it has the advantage of operating on a time scale more closely matching the physiologic dynamics. Results from both research and clinical studies bear out the importance of this temporal difference. Operant techniques lead to small short term changes; continuous, augmented biofeedback leads to large long term changes.

The second conceptual and practical difference between the two methods is the interpretation and verification of "control" over physiologic activities. According to operant tradition, control means that the organism develops differential responses to the conditioning stimuli affecting some physiologic system. The concept that changes in *both* directions are necessary to claim control is an important criterion. However, the impetus for "control" can be either externally determined, as in conditioning, or internally determined, as in augmented biofeedback.

"Control" developed through conditioning remains external to the organism since all conditions for providing the reinforcement are maintained by the experimenter or therapist. Yet, the reinforcement is integral to eliciting the response since failure to provide reinforcement generally results in disappearance of the response (extinction). On a practical level this consequence means that for the patient to sustain control over the physiologic activity, frequent reinforcement must "remind" the physiologic system how to perform. With continuous biofeedback, practice fosters the development of internally generated, *voluntary* control. This effect can be demonstrated by removing the biofeedback signal and asking the patient to perform the task without it. Such voluntary control rarely results from operant methods.

For patients whose symptoms do not require behavior control, voluntary control over physiologic functions is appropriate; patients who require behavior control are not likely candidates for voluntary physiologic control.

The Applications of Biofeedback

The most frustrating problem in collecting information about legitimate applications for biofeedback is the extraordinary number of scientific sources of research and clinical reports. Biofeedback research is reported in as many as 20 different psychologic journals, and in the journals of psychosomatic medicine, physiology, neurophysiology, audiology, vision, physical medicine, psychiatry, electroencephalography, and music as well. For example, a report on the management of migraine through the control of vasoconstriction appeared in the *Journal of Consulting and Clinical Psychology*, a source little used in the field of medicine. Oral reports also are given at meetings of all the various scientific disciplines and at the Biofeedback Research Society. Since these sources cover diverse disciplines, and no comprehensive compendium of biofeedback is yet in the scientific literature, most clinicians may be surprised to learn that biofeedback applications are found in virtually every field of medicine, as well as in psychology, sociology and education.

The beneficial effects of biofeedback have been reported for many emotional and behavioral problems including anxiety, depression, phobias, certain psychoses, insomnia, tension headache, drug abuse, alcoholism, bruxism, learning and perceptual problems, and the hyperkinetic syndrome.

Psychosomatic disorders also respond well to biofeedback treatment. The responding disorders include asthma, ulcers, colitis, functional diarrhea, certain types of cardiac arrhythmias, essential hypertension, Raynaud's syndrome and migraine headache. Biofeedback muscle retraining has been used successfully with the paralysis of stroke, hemiplegia, cerebral palsy, spasticity, spasmodic torticollis, other dykinesias, as well as in chronic pulmonary insufficiency. Other diverse disorders that are positively affected by biofeedback treatment procedures are epilepsy, low back pain, and other types of chronic pain.

It seems quite clear that regardless of how effective it may ultimately prove to be in any of these disorders, biofeedback is capable of evoking the fundamental normalizing mechanisms of the body. Considering its effects, there appear to be two common elements that may account for the remedial effects of biofeedback in such a diversity of psychologic and physical disorders. However, one of these may be a basic mechanism.

From a clinical standpoint, the common element in all successful applications appears to be the ability to learn to reduce tension in all three of the body's major systems: neural, muscular, and visceral. EMG and temperature biofeedback are the primary modalities for inducing tension reduction. Their use accounts for the majority of beneficial effects in the emotional and psychosomatic disorders listed above, although EEG alpha and theta biofeedback also have been reported to be effective. With biofeedback training aimed toward reducing muscle tension—through EMG biofeedback or muscle and visceral tension reduction—neural overactivity in the motor systems and in the autonomic nervous system can be reduced to normal levels with a disappearance of tension symptoms.

The second common element concerns muscle retraining, perhaps epilepsy, and possibly the relief and prevention of migraine headache (through the voluntary vasomotor regulation of the anterior temporal arteries). The underlying mechanism in these cases appears to be the inherent ability of neural structures to adapt to specific circumstances. This characteristic of neural tissue is known as plasticity and means that neural activity can undergo reversible shifts in the direction and the level of activity. In one sense, this capacity can be thought of in terms of a capacity to be shaped into new behavioral modes, a phenomenon similar to that generally conceived of as learning.

The biofeedback modification of overactive muscle and visceral systems indeed may be an exclusive manifestation of neural plasticity, since it reverses an accomodation to a specific circumstance, emotional tension, and social pressure. Theorists may be comforted by opportunities to relate the biofeedback phenomenon to mechanical electrochemical events, or to the roteness of operant conditioning. However, whatever mechanism is assumed to implement the effector phase of biofeedback, one question remains: how are the changes initiated and activated?

The question of how biofeedback procedures elicit learned control over physiologic functions is delineated most starkly by motor unit learning. An individual can learn to control a single motor unit or a complex series of units. This learning, moreover, can occur in an exceedingly short time, facilitated by nothing more than the feedback signal and some instructions. This experiment can easily be repeated in any physiology laboratory. The only observable elements in this learning situation are the perception of the visual/auditory representations of motor unit activity, the perception of the instructions, and the performance. From these elements we can deduce that cerebral processes assimilate, integrate, and associate the input information in such a way as to select and activate effector mechanisms compatible with the projected objective (the control of specific units). The primacy of cognitive mechanisms in biofeedback learning are amply supported by studies demonstrating the importance of the milieu and of the accuracy of the information given to the subject. Inferences about the cognitive, although unconscious, mechanisms involved in the biofeedback learning process have been described. They further indicate that biofeedback and related techniques can be used to isolate and characterize unconscious aspects of the learning process.

There are thus two components involved in the effect of biofeedback on physiologic activity. The first is composed of those complex cerebral processes concerned with the processing of perceptual and cognitive information. The second is the role that the product of this processing plays in influencing in the body's automatic regulation (control) systems. Support for this interpretation also comes from an analysis of the normalizing action of biofeedback learning on the disturbed physiologic activity involved in many stress-related illnesses.

Perspectives on Biofeedback

The extraordinary utility of the biofeedback concept for both medical therapeutics and psychotherapy, as well as for its potential as a preventive measure to preserve states of physical and emotional well-being implies that the fundamental mechanisms of the biofeedback process are concerned with innate processes of homeostasis. When the particulars of effective biofeedback techniques are analyzed and related to the varieties of physiologic and pathologic effects produced, it becomes clear that cognitive factors are integral to both the effectiveness and efficiency of biofeedback.

Ultimately the discovery of the biofeedback phenomenon may rank alongside such medical revolutions as the discovery of vaccines or of roentgen rays. Biofeedback is, however, not only distinctive in that its process involves the more sohisticated elements of the brain's activities, but it is perplexing because of the traditional abyss between medical and psychological therapeutic concepts and practice. The academic and applications gaps between these two disciplines have been the source of a good bit of confusion about what biofeedback really is and how to use it clinically.

There are several very interesting and basic observations about the development of biofeedback which help to understand something of its mechanisms of action and which give direction to effective clinical practice of biofeedback techniques.

Academic and Clinical Concepts of Biofeedback Are Not the Same

The first observation concerns the difference between research and applications concepts of biofeedback procedure. A major share of research effort has come from experimental psychology, and the majority of this research has been rooted in conditioning theory. One difficulty inherent in the conditioning approach is the general failure to document the biological variation of the physiologic parameter under study (as for example, detailing characteristics of excitability and reactivity under both spontaneous and induced activity conditions). Moreover, because many potential influences are not amenable to critical measurement, these are dealt with by means of standard statistical treatments. These pecularities of conditioning behavior research are appropriate for such special circumstances, but are inadequate to offer guidelines for practical applications. The difficulties imposed by methodologies idiosyncratic to a single theoretical approach are clearly seen when results of the laboratory studies, either animal or human, are analyzed by including changes due to spontaneous variation. For example, some biofeedback studies have concluded that a "learned" change in heart rate of 3 beats per minute was significant, or a change of 2 or 4 mm Hg of blood pressure was significant. The biomedical physiologist, on the other hand, determines significance under the contraints of biological variation, normally taken to be 10 to 20 percent of the mean *over time*.

There are striking differences between research and clinical methodologies of biofeedback that are the basis for some confusion to the clinician and these differences also tend to obscure the essential features of the biofeedback phenomenon. The clinician has long become used to the systematic research toward precise clinical use of chemicals, therapeutic. In sharp contrast, the psychophysiological research that led to recognition of biofeedback learning was, and generally still is, directed toward the testing of learning theory or theories of emotion. In essence, these kinds of research activities are designed primarily to determine the relevance of a variable (in this case biofeedback information) to a learning system rather than to maximize or investigate the biofeedback process as an independent phenomenon, and then to determine factors which influence its effectivenss, efficiency, and safety. These latter characteristics are, of course, those required to be identified before medical use can be responsibly undertaken.

There have been two compounding circumstances in the transition of biofeedback from laboratory to therapeutic practice. The first is that psychologic techniques and concepts tended to dominate biofeedback research, yet the effects of the techniques were physiological and normalizing of disordered physiologic function, and thus medical effects. The extraordinary traditional abyss between psychology and medicine has effectively served to maintain a separation between laboratory and medical concerns with biofeedback. Thus the biofeedback researcher was and is often handicapped by inadequate information about the dynamic physiology and pathology of the targets of his research, while on the other hand the clinician was and is relatively unschooled in the concepts and methodologies of experimental psychology. The result of these disparities has been, certainly retrospectively, enormously sloppy methodology on the part of both researcher and clinician, especially when viewed from the standpoint of the other. For example, I cringe at the misuse and misunderstanding of physiologic activities by many experimental psychologists, while at the same time being disturbed by the liberties taken by clinical practitioners with *both* psychologic and physiologic aspects of the biofeedback process.

The second compounding circumstance in biofeedback practice has been the emergence of the unfamiliar role of cognitive processes in therapeutic processes traditionally regarded as in the physical domain. This situation is complicated further by evidence suggesting that the cognitive contribution is largely mediated by subconscious mechanisms. This is a problem unique in formal therapeutics; the apparent primary importance of cognitive processes in the prevention and treatment of physical manifestations of human illnesses.

I feel that we may be better served in developing effective biofeedback treatment procedures if we look at the biofeedback learning process from the very practical standpoint of enumerating and providing exactly what is needed to make the learning the most efficient and effective. Very simply, this means defining the relevant categories of information.

Effective Biofeedback Needs 5 Different Kinds of Information

First, of course is the biofeedback information itself. An analysis of nearly all biofeedback studies indicates strongly that the greater the fidelity of the biofeedback signal to the physiologic activity being used, the faster and more extensive is the learning. The same is true for the amount of information about the selected physiologic activity, function provided, and also for temporal relationship between physiologic activity and biofeedback signal. The most effective biofeedback signal is one in which the signal contains a significant number of "bits" of information (presence of activity, degree of activity, variation of activity, etc.), is a faithful representation of the physiologic dynamics, and is as close to the real time activity as possible.

The learning process obviously needs to be augmented by other, relevant information. The situation is much like any other complex learning situation, such as attempting to derive algebraic concepts from the numbers alone. The augmenting informational channels can be designated as (1) cognitively useful information, (2) strategy information, and (3) psychologically supporting information.

Cognitively useful information is background information which provides an organizational and meaningful framework into which the biofeedback information can be integrated. It provides both the logical and experiential links among the various aspects of the biofeedback learning situation, i.e., among physiologic, subjective, instrumental and instructional aspects, and it consists of providing the patient with some knowledge of the physiologic activity he is working with, some background about his particular disorder of physiology, what the instrument does, and what the objective of the treatment is.

Even with adequate background information, the biofeedback learning situation is a new experience. Most people have little concept about manipulation of internal, unfelt physiologic activities. To bridge this informational gap, most patients require directions, suggestions, or clues about how to accomplish the biofeedback learning. This I've classified as strategy information. For a great part of biofeedback, strategy direction consists of relaxation exercises or autosuggestion exercises. It can also include meditation, home practice, imagery "trips," yogic exercises, or an authoritarian suggestion that the patient can develop his own mental technique.

The psychologic supporting information is directed mainly toward consolidating the patient's learning experience and motivations. It consists of encouraging and reinforcing learning performance and providing assurances about subjective changes.

Biofeedback therapy is fundamentally a learning process, apparently based in complex cognitive processes and can be remarkably facilitated by integrating various channels of information. As such, in clinical practice, it is a treatment process that relies heavily upon patient active participation. As I have often said in biofeedback: The patient is no longer the object of the treatment, the patient *is* the treatment.

Recognition of the underlying importance of cognitive factors to effective biofeedback learning is useful in understanding why many biofeedback treatment modalities are effective in nearly all stress related problems as well as in the understanding of the mechanism of stress reactions themselves.

Biofeedback and Stress

A review of the now vast biofeedback literature indicates a good success rate for biofeedback treatment across the wide range of stress related illnesses, including everything from asthma to tension headache to ulcers and drug abuse problems. This success allows us to view stress reactions from a quite new, precise, and meaningful perspective. This is the obvious identification of cognitive factors involved in reactions to that kind of stress that can be called social stress.

Medically and physiologically we have been concerned chiefly about the physiologic reactions *to* stress and our concepts of the mechanisms and treatment of stress have not been systematically directed toward the role of cognitive factors. Nonetheless, when we casually refer to tension and emotional pressures, we are, in fact, implicating mechanisms concerned with cognition, particularly in the sense that the organism perceives, integrates, interprets, and associates elements of his social environment, and then reacts to the product of such information processing. The difficulty is that few of the elements of this process can be observed in conscious awareness. Another way of stating this is that the bulk of information processing, i.e., mental activity, is implemented by subconscious mechanisms. Even information, associations, and interpretations which are highly significant and meaningful may be largely exclusive to subconscious processes. The same situation applies to the course of biofeedback learning.

When we examine the substance of daily stress or the stress of modern living, it can be characterized as mainly social stress, i.e., the stresses and strains of the social environment and social relationships. The stressors arising from the social environment and social relationships. The stressors arising from the social environment are not discrete stimuli, physically quantifiable, nor even sufficiently systematic to allow for definng precise relationships between stressors and reactions, either cognitive or reflex. Reactions to social stress tend to be idiosyncratic, and dependent upon such factors as genetics, experience, extent and quality of maturity, and particularly upon the adequacy of coping mechanisms.

Thus social stress is largely a mental construction, in which projection or anticipation plays a major role. That is, stressors arising from social environments are mental constructions based on perception of social relationships, special circumstances, and projections of future social relationships. Thus, physiologic reactions to social stress depend upon how mental processes evaluate the social circumstances. That is, stress is not stress until the brain interprets perceptions as indicating stress or disharmony in the social environment and relationships. Only then is the body alerted, and even then, the physiologic system or subsystem and the degree of reaction that occurs is a function of numerous factors such as system susceptibility, prior experience, coping mechanisms, etc. It is, moreover, the interaction among these factors that is the cause of most of man's emotional and psychosomatic problems.

The Mechanisms of Social Stress

The major mechanisms involved in reactions to social stress can be conceptualized as four principal feedback systems, each of which is physiologically complex in itself. These four systems are (1) the perceptual (sensory) input-integrative brain system in which sensory information is processed and interpreted by the complex mental functions of the interpretive or integrative brain, and this result then modifies or modulates the perceptual input; (2) the interpretational brain-physiological feedback control brain systems, in which the result of the interpretation provides one input to the physiologic feedback control centers (the other information input being from internal sensory receptors) and conversely, the status of the automatically regulated physiologic activities is provided to the interpretive brain from the control centers which then can modify or modulate the mental integrative function; (3) the feedback control system for the autonomic nervous system, i.e., the brain control system and the peripheral receptors and effectors; and (4) the feedback control system for skeletal muscle activities with its central control mechanisms and its peripheral receptors and effectors.

Under normal conditions the autonomic and skeletal feedback systems operate more or less autonomously. When normal operating conditions are exceeded, the difference between normal and excessive or deficit activity is communicated to the interpretive brain and gives rise to sensations when the difference is different from threshold for a given situation, and that threshold is determined by the interpretive brain.

Conversely, when a stress situation is perceived, it is the complex of sensory information about an environmental circumstance interpreted as stress by the integrative brain functions that constitutes the perception, and the interpretation concomitantly modifies the information perceived. It is the product of the interpretation of the perceptual data that may or may not activate the neural mechanisms of the peripheral systems, depending upon the significance of the interpretation to the organism's total appraisal of the situation.

The striking characteristic of social stress is that its effects persist long after the actual stressing situation has ended or been removed. The worry about job competition, for example, is perceived only by means of an internal mental construction *about* the social environment, by piecing together elements in certain associations. Indeed, a *direct* social threat may never exist; the interpretation of stress may be an error in mental construction. And in turn the error may be a result of inadequate information about the social circumstances, or lack of appropriate cognitive and experiential mechanisms for processing the social information without stress.

It is the interpretation of elements in the social environment that the individual reacts to as threatening to his personal well-being, and it is the interpreted product that initiates his physiological responses. Direct confrontations with situations in which the majority of elements of the stress construction are present occur rarely, but when they do, the stress reaction is reactivated or at least maintained.

The crucial point is that the stress reaction is maintained in the absence of direct confrontation. There are at least three internal mechanisms which can operate to maintain the stress reaction. These are (1) rumination, that conscious or subconscious activity of recall, mental regurgitation, pondering, or speculation that amplifies and intensifies the effect of the stress. In this actvity the interpretive brain is largely occupied by functions concerned with the stress stimuli, that is, attention is directed toward and on the stress; (2) perceptual modulation, the process by which the perceptual and cognitive concern with the stress are focussed on stress relevance, and environmental factors not originally related are interpreted as related to the stress situations; and (3) feedback action of the physiologic activities reacting to stress, such as muscle tension or increased autonomic activity, reinforcing sensations of stress, such as apprehension or uneasiness. All three mechanisms can operate at the subconscious level.

Under these conditions, the effect of the stress situation is maintained and there are no signals from the interpretive brain to the feedback control centers to indicate that the actual stress situation does not exist and that the defense mechanisms of alerting are no longer needed or appropriate. The muscles and viscera continue to stay tense, and further, they begin to adapt physiologically to higher levels of activity.

To relieve the stress effects, one of these processes must be reversed. Aside from drugs, the chief device which can interfere with the effects which are internally maintained is by redirecting the attention and disengaging the closed loop between the interpretive brain and the perceptual system. Distracting attention is often immediately effective, but since attention shifts only when there is new information to look to, the effect is usually transient. A more lasting effect on attention can be produced by supplying information that can effectively rechannel the information processing activity and intervene in and disrupt the perceptual-conceptual-physiological information loops that have become fixed in their activities.

Information and the Relief of Stress

Stress and stress reactions are, and can be, treated by supplying new information, and there are two major routes to introduce the information. One is conceptual, that is, supplying information for interpreting stress and stress coping and stress reactions differently, as in psychotherapy; the second is by supplying information about the physiologic state, the tension of the muscles or viscera, as in biofeedback.

By supplying information about internal physiologic states and activities, biofeedback shifts attention, and this changing attention initiates changes which ultimately affect all of the internal processes. First, attention is directed toward the physiologic state, and this shifts mental occupation away from stress and toward the result of the stress. This initiates adjustment of the tension reactions via the feedback control mechanisms toward more normal levels, and this in turn allows the cognitive processes to function with less stress impact and more normally, generating awareness of new levels of physiologic activity and a consequent change in subjective feeling states. It is also possible that the integrative brain recognizes the tension of the muscles and viscera as not appropriate defense mechanisms or responses to the present reality, since the substance of the threat is chiefly a mental construction, and thus the integrative brain initiates adjustments to achieve a more stable condition.

The success rate of biofeedback in stress-related illnesses may be attributed to the procedure combining the two informational channels, the supplying of information about the physiologic tensions which shift attention toward internal states, and the supplementary psychotherapeutic support which assists or cooperates in the process by supplying information by which the integrative brain can reinterpret the stress and use alternative coping mechanisms.

In order to appreciate fully the biofeedback process, it is important to catalogue the precise elements in the process which represent departures from procedures dealing with physiologic activities and are quite new elements in therapeutic approaches. The following list describes the majority of new features that distinguish biofeedback from older other approaches.

1. Reliable information about a selected physiologic activity is fed back to the individual generating the activity.
2. The physiologic information is provided in the form of signals that are easily perceived and interpreted.
3. The physiological information is continuously or almost continuously available.

4. These factors allow the individual to interact with and experience internal states.
5. Complex mental events are evoked to exert action on physiologic activities.
6. Conceptual information useful to the control process is provided additionally.
7. The individual learns voluntary control over a physiologic activity.
8. Once learned, the identity and control of the self is shifted from external to internal dependence.
9. Performing control over a physiologic function communicates information about internal states and internal events that are otherwise inexpressible.

All of the above factors constitute a new experience, and experience fosters confidence and development of a new authority, the self, and when such experiences and controls are shared, new belief systems are developed.

Relaxation and Dealing with Stress

The Ubiquitous Muscle

Of all the parts of the body, of all the organs of man's body, the muscles have received the least amount of attention. For most of man's existence, muscles have been regarded solely as man's physical strength, the part of the body that only hunters or athletes or strong men really worry about. For the rest of us, we occasionally exercise our muscles to "keep fit," or to play better tennis or swim better. But until very recent times, human beings, surprisingly, have ignored muscles as truly critical to their health and illness.

This is a curious attitude to have about muscles. If we think about it, we realize that muscles are the greatest mass of the body, the tissue or organ we have the most of. Common sense would suggest that since muscles constitute the greatest part of our bodies, they would be more important than simply serving the function of making the body move the way we want it to.

We have to remember that even in our sophisticated society of the 20th century, we are still learning about the world and about ourselves. And although most of us would like to believe that the medical sciences that study bodies and body functions should have told us about the importance of muscles to health and illnesses, we have to recognize that medicine has been very busy learning how to prevent disease and infection and learning how to repair damaged bodies. And even when the medical sciences have concerned themselves with muscles, their objective has been to recover muscle activity that has been lost or impaired. We now know that unfelt muscle tension is increased in many emotional and psychosomatic problems, and that through biofeedback and relaxation we can learn how to become aware of this tension and how to control and prevent it.

One of the fascinating things that has happened recently in both medicine and in our society in general is the growing awareness and understanding that all body functions have the potential to come under a voluntary control far greater than has ever before been believed. Part of this new understanding has come from rising interests in a variety of things, interest in Eastern cultures that has made us aware of the body and mind control that comes from the practice of yoga and from meditation. The discovery of biofeedback has given us scientific proof for our ability to control any physiologic activity of the body, and this has brought about a revival of older medical physiological techniques for producing relaxation. Even the economics of professional sports have been giving impetus to learning more about muscles, and from the practice of constantly exercising muscles, the experts have found three other ways of working with muscles to improve their functioning. One is learned relaxation, another is mental preparation using mental concentration, and a third is the use of imagery. All of a sudden, we have learned a great deal more about muscles than we ever knew before.

What is it about muscles that can make them so important? The most important, the most critical, the most forgotten things about muscles are not the muscles themselves, but the nerves that go to and from the muscles, connecting muscles with mind and brain. Without nerves, muscles can do nothing. It is only the vital electrical impulse conducted through the nerves to the muscles that can energize the muscles to activity. And like the head bone connected to the neck bone, the nerve to the muscle is connected to the spinal cord, and the nerves of the spinal cord are connected to the brain. It works about the same the other way around. That is, the nerves from the muscles can be traced, via many relays and branches, to the brain, and from the brain the nerve connections can be traced via the nerve bundles in the spinal cord down through nerve fibers to the muscles.

This nerve network is the mechanism by which muscles work and are kept under control. Fine control of muscle activity is carried out from control centers in the middle and higher brain, while innate, reflex activity can be carried out chiefly through connections between muiscles and the nerve fibers in the spinal cord and lower, more primitive, brain. The keys to remember are first, that muscles can do nothing without their nerve supply, and second, that the nerve impulses conducted to and from the brain make many nerve connections within the brain. And because there are so many possible connections between nerves regulating muscle activity and nerves serving other brain functions, muscles can be influenced by many different kinds of complex brain activity, including the brain functions that constitute the mind.

Thus whatever muscles may or may not do, mind activity plays a large role. The person who has a cerebral stroke is an example of the crucial role of nerves in muscle activity. In such cases, the damaged blood supply in the brain can shut off the blood supply to brain areas involved in the muscle activity of certain parts of the body, and the result is paralysis of those muscles. In contrast, the modern day athlete is a good example of how the mind can improve muscle activity. The modern athlete does many things with his mind to make his muscles do exactly what he wants. Some athletes "psych" themselves up, that is, they psychologically make themselves aroused and excited, and this makes the hormones flow that get the nerves and muscles prepared for the effort to come. Other athletes use meditation, say before tennis matches, to calm and rest the muscles, and still other athletes use imagery. That is, they visualize their performance, for example, imagine every movement in the pole vault, and in this way they prepare the muscles for the activity.

The kind of muscle action used in normal, habitual activities is carried out by what are called feedback systems. Feedback systems are systems in which there is some kind of sensor that detects what is going on and sends that information to the control center. The control center compares the information about what is going on with some pre-set value about what should be going on, and automatically makes a correction in action if a correction is necessary. If you want to reach out for a pencil, for example, the brain directs the muscles to move. As the muscles move, sensors within the muscle cells relay information about where the muscle is, how fast it is moving, and other relevant information to central control in the brain, and if any corrections are needed, the control center makes them automatically.

Now, what does all this have to do with health and illness? Once you understand that all muscle activity is under control of nerves, and that the nerve impulses going to the muscles are directed from the brain, then it is fairly easy to understand that other brain activities, such as those involved in emotions and in interpreting the outside world, can influence muscle activity through nerve interactions in the brain.

How Images Make Muscles Mind

Suppose you are watching the Olympics, and your favorite athlete is within 10 meters of the finish when a pursuer starts gaining on him. Your favorite is in trouble, and you can see both runners pushing hard, the second gaining as the finish tape is reached. You become tense, stop your breathing on inhalation. Your favorite wins by a hair's breadth, and you heave a big sigh and relax.

What has happened is that your acute worry about the race, your intense interest in the race has your attention riveted on it so much that unconsciously you identify with your favorite runner. It is you out there, calling on your muscles for more effort. But since your running is all in your mind, all you do is tense your muscles and gasp.

But in everyday life, it *is* you who are involved in all kinds of situations where the outcome is unknown. You are trying to please or perform for your boss, or spouse, or teacher or lover, or for your children or social group, and wherever there is uncertainty and effort needed, you tense your muscles, ready for whatever may come. It is a kind of primitive, animal-like reflex, this muscle tensing which prepares the body to take action.

Theorists in the medical sciences and in psychology call this the arousal reaction. In virtually every situation in life where the future, either the immediate or the remote future is unknown or uncertain, human beings instinctively, reflexly, become tense, prepared to do something. If the situation is threatening, the reaction arouses the entire body. Let's say you are hiking along a lonely mountain trail and suddenly a giant grizzly bear lunges out of the brush just ahead of you. If you're not an experienced hunter, chances are you will go into a vigorous reaction. The muscles tense tightly, ready to burst into activity, the cardiovascular system shifts its activity to help the muscles perform and the heart rate goes up, the blood pressure rises, the respiration becomes irregular, the gut stops its movements, most of the body's secretions dry up, and you are ready in an instant to do something. This extreme reaction is known as the fight-or-flight reaction, meaning that the reaction to a threat to one's own well being and survival is to instinctively, reflexly prepare the body immediately to fight or flee or sometimes just to freeze. All of the body and mind's activities are concerned that the muscles have the first priority, for it is the muscles that can deal with the threat.

Psychophysiologists have found that pretty much the same thing happens in daily life encounters except that the reactions are on a rather mild scale. Remember waiting for the phone to ring with an important message, but you didn't know whether the message would be good news or bad news? The closer the time for the phone to ring, the more tense you got. You become more and more tense. Its basically the same reaction as the fight-or-flight reaction— there is a threat to your immediate happiness or well-being, and you get nervous. The muscles tense, the heart rate increases, breathing becomes irregular, the mouth dry, and the hand sweaty or cold and clammy. You are all ready to take some kind of action. Usually the mind is so occupied with the uncertainty that the body changes are scarcely noticed unless or until the worry becomes extreme.

These are reactions that we generally have some conscious awareness of. But in daily life, there are many, literally innumerable occasions of uncertainty about one's social activities and relationships. For the most part these are often too fleeting or seemingly insignificant to cause any serious conscious worry, yet some part of the mind absorbs the meaning, and if the situations are at all related, or more obvious, the mind continues to accumulate unconscious worry and the body begins to react. This kind of social process is slow and gradual, but insidious changes begin to occur in the body. Every tiny problem causes a tiny bit of tension. But because the tensions do not come to consciousness, the mind does not give directions to the lower brain control centers to relax or release the tensions. The body then undergoes a process of adaptation, that is, it gets used to the state of increased tension. When the next small, related worry comes along, the body is still slightly tense, and the next small surge of tension simply adds to the preceeding tension. It is this building up of body tensions, for the most part unrecognized by conscious awareness, that can lead to all kinds of symptoms of anxiety, such as neuroses, insomnia, headache, and any of the psychosomatic illnesses such as asthma, or essential hypertension, or ulcers, or colitis.

To summarize this process, we can talk in terms of how daily social stresses affect the body, and particularly the muscles. Social stress is really a matter of the way in which we perceive our social situations and relationships.

But if social activity is integral to human life, what happens sometimes to make social life stressful and causes harmful reactions in the body? The answer lies in the way each individual perceives his social world. Social events do not become stressful until mental processes interpret them as stressful. But then why should mental activity perceive something wrong in the social environment and interpret social events as stressful?

How Tensions Begin

It all begins with what the individual expects in his social environment and out of his social relationships. No problem, no social difficulty can be perceived as a problem or difficulty unless the perceiver expects something other than what is happening in his social world and with his social relationships. And what the person expects of his social life depends upon many things, some predetermined, but some that can be controlled if they are recognized. Expectations about what goes on in the social environment and one's role in it depends, for example, on genetic factors such as predisposing factors about illness, health, personality, looks, mental ability, etc. But expectations are even more strongly influenced by one's own life experiences, one's own education, and one's cultural background, which determine how people set their goals and what they expect out of life.

So the first real mental activity in reactions to social stress is the existing expectation set of the individual. The second mental activity is what the individual perceives in his social situations and relationships, and what he perceives is, of course, colored by what he expects to see and hear and feel. More often than not, what a person perceives going on in the social environment doesn't live up to expectations. And that's where the tension begins, because the mind starts asking questions about why not, what's wrong, what did I do wrong, and if the answers are unsatisfactory, the tensions stay and can get worse. This is the beginning of the things that go on in the mind that eventually can lead to emotional and physical problems.

Let's take an example of this beginning of tensions, and then go through the rest of the mental reactions after that. Suppose you are competing for a job, along with 50 other candidates. It is important for you to get the new job, but there are endless forms to fill out, endless tests to take, and personal interviews with personnel, with supervisors, etc. You start out with some confidence that your qualifications are great for the job, but as you go through the hiring process, many questions arise in your mind. You begin wondering if what you've got is what they want, whether you're making a good impression, what the other candidates are doing, and hundreds of other questions. This is uncertainty, and uncertainty becomes insecurity, and when uncertainty and insecurity about one's situation exist, one immediately becomes anxious. The uncertainty, insecurity, and anxiety all lead to body defense reactions, the arousal reaction, with the muscles tense and the viscera in a knot. You are only marginally aware of these body reactions because the mind is completely preoccupied with the mental effort required by this critical social situation. If the hiring process lasts for any length of time, you may develop insomnia, or tension headache, or suddenly become superstitious, which could be the beginning of a phobia, or you may just feel awful or your back may begin to ache. All kinds of physical and emotional and mental symptoms may occur, and one of the most pervasive and persistent changes is the increased muscle tension.

What is happening is, first, that your perception of what is going on around you is certainly not what you expected or had hoped for. In other words, there is an important discrepancy between what you expected and what you think is going on, even though you're really not sure about what is going on. The next mental activity in the process leading to stress reactions is furious mental activity to try to find out how to correct what you think may be going wrong. This is the rumination process, the kind of worry that just won't go away, that insidious mental activity of mentally regurgitating the social situation to find out what is wrong and get some answers. There are two important effects of rumination, that is, of persistent worry, on the body. First, the more you ruminate, that is, the more you worry about the problem, the greater the uncertainty, and this leads directly to the arousal reaction and tense muscles, the primitive defense response to threatening situations. For after all, as you see the social situation, you are being threatened. The second effect of rumination is another very interesting phenomenon of the human mind. You begin to construct images, images about how you did behave, or how you should have reacted, and images about how you should behave in this situation in the future. The images have you moving and sitting and acting out all possible answers you can think of and these imaginary activities involve the body. Now the interesting part is, that when you imagine yourself doing something, the muscles become tense, ready to perform in case you decide to go ahead with the action. After all, for every action, the muscles must first get ready to act before they actually begin to work, and mental images nearly always precede action. So the mental images of the rumination process actually evoke muscle tension, and the more you worry about the social problem, the more tense the muscles become.

Then, with the mind occupied with the problem about the social activity or relationship, there are two more important effects on the body, and especially on the muscles. First, the mind essentially is saying to itself that it is concerned with a social threat to personal well being, and so the higher brain sends messages to the lower brain to keep the muscles uptight, ready to take action if necessary, and this is why the muscle tension continues. The second effect of having the mind so occupied with the problem is that the mind fails to recognize the signals coming from the body and muscles about how uptight they really are. Under normal circumstances, the higher brain and cortex recognizes these body signals and relays messages to the lower muscle control centers to release the tensions and relax if the tension isn't needed for a good reason. But in stress situations, the cortex fails to perform this normalizing function.

In the job competition example, you might go home after a difficult interview and say, "Gosh, I'm getting another headache." This really means that you were so busy with the mental effort of the day that your mind failed to heed the body signals telling you that the muscles of the neck and head were tense and becoming tenser all the time.

One of the reasons that I have spent a good bit of time describing what goes on in the mind that leads to tense states is because the prevention and relief of tension states depends upon working with the mind and conscious awareness.

Treating Tension States

We can now begin to talk about treatments for tension states. There are literally dozens of different kinds of disturbances of mind and body caused by social stress, and since social stress is really a function of mental activity, the most effective and long lasting relief and prevention of stress illnesses and tension states should logically be achieved by using the mind.

One of the sad events in the history of medicine and psychology has been their refusal until so recently to study the role of mind in health and illness. Both medical and psychotherapeutic treatment of anxiety and tension states have relied almost exclusively on treating the symptoms rather than the cause of stress problems. Everyone who has ever been anxious or tense has received tranquilizers or some other psychoactive drug. And the prevalence of tension states and stress disorders is shockingly revealed by the fact that nearly one hundred million prescriptions for tranquilizers are filled each year. And while drugs may temporarily relieve the problem, they can never, never cure or prevent stress disorders. Only the mind can effectively and permanently relieve the problems that the mind has caused.

The discovery of biofeedback has literally hurled medicine and psychology into quite new and effective treatment programs for tension states and all of the discomforts and physical disorders and emotional problems that tensions lead to. What I want to do now is to describe how muscle biofeedback accomplishes its effects, and why it is more of a mind technique than a muscle treatment.

The critical elements of muscle or EMG biofeedback treatment are first that the biofeedback instrument gives the patient specific and immediate and continuous information about this specific physiologic activity. The instrument can reveal muscle tension levels that the person cannot feel and has no awareness of. The second critical element is that the patient pays attention to the information that, as we described earlier, he has not attended to because his mind was so occupied with worry. Now that the patient is paying attention to his muscle tension, two interesting things happen in the mind. First, while he is paying attention to his muscle tension levels via the instrument, he cannot be paying attention to his social problem. In essence, the mind forgets the problem, and slows down the messages to the lower muscle control centers of the brain to keep alert because of the worry and the threat. With fewer alerting messages coming down from above, the lower control centers send fewer and fewer messages to the muscles keeping the muscles tense, and so the muscles begin to relax.

The second interesting effect is that the mind begins to make associations between the information about muscle tension from the instrument and some internal feeling states. In other words, the person begins to develop an awareness about levels of muscle tension he has never had before. Through biofeedback training, the person learns how to increase his awareness of muscle tension levels so that he can detect when tensions are beginning, and then relax them before they cause trouble.

While this kind of learning to be aware of muscle tension and how to relax the muscles can be accomplished using muscle biofeedback alone, the learning how to relax can be speeded up somewhat by using other so-called mind techniques. Some of the additional techniques that are in common use today are the various mental exercises such as progressive relaxation, autogenic training, imagery and meditation.

P.R. and A.T.

The technique of progressive relaxation was developed many years ago by Dr. Edmund Jacobson, and many of the popular books he wrote on the subject are currently available in paperback. The technique is now more popularly known by the name tense-relax exercises. The procedure is simple. First, a specific muscle or muscle group, as the muscles of the forearm, are tensed with as much effort as possible. Then the muscles are allowed to relax completely. The idea is to compare the sensations or feelings of tension with the sensations of relaxation to so that one can begin to detect smaller and smaller levels of muscle tension. It is really a way to gain awareness of muscle tension and how it feels to be truly relaxed. The exercises are systematic, that is, each muscle or muscle group is tensed and relaxed several times, waiting each time long enough to truly appreciate the sensation of relaxation.

Then the same thing is done with another muscle group, and so on progressively around the body, ending with some whole body tense-relax exercises.

Another popular technique used in relaxation training is autogenic training. This is a combination program of mental exercises that uses self-suggestion phrases and some meditation, although usually only the self-suggestion phrases are used. Almost any kind of phrase can be used to suggest to one's self the feelings of relaxation, but scientific work has discovered that there are two sensations critical to the relaxation process. These are the feelings of heaviness and warmth. So the phrases that one says to one's self are something like, "my hands feel heavy," "my arms feel heavy." Phrases for every body part are used, and just as with the tense-relax exercises, the self-suggestion phrases are applied progressively around the body. The first set of exercises deals with the idea of heaviness, then next you go around the body with phrases suggesting warmth, such as "my hand is warm," "my arm feels warm." Then the ideas are combined, and many variations of suggestions can be used. For example, you can say, "my hand feels warm and heavy," "my arm is relaxed, there is no tension," and so on. The phrases are said slowly and for each part of the body, giving enough time between phrases for the desired sensation to be appreciated.

It is important in both the tense-relax exercises and in autogenic training to assume a passive attitude. If any effort is exerted, the effort leads to tension. With a passive attitude, one can just wait for the sensations of relaxation to occur. Once recognized, the state can be achieved when desired by returning to the passive state and feeling the sensations of relaxation.

Imagery and the Relief of Tension

Another helpful mind technique often used in conjunction with biofeedback is imagery. Remember I said earlier that mental images of problems make the body tense? Well, mental images can also be used to help the body to relax. Try visualizing the most peaceful place or situation you know. It might be fishing on a lake far from civilization, or soaking in a hot tub, or possibly sinking down into a feather bed. Visualize the scene completely, then remember how you feel when you are there. This will often help relieve tensions. Or, you can be specific about the mental images, and if the neck muscles, for example, are tense, you might visualize the muscles and how muscle cells might look when they are relaxed, or how the head feels when it is bent forward, relaxed. Any trick of imagination can be used to try to create or recreate feelings of relaxation.

There is technique in psychotherapy that takes advantage of both mental imagery and relaxation procedures to treat emotional problems, particularly anxieties and mild phobias. This is called desensitization, meaning that the procedure is used to desensitize or lessen the effect of those things causing the anxiety of fear. Let's say you have developed considerable anxiety, the exam anxiety that is so common among students. You know the material for the exam fairly well, at least you thought you did, but then the day before the exam, you begin to get sick. You get sweaty, scared, maybe have diarrhea, the heart is racing ... the typical acute anxiety syndrome.

In the desensitization procedure, the patient is first taught how to relax. Nowadays biofeedback is used principally, along with the version various relaxation exercises I described earlier. When the patient has achieved some success in relaxing, he is asked to conjure up mental images about the exam situation. Usually the images are arranged in sequences, from the least anxiety-producing images to the most anxiety-producing images. The first image in the case of exam anxiety might be walking into the building and through the halls to the exam room. The most fearful image might be the time of the passing out of exam papers, or the image of the professor. The patient imagines first the least fearful image, and while doing this he must keep, or learn how to keep, the muscle tension low as in relaxation. When he can keep a mental image of the least anxiety-producing scene in his mind and still keep his muscle tension low, he goes on to the next image, and so on until he learns to stay relaxed while imagining the worst anxiety-producing scene. After this training, he tries out his learned relaxation during each sequence of the real situation, now being aware of the situations causing tension and consciously allowing relaxation to occur.

Training with the biofeedback instrument is very important in attaining the ability for voluntary control of tension and relaxation because it is the only way the learning process can be determined accurately. As a matter of fact, the instrument detects increased tension long before the person is ever aware of increased muscle tension during the image production. But once the person has learned to maintain a good degree of relaxation during imagining the anxiety-producing situations, and learns how to stay relaxed during the real exam time, he no longer develops any anxiety. As I described earlier, with the mind occupied with worry, it cannot function properly. But with the body relaxed and only the mind alert, the mind can exercise its normal capabilities.

As we have seen, the mind and the muscles are intimately related. The problem we have with tense muscles is because when we have nagging worries, we are not aware of rising tension in the muscles. It is the discovery of biofeedback and the use of biofeedback instruments that can give us the information by which we can become sensitive to muscle tension and learn how to prevent tension reactions and maintain a state of physical and emotional well-being.

EEG Biofeedback: Techniques and Applications

As conventionally recorded in the EEG (electroencephalo-gram), the electrical brain activity of human beings and higher animal species exhibits a great variety of patterns. These patterns change when the organism shifts from one state of consciousness to another, from one state of emotion to another, or from one state of mental activity to another. Analysis of this activity shows that the changing patterns are produced by different combinations of and different forms of several specific brain wave types which recur consistently enough in the various brain states to be identified and characterized.

With few exceptions, brain wave components are identified in terms of their rhythmic appearance at different frequencies. The most common brain wave component is alpha activity, now generally characterized as rhythmic activity with a frequency of between nine and 12 Hz. The term Hertz, abbreviated Hz, indicates cycles per second. A cycle is a full wave, measured from any point on the wave to an identical point on the following wave, from peak to peak, for example. Rhythmic EEG activity, like alpha, rarely stands at any one frequency. Instead, it tends to vary within the designated frequency range. For this reason, discussions of EEG activity generally employ averages obtained over suitable time periods. This allows us to track changes within each frequency range for purposes of correlating those changes with behavioral and subjective changes. A significant accessory measure is the degree of variation of the frequency.

Before the advent of biofeedback, information about the significance of alpha activity in behavioral or subjective events was obtained by examining either the changes in alpha activity that followed external stimuli or that resulted from brain injury, or by correlating the presence or absence of alpha with different states of consciousness, with different subjective states, and with different kinds of mental activity. Such studies showed that the best fitting correlate of alpha was a state of relaxed wakefulness.

The development of biofeedback techniques allowed an individual to achieve varying degrees of self-control over the presence of alpha activity in the EEG pattern. This meant that trained subjects could produce a state of alpha sufficiently steady to let them relate certain subjective phenomena to its presence. These subjective reports generally have supported the idea that alpha activity in the EEG does indicate a state of relaxed wakefulness. They also have pointed out that this state is pleasant, calm and peaceful. It should be noted, however, that the subjective states which accompany alpha during biofeedback control may not be precisely the same as those that occur during the spontaneous appearance of alpha activity. One of the major differences between biofeedback controlled and spontaneously produced activity is that controlled alpha generally exhibits a lower average frequency with little variation from the average. Some argument about the mechanism of alpha appearance and its subjective correlates is not in the scientific literature, and will be discussed later in this chapter.

Theta Activity and Other EEG Components

Before we proceed to a discussion of alpha activity and its biofeedback uses, let me quickly cover some of the other EEG components, particularly those currently being investigated for use with biofeedback techniques.

Until biofeedback came along, the normal EEG and the EEG patterns that accompany emotional, behavioral or psychosomatic problems received little attention. Most scientific investigations concentrated on abnormal EEG components as aids to diagnosis, or on neurophysiologic research concerning the mechanisms of arousal and intense emotion. Neither type of study employs the methodology or the recording techniques that are necessary when one wishes to evaluate relationships between the EEG patterns and components and the range of human behavior and emotion which occur in the absence of major pathology. This means that our concepts about EEG and behavior are still evolving and that many of our present conclusions should be viewed as tentative, as subject to further modification and refinement.

Theta activity is a good example. The frequency characteristic of theta activity is generally considered to be between four and seven or eight Hz. However, theta activity is rather rare in the normal waking EEG pattern. Theta waves frequently appear as single waves, rather than in trains of waves, a feature that makes both identification and biofeedback control difficult. In general, the theta frequency is approximately one-half the average alpha frequency. In fact, some neurophysiologists view theta activity as the first subharmonic of alpha.

Through experiments conducted in my laboratory, I have discovered several ways to overcome the problems involved in developing learned control of EEG theta activity. All subjects who learned to control their theta in these experiments had EEG patterns consisting of relatively little alpha activity, faster than expected alpha-beta activity, and a wide variety of EEG components. Those who failed to learn exhibited high levels of alpha, slower alpha-beta activity and mixed background EEGs with virtually no fast activity. Consequently, only individuals showing the low level alpha EEG characteristics can be considered good candidates for theta training.

I also found that theta learners require at least four training sessions—each consisting of two 20-minute theta feedback periods separated by a five-minute rest period—to show significant increases in the amount of theta produced. Theta amplitude also tends to increase, but theta appearances do not increase in frequency to any significant degree. Because faster theta is more often exhibited during periods of intense visual imagery, the effects of this training are enhanced by an ability for imagery. Giving the subjects cognitively useful information about the task of the experiment also significantly increased theta production.

A good deal of unpublished but popularly discussed work with theta biofeedback suggests its role in creativity, particularly creative imagery. On the basis of what is known about the subjective correlates of theta, there may be considerable merit in studying the role of theta in creativity. However, there are certain hazards which can be minimized by understanding the multiple behavioral correlates of theta activity. First, theta activity is a component of arousal and orientation. It also occurs in the brain wave pattern when the individual is assimilating new information about the environment. During the initial moments of EEG recording, for example, theta activity frequently appears. Theta happens during the "Aha!" reaction, at the time of closure when an individual suddenly becomes aware of the meaning of a previously puzzling picture or statement. Finally, theta activity is a characteristic of drowsiness, REM sleep, and dreaming.

There are only two other common, labelled brain wave components. One is delta activity, with a frequency of about one-half to three Hz, which appears almost exclusively during deep sleep. The other component is beta activity, originally defined as low voltage, fast EEG activity with a frequency range that exceeds alpha activity. Many investigators still make no distinction between rhythmic and nonrhythmic beta activity, nor do they describe any exact frequency ranges. Largely because of the design of my first filters, I suggested that beta be defined by frequency range and further qualified as to whether it was rhythmic or nonrhythmic, and as having a frequency range of 13 to 28 Hz. Terminology for other beta frequency ranges has not been explicitly designated.

All varieties of beta activity are present when an individual is alert and attentive, aroused, anxious, or apprehensive. A number of subspecies of beta can be characterized as being rhythmic and having a specific frequency, but few of these have been studied sufficiently for an understanding of their significance. One specific subfrequency is the 12 to 16 Hz wave used by Sterman as a biofeedback parameter in the experimental treatment of epilepsy.

This subfrequency appears to be artificial in the sense that it must be learned since it does not appear in the normal waking EEG. A similar type of beta, a rhythmic frequency of 12 to 14 Hz that appears in bursts during light sleep, is called the sleep spindle because of its spindle-like appearance in EEG recordings. The relationship between the waking and sleeping 12 to 14 Hz rhythms has not yet been investigated.

The only other specific beta frequency that has been investigated adequately is the 40–Hz rhythm. Considerable electronic expertise is needed to extract this rhythm from neighboring frequencies produced by scalp muscle activities and by the environmental electrical noise which can comprise as much as 25 percent of the voltage of high frequency EEG signals. The assumption underlying work with the 40–Hz rhythm is a presumed relationship with states described as circumscribed cortical excitablity or focused arousal. The behavioral inference is that this rhythm accompanies conditions favorable to short-term memory consolidation and problem solving. Extensive studies by Sheer suggest that biofeedback training of the 40–Hz rhythm does increase problem solving capacity to *some* extent in *some* individuals. However, Sheer cautions against generalizing these findings.

These results and the premise that electrical brain activity reflects brain functioning which in turn reflects subjective and mental states are the reasons why EEG biofeedback holds considerable promise for the future. Still, it must be realized that EEG biofeedback is in its infancy. Because of the complexity of the EEG and the difficulties entailed in proper recording and analysis, precise information will be sparse for some time to come.

On the other hand, the current status of EEG knowledge and research offers both the researcher and the clinician considerable encouragement for working with EEG biofeedback. There are obvious advantages to using the relatively general frequency ranges, such as alpha, beta or theta. The first advantage is that learning their control offers the first technique which produces reasonably steady brain states, and hence reasonably steady, though rather general, subjective states. Since alpha activity, for example, accompanies a state of relaxed wakefulness which minimizes distractions and makes the mind/brain more accessible to information input or to awarenesses, the general therapeutic usefulness of alpha biofeedback is of considerable importance. In a large degree, alpha represents the opposite of beta activity. Since beta (particularly low voltage, mixed frequency, nonrhythmic beta) is associated with anxiety, fear, and generalized arousal, biofeedback's ability to produce fairly sustained alpha activity has applications in all conditions where anxiety and CNS arousal are major contributors to illness.

Another advantage of EEG biofeedback lies in its abilities to capture and retrieve infrequently occurring brain and subjective states, and to isolate components of mixed brain and subjective states.

In the assimilation of information about a new situation, for example, much emphasis has been put on the appearance of theta activity. But, if the complete EEG pattern is inspected, then one sees that the pattern is quite mixed, showing a great variety of brain wave components. It is the appearance of theta that has been stressed. That is, theta seems to be important here because it appears in these situations and not in other situations. However, theta waves actually are quite infrequent even while assimilating new information, during recall, during moments of closure, during drowsiness, and even during dreaming. Here biofeedback has allowed us to capture and sustain an infrequently occurring wave form. So it seems that in the future, learned control of theta activity may have uses related to one or all of the behaviors which it accompanies.

EEG Procedures

Let's now take a look at biofeedback procedure. There are four elements in this procedure: the electrode placement, the instrument, the training program, and the goal. All of these elements are equally important.

Appropriate electrodes and placement are necessary for accurate feedback information. Reputable manufacturers of biofeedback instruments generally supply good electrodes with their instruments. Where there are questions about electrodes, it is advisable to consult an electroencephalographer. A standard 10–20 system for electrode placement is used in research studies. For clinical use, electrode placement is less critical if the same placements are used with the same patient during each session.

The most convenient electrode placement for general biofeedback purposes puts them in the parietal region—roughly midway along a line drawn from the intra-aural plane to the cranial midline—and near the inion in a line starting at the parietal electrode. This general placement is desirable for alpha recordings. For theta biofeedback, a different placement is necessary because some individuals do not exhibit theta in the parietal-occipital areas. In this case, it is wise to shift the occipital electrode to a more frontal position, perhaps three inches in front of the parietal electrode. Proper grounding, of course, is important. The most frequently used reference is a clip on the earlobe.

The second element, the EEG biofeedback instrument, plays the crucial role in training. Therefore it is desirable to use a high quality machine. Some of the most important features of a reliable EEG biofeedback instrument are high impedance input, low noise level (no more than one microvolt), moderately narrow band filters with sharp edges or a variable filter with sharp edges, and a display of the biofeedback signal, via lights, tones or meters, that faithfully follows the designated EEG component.

One cannot check the accuracy of an EEG biofeedback instrument through the display. Therefore, it is advisable to take recordings from the instrument. It is particularly important to inspect an EEG recorded through the amplifier section of the instrument to make sure that the amplifier only records electrical brain activity and is not contaminated by artifacts, such as ambient electrical noise. The filter stage then should be inspected via a recording that's compared to the "raw" EEG, thus ensuring that the filtering is sharp and contained within the proper limits. Next, the electrical signal activating the display should be recorded and compared to both the original EEG and the filtered signals to check the fidelity of the biofeedback signal.

The third element of the biofeedback procedure is the training program. A number of research papers describe the method of alternating periods of reinforcing production of alpha with periods of reinforcing suppression of alpha. The periods are from 30 to 90 seconds in duration. This kind of procedure has been used to investigate certain theoretical points concerning conditioning theory, and has been found to result in either a slow rate of learning with only modest learning gains, or in no significant learning. In clinical applications, fair to excellent results have been obtained by providing continuous feedback about only one direction of change. That is, the patient works toward a single objective, such as increasing their production of alpha.

Some researchers and clinicians prefer to leave the patient alone with the instrument, and to let them work on their own; many others have reported that biofeedback learning proceeds more rapidly and efficiently when accompanied by psychologic support techniques. Since complete relaxation is not usually an objective, neither progressive relaxation nor autogenic training has been found useful, and appropriate auto-suggestive exercises evoking imagery of the objective and of the processes involved can be designed easily for individual cases. The communication of ancillary information also facilitates learning, particularly information about brain waves—what they look like, what they are related to, how they are recorded, etc.

Some of the most successful EEG biofeedback results from clinical cases have been obtained by following the training with sessions of psychologic counselling or psychotherapy. Here the images, thoughts, emotions, and insights that accompany the feedback training are reviewed and suggestions for improving the patient's learning strategy are offered.

The fourth and last major element of the biofeedback procedure is the establishment of well-defined goals for the training. These goals define the criteria to be met and the number of training sessions involved. Except in specialized programs used with epilepsy, EEG biofeedback procedures concentrate on learning to increase the amount of a specific EEG component. There is an obvious rule about EEG components which says that the more desirable a certain EEG activity is in a particular individual, the rarer that activity will be in that individual. If it is desirable, for example, that an individual produce more alpha activity as a way to relieve anxiety, then the less alpha that individual will have, and the more work it will take, on the part of both the individual and the therapist, to elicit a production of alpha. For this reason, it's better to define the goal for increased production as a series of progressive objectives, each requiring a moderate gain over the preceeding one. The maximum possible increase differs considerably from individual to individual for many reasons, including inherent EEG pattern, inherent arousal level, personality, and intelligence.

The second goal to be established concerns the degree of subjective change. A variety of psychological tests offer objective and subjective ratings for subjective phenomena. Because of individual differences and the possibility that the objective EEG measure and the subjective measure may not be strictly associated, both measures are needed in order to evaluate progress and to monitor the effectiveness of the biofeedback training. One of the most critical measures, in fact, is the usefulness of the training in the patient's life outside the laboratory.

It is important to remember that the changing awareness which generally occurs with biofeedback training may also alter the patient's concept of the treatment and his dependencies. This new awareness may require special psychologic attention. Moreover, both the changing awareness and the therapeutic benefit of the biofeedback treatment can modify the effectiveness of concurrent medication, sometimes rendering the dosage excessive and resulting in side effects.

EEG Applications

No aspect of biofeedback has generated more general interest than the possibility that human beings can learn to control their own brain waves. Yet despite the interest and a good deal of research activity, the state of the art of EEG biofeedback has not advanced significantly in the area of clinical usage. This should not, however, detract from the potential of EEG biofeedback to contribute to improved therapy and therapeutic approaches. In support of this position, I would like to point out some of the reasons behind the mixed opinions about EEG biofeedback and the existing confusion concerning its real potential.

First, we must remember that there has been a dearth of qualified EEG researchers, particularly those with expertise in both neurophysiology and psychology. Moreover, the traditional isolation between psychologists and physiologists has resulted in the publication in specialty journals of many reports that are inaccurate, incomplete, or actually misleading.

A second factor causing confusion about EEG biofeedback, and particularly about alpha biofeedback, has been the great variety of experimental and clinical approaches. Following the initial alpha biofeedback work, most research studies have concentrated on three areas: (1) the relationship between alpha and visual mechanisms; (2) the study of similarities between alpha biofeedback and meditation; (3) the effect of alpha on experimental anxiety. In each of these areas, the roles of alpha and of the other variables under study are extremely complex. Yet, the rush to explore biofeedback potentials, coupled with the constraints of systematic research, has tended to produce an oversimplification of the role of alpha, particularly in non-professional discussions of this phenomenon.

Few of the recently reported research studies of alpha activity have attempted to explore its potential for clinical application. Overall, the number of definitive studies on the clinical uses of alpha biofeedback is small. This lack of clinical data seems primarily due to the relative complexity of the disorders being treated. While informal reports by clinical investigators indicate considerable success with alpha biofeedback, details about patient selection, methods, and results are lacking, as is information about the relative effectiveness of alpha feedback when compared to other treatments.

Most scientific reports on alpha biofeedback exhibit a number of deficiencies. The roles played by the brain mechanisms subserving subjective states, mental activity and emotion in the appearance and disappearance of alpha within the EEG pattern are often misunderstood. Too often arousal and attention are equated with the disappearance of alpha, and the assumption is made that the presence of alpha is inconsistent with arousal and attention. It is also frequently assumed that subjective reports of a relaxed state during the presence of alpha indicate general body relaxation. And, because anxiety is rarely found in relaxed states, it is inferred that the presence of alpha means the reduction of anxiety. There are few, if any, data that support this contention; instead research studies report a state of relative *mental* relaxation toward external stimuli that occurs simultaneously with a state of inwardly directed attention. This association, which has been demonstrated experimentally, is paralleled by the occurrence of steady, slow alpha during certain meditational exercises, like transcendental meditation, and during certain states of zen and yogic meditation. It is likely that such inwardly directed attention indicates a shift in the relative significance of external and internal events.

Nonetheless, the bulk of the neurophysiologic, psychophysiologic and clinical data reported to date constitute a very strong rationale for using alpha biofeedback with a wide variety of conditions.

To date, seven reports of clinical trials using alpha biofeedback are available. Two interesting and significant themes are present in all of these studies. First, as indicated earlier, attention to or awareness of interior activity (that is, turning the attention inward) reduces the attention paid to external stimuli. This shift diminishes mental tension and preoccupation with environmental or social factors, a decrease which alters the significance attached to external stimuli. Such an association suggests that a state of inwardly directed attention is perceived as more pleasant, possibly because it excludes the perceptual triggers of emotional memory. If this is the case, then alpha biofeedback might produce a substitute for the euphoric states induced by drugs or neurotic behavior. The second theme in these clinical reports is the strong suggestion that the *idea* of self control may be the important element in therapy because it supplies the motivation necessary to develop control disorder via obscure processes.

Let me review these clinical reports individually before returning to the research reports which may further clarify the rationale for the clinical use of alpha biofeedback.

In 1971 J. Korein and his colleagues presented a preliminary report on eight patients with psychogenic and systematic disorders who learned alpha control within two weeks. A majority of these patients also gained control of their symptomatology. The patients described the alpha training experience as tranquil. To my knowledge, no written report of this study has appeared in any biomedical journal.

A report by G.K. Mills and L. Solyom (1974) described the use of alpha biofeedback in the treatment of ruminating obsessives. These investigators reasoned that mental relaxation might inhibit the ruminating activity that characterizes the obsessive neurotic. In this study, five patients received between seven and 20 biofeedback training sessions with extremely encouraging results. Briefly, they showed that some obsessives can learn EEG control, that augmented instructions concerning the learning process were no more effective than minimal instructions, that the subjective states occurring during alpha production were labeled "relaxed," "daydreaming," and "not thinking," and that no ruminations occurred during alpha, regardless of the amount of alpha produced. Apparently, this elimination of rumination did not persist after training. Still, the dramatic success of alpha feedback with these neurotic patients seems to warrant further study.

At the 1975 BRS meetings, C.A. Childers reported on the use of alpha biofeedback for treating severe social problems in five patients classified as psychopathic. Four of the patients showed long standing severe symptomatology: a convulsive disorder and antisocial personality; an organic brain syndrome (secondary to psychosis) with brain trauma; a toxic psychosis and pain with a diagnosis of paranoid schizophrenia; a chronic undifferentiated schizophrenia. The fifth patient, a 13-year-old, was showing an adjustment reaction to adolescence.

All patients received ten 45-minute sessions of alpha biofeedback training. By the sixth session, "assaultive, abusive behavior had completely ceased with a dramatic change in their behavior and appearance on the ward." All patients were discharged within two to three weeks, and two of the four adults became gainfully employed. Dr. Childers cautioned that this was a preliminary study, and that quantification of changes in EEG alpha was not made. Consequently, no statement can be made about the relationship between the learned control of alpha activity and the behavioral changes occurring in the patients. Even though the behavioral changes were dramatic, Childers warns that the possibility of a placebo effect cannot be ruled out. Nonetheless, the substantial changes in psychotic behavior that occurred with only ten biofeedback training sessions, strongly suggest a causal relationship between the biofeedback therapy and the therapeutic result.

Another paper presented at the 1975 BRS meetings reported on the use of "alpha-theta" biofeedback in chronic alcoholics. The EEG frequency range indicated by the term "alpha-theta" is roughly six to nine Hz, that is, slower than alpha, but not as slow as theta activity. Apparently following the earlier interpretations of E.E. Green, J.D. Sargent, and others at the Menninger Clinic, Twemlow and his colleagues in this study attempted to use alpha-theta biofeedback as "a psychophysiological growth process, enabling psychological maturation to occur in a nonverbal milieu." (This projection of the possible relationship between complex electrical brain activities and subjective states may have considerable merit in the psychotherapeutic situation.) The study used 60 alcoholic patients in a Veteran's Administration hospital. The patients received five hours of biofeedback training per week for five weeks. This treatment regimen was supplemented by intensive support programs that encouraged meditation and reflective reverie as problem solving devices. Results from the variety of personality and behavioral tests used to evaluate the effects of these treatments described a number of significant trends. Both personality and emotional profiles showed a reduction in depressive affect, a reduction in the fear of emotional situations, an improvement in impulse control, an increased sensitivity to personal needs and feelings, and a better ability to handle aggressive feelings.

The four clinical studies just discussed have used alpha biofeedback in the treatment of serious emotional or behavioral disorders. In addition to these studies, at least two pilot studies using EEG alpha biofeedback in the treatment of heroin addiction have reported encouraging results. Moreover, I am familiar with the clinical work of two psychiatrists who have used EEG alpha biofeedback with a variety of emotional problems with considerable success.

R. Barnes, for example, describes the successful use of alpha biofeedback with anxiety, with certain psychosomatic problems, such as colitis, and with headaches. In a 1974 report to the journal *Headache*, McKenzie, R. Barnes, and their co-workers report their use of alpha biofeedback in cases of tension headache. When compared to relaxation training, alpha training provided considerably more and longer lasting relief—the average incidence of headache was reduced to approximately 20% of baseline by the fifth week of treatment. In personal communications, the authors also have reported that they found alpha training to be similarly effective with migraine headache.

Such a spectrum of clinical effectiveness for alpha biofeedback is compatible with the majority of research studies suggesting that EEG alpha activity is related to calm states and to relief from anxiety. A review of the literature on this point shows that some 40 reports confirm the relationship between the presence of alpha activity in the EEG and relief from anxiety, as well as the relative absence of alpha in anxiety states. In contrast, only two reports suggest that alpha has little to do with apprehension, arousal, or anxiety; both come from laboratory studies conducted under highly artificial conditions (such as being conducted in total darkness or using electrical shock in alternating 30-second trials with alpha feedback training).

The one study of this type that has been published contains numerous methodological and interpretational errors. The experimental objective of this study was measuring the arousal responses, particularly skin conductance, heart rate, and alpha blocking, which anticipate the forthcoming shock. The results showed that while spontaneous skin conductance and heart rate were accelerated, no significant change occurred in the level of EEG alpha. Because the subjects reported feelings of apprehension during the trials signalling shock while alpha persisted in the EEG, the authors suggest that there must be little relationship between alpha and relief from anxiety. Curiously, alpha content in this study was maintained between 50 percent and 60 percent abundance, regardless of the experimental conditions. This suggests that either the subjects learned to sustain a steady abundance of alpha or that they learned to ignore external distracting stimuli. If the second alternative is correct, then it points to a relationship between alpha and inwardly directed attention, and thus between alpha and decreased perceptual awareness.

One primary report from M.T. Orne and D.A. Paskewitz has been interpreted to mean that alpha biofeedback training is probably ineffective in the treatment of anxiety. However, a critical analysis of their report that appeared in *Science* reveals a number of methodological and interpretational flaws. For example, the experiments were conducted in total darkness without conducting tests to determine whether the reactivity of alpha is similar under light, eyes open conditions and dark, eyes closed conditions. Both T.B. Mulholland and I have argued that eyes open alpha and eyes closed alpha are two quite different species of alpha, exhibiting different characteristics of frequency, amplitude, topographical distribution, phase relationships and reactivity to stimuli.

The crux of the Orne and Paskewitz argument is that alpha training in total darkness resulted in an EEG condition which failed to respond to a noxious stimulus, though many other studies have found that any alerting stimulus, such as the electric shock used in this study, causes a disappearance of alpha from the EEG pattern. Unfortunately, the critics failed to provide evidence that such a response occurs with the eyes closed in total darkness, and to provide evidence that alpha blocking occurs in response to an electric shock in either lighted or eyes open conditions *after* biofeedback training. Moreover, Orne and Paskewitz gave no data on the degree of alpha control during training, on the actual change in alpha abundance, or on a possible relationship between the degree of alpha control and the degree of alpha response to the electric shock. The fact that apparently little, if any, change in alpha abundance occurred during electric shock after biofeedback training in total darkness strongly suggests that either the relationships between alpha activity and visual mechanisms differ radically under different conditions of lighting or that learned control of alpha constitutes a remarkable prevention technique against apprehension and anxiety. Orne and Paskewitz argue that this cannot be the case because they found normal GSR (galvanic skin response) patterns and heart rate responses to the electric shock, and because subjects reported high levels of apprehension during the "jeopardy" trials.

There are several problems with this argument. First, there is little reason to believe that apprehension about electric shocks has much to do with clinical anxiety states. Second, the results clearly show a dramatic dissociation between brain wave patterns and peripheral (or autonomic) responses to noxious stimuli after alpha biofeedback training. It seems incontrovertible that the alerting mechanisms associated with brain wave reactivity—namely alpha blocking and shift to a low voltage, fast frequency EEG pattern— did not occur. So, we can conclude that while the major cortical and limbic systems did not react, the noxious stimulus did evoke activity in the more primitive defense mechanisms which alert the body to action. This suggests that the significance of the stimulus either was no longer appreciated or was related to normally responding brain mechanisms.

The subjects' reports of uneasiness and apprehension while anticipating the electric shock appears to be mostly a component of defensive arousal, a response which psychology explains by theorizing that the sensation of emotion is the cortical appreciation of the body's arousal reactions or that the sensations of emotion at least occur simultaneously with body reactions. The fact that cortical activity failed to respond—while both the body and the feeling state did—in turn suggests three possibilities. Either the cognitive significance of the stimulus was not retained after alpha biofeedback training, or clinical EEGs do not reflect altered states, or the cerebral and autonomic arousal systems are mediated through different CNS processes.

The authors of this study suggest that the research reports of calm and pleasant states in the presence of increased alpha activity might be accidentally describing the results of learning to ignore distracting influences. But, they do not suggest the obvious, that their subjects learned to ignore the apprehensive significance of the noxious stimulus. Learning to ignore distracting influences may result from altering the focus of attention, and many studies have indicated that abundant alpha is an index of internal attention. If the attention is turned inwardly during alpha production, then external stimuli would receive little attention and so would cause little cerebrally recognized apprehension.

There are two reasons for this long discourse on the Orne and Paskewitz paper, aside from its prominence in the scientific literature. First, I want to indicate the complexity of both EEG patterns and EEG biofeedback as they are related to any specific subjective activity. Second, I want to point out the important discrepancies between basic research conditions and those that obtain in clinical applications. Any study done in total darkness fails to consider the fact that our anxieties and apprehensions are triggered chiefly by perceptual input, or by recall evoking the same or similar neural mechanisms used in processing the original perceptions. Thus real apprehension and anxiety tend to occur in lighted conditions where triggering events are abundant, rather than in totally dark environments. On balance, the evidence from both research and clinical studies favors the concepts that EEG alpha is a reliable index of relief from apprehension and anxiety.

When evaluating the results of any alpha study, it should be remembered that alpha is only a single index of EEG events. Both the incidence and specific wave characteristics of alpha are related to other EEG activities happening at the same time. In other words, alpha is only one of many electrical brain events occurring during the observations. Yet, because it is an obvious activity and one that is relatively simple to measure, its role and relationship to subjective phenomena have been over-emphasized, while the role of the remainder of the brain wave pattern has been neglected.

The EEG literature also contains numerous reports indicating relationships between personality traits and specific characteristics of alpha, such as its frequency, amplitude, or topography. For example, slow, regular abundant alpha is found with a passive personality and underachieving, while rapid alpha frequencies occur in neurotics and individuals with high intelligence. Different amplitudes of the overall EEG pattern and of specific EEG components relate to subjective states. For example, a low voltage, fast frequency EEG pattern characterizes anxiety or alertness, while a high voltage, slow frequency EEG pattern tends to occur with states of relaxation and inattention to the external environment. In addition to these relationships between gross measures of the EEG pattern and subjective states, there are many more subtle relationships that pertain to more specific forms of emotional and mental expression. Obviously, considerable care should be taken in making EEG/subjective state correlations.

EEG biofeedback research efforts have tended to concentrate on discrete EEG components and interesting results have been obtained. However, in view of the complexity of the EEG and the host of unknowns it contains, the positive results obtained from working with discrete factors, such as alpha or theta, might suggest that EEG biofeedback training simply indicated a direction for change in EEG pattern. In other words, when we train people to produce more alpha, then the best explanation of the effect we observe may be that we are providing a direction for altering the *total* brain state. The relative percentages of the specific component may change, but this is merely the result of a change in the total activity of the EEG. And since the entire electrical brain pattern is what allows for shifts in awareness, concentration, direction of attention, etc., it seems likely that in EEG biofeedback we are dealing more with the phenomenon of change toward a particular pattern than with change within a specific component. This interpretation offers a more reasonable explanation for the effectiveness of alpha biofeedback in such diverse conditions as ruminative obsession, alcoholism, psychoses, tension headache, and anxiety.

Two other clinical studies tend to support this interpretation. J. Stoyva and colleagues reported a preliminary study on the effectiveness of EEG theta training with insomnia. Of the 12 patients studied, they found theta training resulted in marked improvement for six of them. Three others report faster falling asleep rates after nocturnal awakening; three reported no improvement. In another study using the rhythmic 12 to 16 Hz activity which is frequency-related to sleep spindles, B. Feinstein found that training with this

EEG rhythm produced significant improvement in sleep EEG patterns and in subjective sleep quality.

Further support for the brain wave pattern shift comes from scattered reports on the effectiveness of alpha biofeedback training in the treatment of epilepsy. The use of EEG biofeedback in the treatment of epilepsy may be as complicated as alpha training. There are three major procedures: one using feedback of the 12 to 14 or 12 to 16 Hz rhythm; one teaching the control of alpha or any EEG component; one teaching the suppression of specific seizure wave activity in the EEG.

The 12 to 16 Hz rhythm was first observed in the cat. There M.B. Sterman and colleagues found the rhythm to be associated with relaxation and with the absence of movement. The rhythm was called SMR because of the sensori-motor cortical site where it was recorded. However, research has yet to determine whether SMR is different from the pre-central fast alpha activity called the mu rhythm. Cats trained to produce more of this rhythm were found to be resistant to seizures induced by convulsants. A variety of neurophysiological observations suggested that increasing the production of the SMR could lead to significant neuronal reorganization and so a search for an analogous rhythm in human beings began.

Primarily because of its very low voltage, 12 to 16 Hz rhythm can be observed only by means of electronic filters. Optimal electrode placement is obtained through the use of bipolar leads positioned over the left and right central cortical areas from a point 10 percent off the vertex to a point 30 percent off the vertex, with reference to the total interaural distance. Sterman's feedback devices have employed a variety of signals, such as rows of lights which display increments of production of the SMR rhythm, or a projector showing the sequential steps of completing a picture puzzle.

Biofeedback training of the 12 to 14 Hz rhythm (reported as the filter peak of the 12 to 16 Hz filter) resulted in the emergence of clear trains of this rhythm. The appearance was clearest in the hemisphere rewarded for increased production of the rhythm. The subjective states occurring during this training tended to be relaxation and attention. However, all patients experienced drowsiness which interfered with their performance. Interestingly, the control subjects performed much better than the epileptic patients.

Because of the success of his early attempts, quite a number of epileptic patients have now received treatment via this biofeedback technique in Sterman's laboratory. Though most of these were considered unmanageable by drug treatment, the biofeedback results generally have been excellent—ranging from a significant reduction in seizure activity to complete freedom from seizure and a normalization of EEG patterns.

One other study has reported similar effectiveness with SMR training. This study, however, used simultaneous training to block theta activity. And, two investigators have reported failures in preliminary studies. Patient selection or persistence in training may account for these differences in results, yet one study devoted to confirming Sterman's report that normal subjects can enhance the production of SMR was completely negative.

The reports dealing with the use of alpha biofeedback in the treatment of epilepsy may be more interesting here. Four reports—two from the United States, one from Canada and one from India—have reported that alpha biofeedback dramatically reduces seizure activity in epileptics. At the 1974 BRS meetings, B.J. Kaplan interpreted her positive results as indicating a learned ability to function at a lower level of arousal.

The effectiveness of alpha biofeedback in treating epilepsy supports the interpretation I offered earlier, that EEG biofeedback may be primarily a process of learning to shift brain states in a directed manner. Further support for this concept comes from the work of F. Poirier, a Montreal electroencephalographer and neurologist who specializes in epilepsy and seizure disorders. Poirier reports that patients who choose which brain wave they wish to control make progress equal to those who learn to suppress the epileptic brain wave forms. Both approaches result in considerable success. These results indirectly support Kaplan's contention that the shift in brain wave activity represents a shift in the threshold for arousal. If this interpretation is correct, it poses some problems for current concepts concerning the etiology of epilepsy because it opens up the possibility that some epilepsy, or some components of epilepsy, result from emotional disturbances.

The therapeutic studies described here represent the total reported experience with the clinical use of EEG biofeedback. Research reports exploring many different uses for EEG biofeedback suggest that the near future will bring several new applications. These reports include, for example, the hemispheric synchrony studies reported by Galin, R. Ornstein, and others. Based upon neurophysiologic studies showing that the two hemispheres process different kinds of cognitive information, investigations attempted to determine whether these differences could be detected under laboratory conditions. The ultimate objective here was using biofeedback techniques to alter hemispheric relationships with respect to EEG activity. It was found that the mental processing of information classified as analytic, such as that involved in language or arithmetic tasks, produced a relatively greater suppression of EEG activity in the left hemisphere; mental processing of information classified as intuitive, such as that involved in spatial or music tasks, produced a relatively greater suppression of EEG activity in the right hemisphere. A follow up study found that the primary difference in activity between the two hemispheres occurred in the alpha frequency range.

Another exploratory experiment gave alpha synchrony feedback to subjects during different types of mental activity. Subjects did not see the feedback signal as integral to the experiment, presumably because it was not measured precisely. Subjects were asked to perform two different tasks. One asked them to focus on some activity, like performing mental arithmetic or clenching their fist. During this task the alpha was not synchronized between the hemispheres. The second type of task asked subjects to maintain a stabilized field of awareness by becoming deeply involved in focusing on an object, a mental concept, a perceptual memory, or an image. These circumstances produced maximal alpha synchrony between the hemispheres. The authors concluded that these results show a distinction between the exacting process attending to performance and the apparently effortless experience of focusing upon an internal image.

The numerous potential applications of alpha hemispheric synchrony biofeedback are obvious. First, since the two hemispheres process different kinds of information—handle different kinds of tasks—the manipulation of the electrical relationships between the two hemispheres may alter the relationships between intuitive and analytic processing. This possibility has special applications in certain types of learning disability. Changes in one's ability to communicate also may result from such training, since the nondominant hemisphere appears to be more concerned with subconscious mental activities while the dominant hemisphere seems to focus on the aspects of conscious awareness that may be verbalized.

Another EEG synchrony study points to further clinical applications. In this experiment I trained pairs of subjects to synchronize the occurrence of alpha activity. This learning was done with the eyes open, and subjects learned to produce abundant alpha in complete synchrony with each other. The rationale behind this experiment comes from the fact that when two individuals establish a rapport with each other, their physiologic responses to emotional stimuli occur at the same time and in the same direction.

The degree of synchrony control was tested by asking each trained subject to signal when he thought his partner had alpha activity in his EEG pattern. After training, subjects were approximately 75 percent correct in their predictions. This accuracy was interpreted as evidence of entraining a biological rhythm. The use of the synchronized biofeedback may accelerate the development of empathic states and so facilitate communication between two people. The study now continues using pairs made up of one psychiatrist and one patient in the hope of finding ways to increase the effectivenss of therapeutic relationships. Early results suggest that synchrony is more difficult for the psychiatrist, who, of course, is responsible for analysis of the relationship between himself and the patient.

In summary, let me suggest some appropriate criteria for scientific reports on EEG biofeedback. One important requisite is the reporting of whether or not control of an EEG component or wave was attained. Few investigators test for degree of control, and this poses some difficulty in accepting interpretations. Another difficulty arises from the fact that some studies employ a technique in which brief training periods alternately focus on production and suppression. This technique is not appropriate to the EEG studies since the mechanisms involved are not opposites. Also, the training times are generally insufficient to ensure any kind of true learning. The same holds true for studies which use one brief training session. Learning does not usually occur before the second session, and control does not become precise until the fifth session or later. Because the literature is replete with instrumental and methodological errors, I suggest a discriminating reading of scientific reports and a delay in forming conclusions until confirming studies are reported.

Recognition of Aspects of Consciousness through Association with EEG Alpha Activity Represented by a Light Signal

The reported study is part of a program designed to attempt identification of aspects of consciousness (as mood and feeling states) by means of specific components of EEG activity. The EEG parameters generated by the individual are externalized in the form of visual displays (attributes of colored light.) No external stimuli or reinforcement are used.

In the present experiment subjects were asked to attempt identification of a feeling state which would be successful in keeping a small blue light turned on. The light was operated by the presence of alpha activity in the EEG, and its intensity was proportional to the amplitude of the alpha waves.

Experimental work has been reported for the obverse situation. Attempts to induce "control" of alpha have, until recently, been concerned with conditioning desynchronization of alpha activity (Jasper & Shagass, 1941a, 1941b; Albino & Burnand, 1964). Current investigations being conducted to determine the degree and mode of voluntary control of alpha are of two types: control of short bursts of alpha activity and no-alpha, by means of manipulation of oculomotor configuration and accommodation (Dewan, 1967; Mulholland & Evans, 1966); or by employing brief periods of an auditory "feedback" signal augmented by informing the subject of his progress (Kamiya, 1962; Stoyva & Kamiya, 1968; and Hart, 1968). These studies have not employed feeling state association as the experimental objective.

Method

Subjects

Subjects for the study were recruited from hospital and volunteer personnel and from nearby colleges. Ages ranged from 21 to 60. Twenty-three subjects (10 males) completed 1 practice session only, 14 completed 2 practice sessions, and 10 completed 4 sessions (6 males). Two additional subjects each completed 1 practice session but neither contained quantifiable alpha activity in the EEG during the entire practice session and were not included in the results. Intervals between successive practice sessions ranged from 7 to 90 days.

Procedure

The procedure for each practice session was the same; after a relaxation period of 10-15 min, EEG activity was recorded for periods of 5 min each with the subject's eyes closed. The practice session followed and consisted of experimental periods of 10 min, during which a light circuit was operating, alternating with 3 min rest periods during which the light circuit was not operating. There was a total of 5 experimental and 5 rest periods. The eyes were kept open for all experimental and rest periods.

Instructions consisted of informing the subject that portions of his thinking and feeling activity were mirrored by brain wave activity, and that as the brain wave activity was recorded, a part of it was converted to a form that could turn on a blue light. The subjects were requested to attempt to identify or isolate, nonverbally, a feeling state which would keep the blue light turned on, and were told that the intensity of the light represented the strength of the activity representing the feeling state which operated the light. The subjects were told that during rest periods the light circuit would not be operating but they were to keep their eyes open, and that they would be informed of the beginning and end of each rest and experimental period.

The subject's environment was a small room with moderate ambient lighting and isolated from the recording room. A speaker and microphone were mounted on the subject's chair and were always open for communication with the recording room. The blue lamp was approximately 1/2 inch in diameter, and was placed at the small end of a cone encased in a square styrofoam box (5 x 5 x 5 in.), which was covered by heavy tracing paper and contained a magnifying lens in the front of it. This unit was placed 5 in. from a large (3 x 2 ft.) diffusion screen placed 3-1/2 ft. in front of the subject. The diffused light occupied an area approximately 6 in. in diameter in the middle of the diffusion screen.

Instrumentation

EEGs were recorded bipolarly from temporo-parietal, parieto-occipital and occipital sites of the right hemisphere. Eye movements were also recorded continuously using disc electrodes supraorbitally and at the external canthus of one eye. Activity from the parieto-occipital placement was used routinely for the feedback signal and for analysis. The EEG signal was recorded on and amplified by 1 channel of a Grass Model 6 EEG. The amplified output was fed through a 7-15 Hz active band pass filter, the output of which was again amplified by the EEG machine to produce a sufficient level to drive an RC filter circuit which produced a smooth output voltage proportional to the envelope of the alpha voltage. The time constant of the RC filter was set to require 2.5 alpha waves of at least 15 μV for activation. The smoothed voltage was then amplified by a special double Darlington power amplifier circuit which drove the 6 volt blue lamp bulb in the subject's room.

A photoresistive cell located adjacent to the lamp monitored the lamp activity and brightness. The photocell circuit produced a de voltage proportional to the brightness of the lamp. To provide a graphic record of the monitored output it was necessary to gate the signal with a 10 Hz pulse signal from a Tektronix pulse generator. The gated output was displayed on one channel of the EEG machine, and was also fed to the input of the amplitude discriminator accessory unit of the C.A.T. 400, triggered by each of the gate pulses, and these pulses were automatically counted by a sweep counter.

Scoring

Each 10 pulse counts represented 1 sec of lamp-on time. Samples for abundance of alpha activity present in the EEG were therefore derived from the counts since the lamp was on only when alpha activity was present. The total amount of time that alpha activity was present was determined for the total duration of each rest and of each experimental period, and was expressed as percentage of the time that alpha activity was present in the EEG.

Frequency and amplitude values of alpha activity were measured directly from the written EEG records. Average values for each rest and experimental period were obtained from measurements made for the last 10 sec of each min throughout the entire practice session.

Immediately after each practice session each subject completed, in writing, a questionnaire of 3 questions: (1) what did you experience during the practice session?, (2) did you use any special technique to control the light, and if so, can you describe it?, and (3) what was your concept of time during the practice session? No assistance was given to the subject for answering the questions and all comments about the experiment were confined to generalities. Answers to the questions evidenced many similarities, therefore it was most convenient and relatively simple to establish categories of answers. This was done by 3 judges who had no knowledge of the EEG changes. The 3 judges then independently sorted the answers to each question into 1 of 3 categories (see below, Table 3).

All data, i.e., 3 leads of EEG, filter output, eye movements, and lighting monitor signal, were simultaneously recorded on analog tape as well as on the EEG machine.

The criterion used to evaluate the subject's ability to reproduce and/or sustain feeling activity was abundance, measured as percent, of alpha activity in the EEG.

Results[1]

Abundance of Alpha Activity

Intra-Session Changes. In order to simplify expression of the results, the percentages of alpha activity present during the first 2 of the 5 experimental periods were averaged to give a value representing abundance during the initial part of the practice session (E_i), and the percentages for the last 2 experimental trials were averaged for abundance during the final part of the practice session (E_f).[2] Values for the rest periods were treated similarly (R_i and R_f). These were obtained for each subject and then were averaged across subjects.

Results (Table 1) are given for all subjects who participated only in practice sessions I and II, and are compared to results obtained for 10 subjects who completed 4 practice sessions. There were no significant differences between average values for the 2 sizes of samples for the 2 practice sesssions; therefore, the remainder of

---

[1]Since many approaches to the reported study are possible, briefly summarized results of several preliminary experiments are noted here which may clarify aspects of the present report but which do not warrant detailed reporting. (1) Continuous 90 min experimental trials (10 subjects) without rest periods yielded no consistent changes in alpha activity, and after approximately 60 min, 6 subjects showed change to low frequency, large amplitude activity (dominant frequency 3 to 8 Hz) resembling a drowsy pattern, but in 4 subjects no increase in alpha content was observed and 2 of these subjects actually developed predominantly desynchronized EEGs. (2) A reinforcement technique was employed in an experimental design using 5 min experimental trials alternating with 5 min rest periods (10 subjects). A count of alpha waves was given to the subject at the end of each 1 or 2 min. Either interval of reinforcement resulted in EEG activation (desynchronization) following announcement of the count such that no consistent change in alpha abundance occurred. (3) The same experiment without reinforcement (5 min experimental and rest periods) yielded data similar to that being reported.

[2]A detailed analysis of the first and last minutes of each experimental or rest period revealed that the differences between these 2 periods were consistently evident as early and as late as the first and last minutes of each succeeding experimental-rest-experimental sequence. Presentation of these data was omitted in favor of the more comprehensive analysis over long periods, but the phenomenon is noted to indicate timing of the changes in alpha activity.

TABLE 1

Means for abundance of alpha activity during 4 sessions of practicing voluntary control of alpha

Practice Session	N	Mean No. days from preceding session	Mean % alpha activity present in EEG		Period	Mean % alpha activity present in EEG		Ratios of Means[1]		
			E.C.[2] %	E.O.[2] %		Initial (i) %	Final (f) %	R_f/R_i	E_f/E_i	E_f/R_f
I	23	—	54	15	Rest (R)	14	17	1.22		
					Exptl. (E)	25	36		1.46*	2.10*
II	14	14	60	27	Rest	24	35	1.46		
					Exptl.	33	44		1.33**	1.25**
I	10	—	55	14	Rest	14	14	1.00		
					Exptl.	26	33		1.27***	2.36*
II	10	12	56	27	Rest	21	24	1.14		
					Exptl.	31	41		1.32*	1.71*
III	10	28	64	30	Rest	32	45	1.40		
					Exptl.	28	57		2.04*	1.26*
IV	10	16	59	32	Rest	30	40	1.33		
					Exptl.	32	53		1.65	1.32**

[1]Significances of the differences expressed by the ratios were determined by the Wilcoxon signed-ranks test.

[2]E.C., eyes closed; E.O., eyes open.

*Significant at $p < .01$ (2-tailed test).

**Significant at $p < .02$.

***Significant at $p < .05$.

results are given only for those subjects who completed 4 practice sessions.

The amount of alpha activity increased continuously in each succeeding experimental trial in each of the 4 practice sessions and always exceeded that occurring during the successive rest periods. By the last 20 min of the first practice session, 50% of the subjects had shown at least a two-fold increase in abundance of alpha activity as compared to the interspersed rest periods. The average increase of alpha activity from the initial to the final portion of each practice session is summarized by the ratio E_f/E_i in Table 1.

The largest increment of enhanced alpha activity occurred during the first practice session with successively smaller increments occurring during practice sessions II and III. Within any one practice session there were no significant changes in the amount of alpha activity during the 4 rest periods, although the average always increased in the first 3 intrasession rest periods followed either by no further change or by a small decrease in the last rest period. The average change from initial rest to final rest period is indicated by the ratio R_f/R_i in Table 1.

The effect of practicing identification of subjective feelings for each practice session was expressed by comparing the averaged percentages of alpha activity present in the EEG during the final experimental and final rest periods, i.e., by the ratio (E_f/R_f (Table 1). The difference indicated by this ratio was statistically significant for each practice session at $p < .01$. In the following discussions the term *EEG discrimination* will be used to indicate specifically a large difference between the abundance of alpha activity during experimental trials and that during rest periods for the final portion of a practice session.

Intra-Session Changes. The amount of alpha activity increased successively from practice sessions I through III during all experimental conditions (Table 1). There were no significant differences among any of the parameters between sessions III and IV, although the comparison of averages indicated that a small decrement occurred in each of the parameters. The discussion of this section is therefore limited to inter-session changes from I to III.

The Wilcoxon signed-ranks test was used to determine the levels of significant differences in alpha abundance across practice sessions for the 4 experimental conditions (Table 2). Both the E_i and E_f averages were significantly different between practice sessions I and II and session III. An over-all increase in alpha content over sessions was shown by the R_i average for the first 3 practice sessions. Similarly, the difference between the R_i average as of one practice session was significantly different from the R_f average of the immediately preceding session. In contrast, the initial experimental (E_i) average always showed a slight decrement from the E_f

TABLE 2

Levels of significance for inter-session changes in conditions of alpha activity possibly related to change in the experimental variable (E_f)

Condition Examined for Abundance of Alpha Activity	Probability Levels of Significance for Differences Between Practice Sessions Determined by the Wilcoxon Signed-Ranks Test				
	Practice Session Numbers				
	I to II	II to III	III to IV	I to III	I to IV
Eyes open	NS	NS	NS	NS	NS
Eyes closed	NS	NS	NS	NS	NS
R_i*	NS	NS	NS	.05	NS
E_i	NS	.01	NS	.02	.05
R_f	NS	NS	NS	NS	.05
E_f	NS	.01	NS	.01	.01
R_i/prev. R_f	NS	.05	NS	—	—
E_f/ R_f	NS	NS	NS	NS	NS

*E, experimental, and R, rest periods; i, initial, and f, final portions of practice session

average of the preceding session. Although the E_f/R_f ratios always indicated a significant difference within practice sessions, they did not differ significantly between successive sessions.

The abundance of alpha activity during both the eyes open and eyes closed control periods also increased successively from one practice session to the next, but this change was not statistically significant. *Differences* between alpha content during controls with the eyes closed and the E_f averages, however, decreased successively over the practice sessions.

Verification of Voluntary Control. Three subjects, all with high E_f/R_f ratios, were available for further study. They were asked to signal (via a switch in a circuit to a light indicator in the recording room) when they recognized the feeling state selected to operate the light, and thus alpha activity would occur in the EEG. Trials of 10 each were conducted when the blue light circuit was and was not operating. Subjects' scores for accuracy were 100%, 90%, and

75%. Recorded eye movements showed absence of eye movement activity.

Types of Responses. Four types of responses could be identified: increased alpha activity to high levels (>50%), or significantly increased alpha activity but reaching a maximum at relatively low levels of abundance (20-30%). Either type exhibited either retention of the new level of alpha activity during rest periods, or showed a marked and significant reduction of abundance during the rest periods.

Subjective Data

There was a surprising and striking similarity among the voluntary written responses of all subjects to the first 2 questions (see Method). Answers to the questions were relatively constant over the 4 practice sessions but were best defined for practice session III; therefore comparisons between subjective data and enhanced alpha activity were made for this session only.

The ranked values for absolute abundance of alpha activity (E_f) and for E_f/R_f ratios were paired with appropriate categories from each subject's subjective responses.

Despite the small sample size, results (Table 3) suggest that subjects who lost awareness of all environmental factors except the light, or who felt "dissolved into the environment" tended to have higher levels of alpha abundance (low ranks), whereas subjects who remained aware of the environment were those with the lowest levels of alpha activity in the EEG. When compared to the E_f/R_f ratio, indicating discrimination, no obvious relationship to type of awareness appeared, although the 2 highest discrimination scores occurred for those subjects who expressed the feeling of floating or dissolving into the environment.

Half of the subjects either felt relaxed by the experience or attempted actively to relax, but use of this technique to maintain a selected subjective state was *not* necessarily accompanied by the higher levels of alpha abundance for the subject group. Subjects who concentrated on imagery tended to be ranked high with respect to absolute abundance of alpha (E_f) but ranked low with respect to discrimination (E_f/R_f).

TABLE 3

*Relationship between degree of absolute enhancement of
alpha activity (A), degree of specificity of enhancement of alpha to the experimental
situation (B), and subjective response*

Question	Categories of Answers to Questions Session III[1]	Associated ranks for Session III[2]	
		A Absolute Abundance	B E_f/R_f Ratio (Discrimination)
1 (subjective experience)	a) remained aware of environment	8, 9, 10	3, 6, 9
	b) lost all awareness except of light signal	1, 2, 5, 7	5, 7, 8, 10
	c) drifted, floated	3, 4, 6	1, 2, 4
2 (technique used)	a) felt relaxed by experience	6, 10	4, 9
	b) actively attempted to relax	3, 8, 9	2, 3, 6
	c) concentrated on mental imagery	1, 2, 4, 5, 7	1, 5, 7, 8, 10
3 (concept of time)	a) felt experience was a long time	3, 4, 9, 10	6, 7, 9, 10
	b) felt experience was a short time	1, 6, 7	1, 4, 8
	c) no awareness of time	2, 5, 8	2, 3, 5

[1]Representative excerpts of exact words of the subjects.
[2]Where the largest value = 1 and the smallest = 10.

There was a wide distribution of levels of abundance of alpha activity as related to the type of appreciation of time; however, the majority of higher levels of discrimination were paired with reports of either no awareness of time of the session or to the feeling that the elapsed time was short.

Discussion

It is apparent that when individuals can perceive information about their own physiology (see also Levene, Engel, & Pearson, 1968; Stern & Kaplan, 1967; and Delse & Feather, 1968) they can experience interacting with specific components of their own physiology and then develop voluntary control over these functions.

The fact that reports of the subjective aspects of the practice sessions were uniform suggests that the feeling states associated with alpha activity were of a quite general nature. This was also indicated by a relative predominance of high absolute levels of alpha activity over EEG responses showing discrimination between experimental and rest periods. Moreover, effective enhancement of alpha activity was more regularly associated with pleasant thoughts or feelings.

Several features of technique, experimental design, and results are emphasized to indicate that the process investigated is unique. First, *no* stimuli or reinforcement external to the subject-instrument feedback circuit were employed. Moreover, no stimulus or response *within* the feedback circuit can be isolated as such, i.e., any identifiable "relay" of the circuit can be considered as both a response *and* a stimulus.

Second, the time to optimize operation of the feedback circuit is very short, and is more suggestive of an insight function than a conditioning function. Events leading to successful feedback operation might be visualized as follows. In the reported experiments, only 2 conditions can exist: circuit complete (operating) or circuit not complete (not operating). Initially the circuit is completed randomly, but with practice the subject isolates characteristics of the circuit indicator (light). This constitutes his perceptual data. At the same time, the subject's *task* is to identify feeling state activity related to the on-ness of the light, and this supplies data about feeling states.

The subject therefore has 2 streams of information, previously unrelated, which must now be related in order to complete or operate the feedback circuit. Successful operation of the feedback circuit occurs only when the 2 sets of information have been sufficiently organized or structured such that verification of the relatedness between them can occur. The light operates only when some shift in a physiologic activity (to produce alpha) occurs. Results indicate that this is at least a 2 stage process: pre-conscious and volitional. The concept that a preconscious mobilization of biologic activity occurs which generates the appropriate signal (alpha) to operate the light successfully is supported by the evidence that subjects markedly increased their alpha activity both (a) before the EEG response became differentiated between experimental and rest periods and (b) before they formed a concept about how to keep the light on. Results of a study documenting feeling state-EEG associations using alpha, beta, and theta frequency possibilities simultaneously confirmed this latter point (Brown, 1969).

Third, no decrement in ability to produce alpha occurred even when the interval between practice sessions was quite long (see Table 1).

Finally, voluntary control implies an awareness of a biologic activity which is successful in keeping the light on. When awareness of the relationship between a feeling state—biologic activity—light signal occurs, the external portion of a circuit becomes unnecessary. At this point the process becomes internalized, and voluntary control can be exerted exclusively with respect to the subconscious activity; the physiologic parameters becoming a consequence of the phenomenon rather than components necessary for optimal functioning of the feedback circuit.

Neural mechanisms effecting enhancement of alpha activity are unknown (see discussions by Kreitman & Shaw, 1965; Brown, 1966). Kreitman and Shaw offered two possible explanations: the relative dominance of processes inhibiting activation or a rebound effect following activation of the EEG. Either could adequately explain the present result, particularly since EEG activation during rest periods tended to accompany high levels of voluntary control during experimental periods (process of active inhibition of activation).

On the other hand, activated EEG patterns might be expected as a result of the attention required while the subject was trying to perceive meaningful attributes of the light signal. The fact that drowsy EEG patterns did not occur and alpha actually increased during the experimental trials demonstrates that the type or quality of the attention employed (to internal activity) functions in the absence of EEG activation.

Both the techniques and the results of the study reported here differ considerably from the 2 types of studies recently reported which relate to control of alpha activity. The experiments of Mulholland and Evans (1966) and Dewan (1967) were concerned chiefly with the relationship between oculomotor activity and the EEG activation cycle. In the present experiments voluntary control of alpha activity occurred in the absence of eye movements.

Kamiya (1962) and Hart (1968) employed a tone signal for feedback and found that the majority of subjects significantly increased alpha activity within 10 practice sessions. The relatively slow progress of the subjects, as compared to the rapid and marked change shown by our subjects in the first practice session, might be attributed to inherent cyclic and latency characteristics of alpha activity. It also seems likely that the reinforcement used amounted to an arousal signal, and exerted an inhibitory effect on alpha production, as our preliminary experiment indicated.

An additional difference is that our experiments were conducted entirely with the eyes open whereas the 2 types of studies cited above were conducted with the subjects' eyes closed.

References

Albino, R., & Burnand, G. Conditioning of the alpha rhythm in man. *Journal of Experimental Psychology*, 1964, *67*, 539-544.

Brown, B.B. Specificity of EEG photic flicker responses to color as related to visual imagery ability. *Psychophysiology*, 1966, *2*, 197-207.

Brown, B. B. Recognition of associations between aspects of consciousness and EEG frequencies using colored lights operated by specific EEG components. *Psychophysiology*, 1969, *5*, 574. (Abstract)

Delse, F. C., & Feather, B. W. The effect of augmented sensory feedback on the control of salivation. *Psychophysiology*, 1968, *5*, 15-21.

Dewan, E. M. Occipital alpha rhythm, eye position and lens accommodation. *Nature*, 1967, *214*, 975-977.

Hart, J. T. Autocontrol of EEG alpha. *Psychophysiology*, 1968, *4*, 506 (Abstract)

Jasper, H., & Shagass, C. Conditioning the occipital alpha rhythm in man. *Journal of Experimental Psychology*, 1941, *28*, 373-388. (a)

Jasper, H., & Shagass, C. Conscious time judgments related to conditioned time intervals and voluntary control of the alpha rhythm. *Journal of Experimental Psychology*, 1941, *28*, 503-508. (b)

Kamiya, J. Conditioned discrimination of the EEG alpha rhythm in humans. Paper presented at the meeting of Western Psychological Association, 1962.

Kreitman, N., & Shaw, J. C. Experimental enhancement of alpha activity. *Electroencephalography & Clinical Neurophysiology,* 1965, *18,* 147–155.

Levene, H. I., Engel, B. T., & Pearson, J. A. Differential operant conditioning of heart rate. *Psychosomatic Medicine,* 1968, *30,* 837–845.

Mulholland, T., & Evans, C. R. Oculomotor function and the alpha activation cycle. *Nature,* 1966, *211,* 1278–1279.

Stern, R. M., & Kaplan, B. E. Galvanic skin response: Voluntary control and externalization. *Journal of Psychosomatic Research,* 1967, *10,* 349–353.

Stoyva, J., & Kamiya, J. Electrophysiological studies of dreaming as the prototype of a new strategy of consciousness. *Psychological Review,* 1968, *75,* 192–205.

Identifying One's Own Brain Waves: A Trial Run to the Subconscious

In Western civilization the comfort of the self has been troubled for many centuries by a bewildering polarity cultivated by those who claim wisdom and the ability to offer us advice. We have been torn between the gurus of science and the gurus of the soul. Both have persuaded us to believe their wisdom separately. In the experiential life the division between physical and mental being is not clearly defined. We may now be on the threshold of experiencing an inner wisdom that may heal the breach between science and the spirit.

Recognition of Different Waves in One's Own EEG

Not all work with brain wave biofeedback need be exclusively learning how to control different brain components. With biofeedback also came the opportunity to explore whether sensations and feelings and thoughts actually did have some relationship to the mysterious brain waves. The only information we biological scientists had about the correspondence between brain waves and mental activity had been learned most indirectly. Before biofeedback no scientist pulled out certain brain waves, held them up for view, and asked, "Here's alpha, how do you feel now?," or "Here's beta, what sensations do you have, what mood?"

I took advantage of my early entry into biofeedback, and of the laboratory of special instruments built for me, to see whether it might be possible for human beings to identify various brain waves of their own directly, and in terms of their feeling states or thoughts. It seemed to be a straightforward task: let people watch their brain waves and let them describe their sensations or thoughts that seemed to go along with each different kind of wave. Now that part actually is easy; what complicates the problem is making sure that any correlation between subjective activity and EEG components is so accurate and reliable that other scientists will believe you. Scientific procedure is very rigid and that complicated my project enormously.

Nonetheless, the experiment was fairly simple, although the instrumentation was considerably more complex than in the alpha work. The same EEG activity was used: that recorded from the parieto-occipital area (from midway on one side of the skull to a midpoint on the back of the skull). This time the EEG activity was fed into three filters simultaneously, so that alpha, theta and beta frequencies were simultaneously being filtered throughout the experiment. The beta activity in this case was specifically a frequency between 13 and 28 cycles per second; the theta was 4 to 7 cycles per second.

These three EEG frequencies were used to operate lights of three different colors. Again, electronic circuitry was used so that recognizable trains of waves of adequate amplitude were required to be present in the EEG in order to activate the lights, and once on, the lights remained on for the duration of the rhythmic burst. As in the alpha experiments, the intensity of the lights was proportional to the amplitude of each of the signals.

The experimental situation was similar to that of the previous one with a few exceptions. The only instructions to the subjects were to keep their eyes open but this time they were asked to try to identify feeling states which they felt were related to any particular color of light. Red, green and blue lights were used and were paired, in random fashion, to one of the three EEG frequencies, alpha, beta or theta. The subjects, all completely naïve about brain waves, were told that the lights were being operated by their own brain waves, and that it was believed that these mirrored feeling states in some way.

In this first experiment using three colored lights to feed back information about the three most commonly occurring brain wave frequencies, the subjects were simply allowed to watch these light indicators of their own brain wave activity for about an hour. Nothing else. Afterward they were asked to write a description about what feelings or moods or thoughts states they related to the different light colors.

The experimental subjects of course knew that the different colored lights represented different brain waves, but they didn't know *which* colors represented *which* waves. Moreover, for some subjects theta waves were displayed via a green light, others were displayed by a red light, etc. Because the brain waves of different people were being fed back by different colored lights, in order to prove that particular subjective feelings related to specific brain waves, all of the different people would have to discriminate and describe similar feelings or thoughts for each brain wave regardless of the color of light used to display those waves. This was a large request to make of a bunch of normal human beings who didn't know an alpha wave from a hole in the wall and cared little about brain waves anyway.

After the entire study had been completed, my assistants and I had before us a stack of written experiences about the biofeedback experience. As we analyzed the descriptions, we had to decode the color the subjects were talking about as to whether the color had represented alpha, beta or theta brain wave activity. We were surprised to find that regardless of the color of light used to indicate any particular brain wave, the descriptions of subjective feelings and thoughts tended to be quite similar for any particular brain wave.

In describing alpha waves, regardless of light color used, the experimental subjects tended to use quite similar phrases. fourteen of twenty-six said that the light gave them feelngs of "pleasantness," or "well-being," or "pleasure," "tranquility," or "relaxation"; and there were seven subjects who described alpha as giving them "an increased awareness of thoughts and feelings." Two reported that during alpha they were reviewing personal experiences and only three had nothing to say about alpha. On the other hand, in describing their feelings about beta activity (again regardless of light color used), there was general agreement among subjects, nine reporting "worry," "anger," "fear," or "frustration" while five reported "tension, alertness, excitement." One said it gave a feeling of hunger and surprise, while eight subjects had no particular sensations. There were, interestingly, three people who said that the beta lights gave them feelings of contentment, warmth, and love.

The feelings and thoughts described for theta activity were quite different and strongly reflected the influence of more thought than feeling activity. These descriptions were chiefly "memory of problems," "uncertainty," "problem solving," "future planning," "switching thoughts," "solving mechanical or financial problems," and "daydreaming." There were ten such reports, but there were also thirteen subjects who could recall no specific feelings or thoughts that related to the colored light that had represented theta.

One can easily see a conceptual unity among the descriptions noted above for each different brain wave. For alpha, for example, most descriptions implied an awareness of body feeling, while other descriptions implied less attention to body and somewhat more attention to an experience of consciousness. By contrast, the descriptions of feelings produced by the lights representing beta, i.e., fast brain wave activity, appear to be directed toward unpleasant feelings and thoughts. Those few indicating a pleasant experience cannot be explained at this time.

When theta activity was observed, the agreement between brain wave and a subjective state was less clearcut. Nearly one-third of the subjects related theta waves to feelings and thoughts suggesting the thinking process, while the majority were not able to identify any relationship between the theta light and subjective experience. Even though success in identifying theta was just 30 percent, we had expected much less success than this because very little theta activity is normally present in brain waves during quiet, awake states. We know, moreover, that two almost diametrically opposed feeling states can relate to theta: drowsiness and serious thinking.

With so little theta present in the EEG, trying to identify a feeling or thought state for theta might be quite a confusing task.

The first experiment with the three-light system demonstrated the obvious ability of human beings to identify specific components of their own brain waves. If indeed brain cell activity does reflect our mental functioning, then the result is not surprising. It simply hadn't been done before.

Toward Identifying the Subconscious

A second experiment using the three-light system was much trickier. The objective was to attempt to identify any subconscious influences or elements that might be used in the ultimate process of learning to control different specific brain wave components. This presented a difficult task since, after all, we have not yet been able to identify any physical monitors of mental activity let alone subconscious activity. It seemed to me that the experiment might be valuable since a great deal of our thinking and feeling activity takes place when we are not consciously aware of it. Although the mission seemed impossible, my own subconscious momentum to experiment took over and I didn't argue with it.

I was using colors to feed back to three dominant brain wave activities, and this meant that a person's feeling about a particular color might influence or dominate over the feeling he could develop about a certain brain wave. This problem was solved in part by the procedure used in the first experiment—that is, changing the pairing between color and brain wave component in a scientific, random fashion such that one subject might see his alpha activity as a red light, beta as a blue light etc., while another subject might see *his* alpha as a green light, his theta as a red light and so on. This arrangement meant that the consensus of a large group of subjects about the feelings and thoughts they related to a specific brain wave component would not be influenced by the feelings they had about the specific colors.

But this, of course, raised another problem. In some circumstances the feelings and thoughts they related to a specific color might be exactly the same as those feelings and thoughts related to a specific brain wave. Now this is the sort of thing which complicates science and the reason that biological scientists are so often hung up on the concept of control. How could I control for this contingency—that the feelings and subjective response to colors might be the same as that to certain brain waves?

The answer is surprisingly simple. First, let me restate the problem. If we want to know what feelings relate to a specific brain wave, and the brain wave is represented by a color and yet the feelings that relate to brain waves are unknown, then what items in this formula do we already know? Simple: We know how we feel about colors. If we feel that calmness is a blue word and if we should find that calmness is also an alpha brain wave word, then shouldn't we get some indication of this if we represent alpha waves by some color *other* than blue?

So the first procedure was to survey average people about their feelings about colors. First I prepared a list of words which are descriptive of feelings, thoughts, moods and emotional responses, such as happy, distracted, tired, excited etc.—150 of them—and printed these on cards. Then I prepared four colored boxes: red, blue, green and white. Nearly a hundred people were surveyed for how they related feelings and colors. They were asked to sort all of the cards with descriptor words into the colored boxes as fast as they could. The faster the sort the more possible might be the representation of subconscious influence. The white box was for descriptor words for which they had no color-feeling relationship. After the survey I had quite specific data about how most people felt abut colors and was in a position to go ahead with the experiments.

Relationships between feelings and color are very strong. In general most people feel that angry is a red word, frustrated is a red word, or that peace is a blue word. Naturally people differ in some respects, but the majority agree about many relationships between feelings and color.

The biofeedback experiments were exactly as they had been for the people who wrote descriptions about how they felt watching three colors of lights signaling their brain wave activity. The subjects sat watching the colors displaying their different brain wave components for an hour. Immediately after the biofeedback experience they were asked to sort the descriptor cards to the same red, blue, green and white boxes, just as the people had done for the control data who didn't have the biofeedback experience.

The results were quite astonishing. An analysis of the card sorts to color by the subjects who had just had an hour of watching their brain waves represented by colored lights revealed totally different relationships between feelings and colors from people who hadn't had the experience. No longer did all of the subjects feel that angry was a red word. If their *beta* brain wave activity had been displayed by a green or blue light, they now tended to relate the concept of angry either to green or to blue. Or, for example, they related the words peace or calm to red or green instead of to blue—provided their alpha activity had been represented by a red or a green light.

What this meant was that the hour's experience of watching their own brain waves had not only reorganized their usual feelings about color, but had given them an awareness of those feelings that were specifically related to certain brain waves. The way in which different brain wave patterns, containing different amounts of alpha, beta and theta relate to subjective feeling states is illustrated in Figure 1. There is an interesting point that I will discuss later concerning the question of whether feelings about color modify brain waves or whether brain waves are first affected by colors and then feelings developed later.

In any event, we had now found that as human beings we could identify different elements of our own brain wave activity if we were given a suitable indicator of that activity. But the exciting aspect was that this identification appeared to take place largely on a sub- or pre-conscious level before becoming consciously aware of the association between brain wave and feeling or thought. The reason for deducing this was that the associations between feelings and brain waves overrode normal, deeply entrenched associations between feelings and color. There was other evidence for the conclusion because the cards describing feeling and thought had been sorted as quickly as possible (150 into four colored boxes) and virtually no contradictory synonyms of varieties of mental activity

Figure 1. A graphic representation of the relationship between subjective feeling states and the relative amounts of alpha, theta and beta found in the EEG as obtained in the experiment described. The descriptors of subjective feeling shown for each point around the circle are those selected by a statistically significant number of people with similar quantities of the three major EEG frequencies. The midpoint of each segment of the circle indicates that the EEG contained relatively large amounts of the frequencies noted, while at either side of the midpoints the respective frequencies occurred in smaller quantities.

It should be noted that although the results represented here have been replicated in other studies, they are by no means intended as conclusive.

were found when the card sorts were analyzed. Moreover, the feeling states that the card sort data indicated as being perceived were *not* found to relate to any change in the *amount* of the brain waves with which they were associated, as has been found for conscious feeling states induced by experimental procedures. There were some marginally significant changes in the *amplitudes* of alpha, beta and theta in subjects who agreed about related subjective feelings but they pertained more to rather general mood and feeling states. All in all, the two experiments indicated that we had the prospect of having actual physical and/or physiological indicators of aspects of pre-conscious activity.

A Concept of How It Happened

The unique characteristics of the experimental situation were that they allowed the subjects to interact with aspects of their own physiologic functioning in the *absence* of either directed or pre-formed concepts. (In psychologic experiments, particularly conditioning experiments, the experimenter or the experimental situation directs the behavior and programs the number and type of behavioral responses allowed.)

The colored light monitors of the individual's own EEG activity (i.e., of the three major frequency components of the EEG) provided continuing perceptual information about the electrical activity of the brain's functioning. We all know how difficult it is to sustain a single thought, or even to sustain a single feeling state. Conscious awareness, particularly conscious awareness of directed thought and feeling activity, is continuously varying both in degree and direction and in content and range of perspective. Brain electrical activity is also a continuously varying activity and is a reflection of the continuously varying dimensions of mental or subjective states. If a relationship between subjective and brain electrical states is even approximately true, than the *temporal* characteristics of both elements of the relationship constitute the most important aspects requisite for establishing associations between these two variables. That is, the feeling state should coincide with the presence of the particular brain wave in the EEG. The more frequently this occurs the more opportunity there is to identify a particular feeling or thought to a particular brain wave.

If the information from the alpha learning experiment and from the experiment demonstrating ability to identify subjective relationships to specific brain wave components are combined, one can conjecture on the role of mental activity in the biofeedback control system. Because the subject is allowed to interact with aspects of his own physiologic functioning without either direction or conceptual information, the experiment cannot proceed unless the subject generates the specific physiologic activity (such as alpha or beta) which will activate the machine. Activation of the biofeedback display occurs only when a specific brain wave is present in the total brain wave pattern. It thus monitors precisely the selection of the appropriate brain wave, and this selection evolves from mental effort by the individual. During the first minutes of such a biofeedback experience, the feedback monitor (the light signal) operates strictly according to the probability for occurrence of the desired brain wave in any individual. When the desired brain wave occurs, the monitor faithfully signals its presence. At this point in time the subject has no prior knowledge of how that particular brain wave relates to his subjective feelings. He does, however, have a store of memory information by which he can relate the subjective feeling state present to previous similar subjective feelings when the light signal is on.

Thus, during the biofeedback training, the subject is receiving two different sets of information about himself. He is receiving perceptual data via the light monitor which tells him many characteristics about the brain wave in question: its rate of occurrence, how long it is present at any one time, how fast it appears and disappears, etc. At the same time the subject is undergoing the experience of interacting with specific aspects of his own physiologic substrates of emotion and with past experience. He has been instructed to try to identify his feelings and thoughts at those specific moments when the monitor light signals the presence of a certain type of brain wave. The second set of information available during the feedback experience is thus experiential data which, either because of the instructions to the subject or because of the nature of the feedback system, generate subjective exploratory activity. The individual searches his memories of experiences first in order to identify his present state and then to verify whether the subjective state is similar each time the monitor signals the selected brain wave.

During the biofeedback learning experience the subject thus has two streams of information available for subsequent integration: the perceptual data and the experiential data. As the training continues, the repeated availability of these data provides the opportunity to verify the characteristics of their relationship over time. The individual continues to perceive the experience of interacting with specific aspects of his own internal experience and is able to verify the relationships of the experience such that subsequently he is able to form a concept about it.

The verification of perception of the experience implies that some organization of data has occurred. In this case we are talking about the association, organization, or structuring between two sets of internally originating information, one set of which has been externalized and has been perceived as part of the external environment.

My conception of the phenomenon is represented by the diagram in Figure 2. First, unelicited random brain wave activity produces a response of the instrument. Now, because of instructions to the subject, two quite different processes begin: the subject becomes aware of certain patterns, or repetitions of patterns, of the lights coming on and staying on, which is, or represents, the perceptual data; and at the same time he is undergoing the normal ranging of subjective thought and feeling, which provides internal orienting and memory experiential data. At some point he begins to generate appropriate signals, i.e., signals that are appropriate to the instrument's ability to respond. It is at this time that the gap between the two streams of information has narrowed sufficiently

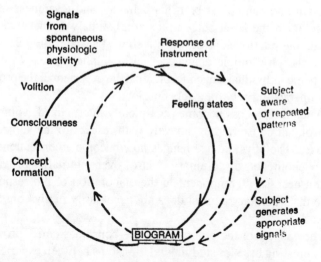

Figure 2.   Diagram of possible events occurring during biofeedback learning.

for some type of associational structuring to occur between the two types of information.

In order to refer conveniently to this point, I have proposed the term biogram. Although the term has been used elsewhere to describe a relationship between an individual and his biologic environment, it is a useful temporary term in biofeedback because it relates semantically to the word engram, denoting a memory trace. Some kind of memory record has to have been made of the association between the perceptual and experiential data, and this memory record is the result of internal biologically originating experience. It is essentially now a subconscious representation of an experience, hence the name biogram.

Since the two previously unrelated sets of information have at this point now been brought into a relationship with each other and have some type of structure, verification of the experience becomes possible. During verification the mind becomes aware of the organized perceptual and memory data, and continued verification of the biogram leads to conscious recognition and finally conscious voluntary control of the now internalized relationship between mind and body activities. With this information in consciousness, the subject can voluntarily retrieve components of the biogram and can adjust both his behavior and awareness of his behavior. In the latter stage no external signals are necessary to sustain the relationships between feeling states and EEG activity. Since the physiologic changes, such as alpha, appear to occur before the individual can conceptualize the experience, the process may operate entirely on a subconscious level.

When the process becomes completely internalized, voluntary control can be exerted exclusively with respect to the subjective activity. The physiologic changes now become a consequence of the phenomenon of voluntary control over internal states rather than a necessary component in the elaboration of the response. Note that voluntary control does not necessarily imply conscious control.

The concept of the biogram as a pre-conscious entity provides an interesting base for studying relationships between experiential and perceptual data. Variations in the degree of organization of the biogram may account for differences in ability to conceptualize the relationships between mind and body activities.

Color, Brain Waves, and Feeling States

In addition to the information which related feeling states to brain waves obtained during the three-light, three-brain-wave experiment, substantial information was accumulated on the relationships between color and brain waves.

These fascinating interrelationships are easily illustrated using Venn logic diagrams as in Figure 3. There are three primary variables of color, feeling state, and brain wave represented by the circles. Each variable relates to each other in varying, unknown degrees. If we say, as we have found, that some colors relate to some brain waves and that the *same* colors relate to some feeling

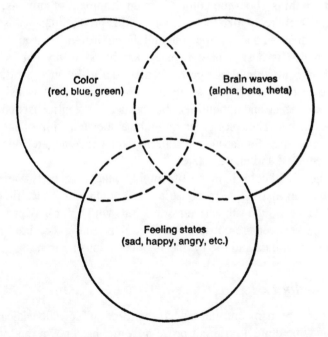

Figure 3. Venn diagrams to illustrate the syllogism that if some colors relate to some brain waves and the same colors relate to some feeling states, then some feeling states relate to some brain waves.

states, then we can conclude that some feeling states relate to some brain waves, and this is exactly what the experiments revealed.

The overlap between the associations between color and feeling states and the associations between color and brain waves, shown by the overlapping circles, suggests the possibility that subjective activity relating to colors may originate from the same underlying neuronal processes as do the brain waves. We will probably never know exactly which came first, the relationship between brain waves and feeling states or the relationship between brain waves and color, but we can make a number of conjectures about it. I tend to favor the concept that the brain cell, neuronal, response to color came first, since in my studies and those of others the brain electrical response to red is one of alerting or arousal, whereas the brain electrical response to blue is one of relaxation. This happens in animals as well as man.

If we think about the color of the environment of animals, we immediately recognize that the color red is predominantly associated with blood that is spilled out into the environment during a kill and which is a sign of danger. When blood is present in the environment, animals are probably alerted. On the other hand, the presence of a perfect blue sky in the environment might well signal a time of peace and tranquillity, the absence of potential harm from the elements. The color green might be associated with foliage for hiding or grass for eating and stalking, and hence be intermediate between rest and alerted states.

One role of color in man's life might be that of an early warning system, an instinctive response to be modulated by specific circumstances. Such subjective associations with color may provide a bridge between pre-conscious associations among perceptual and experiential data and the synthesis of conscious awareness.

Biofeedback Is a Different Way of Learning

There are many unusual aspects that suggest biofeedback learning may be quite a different process from other known modes of learning. In general, learning theories must rely on evidence for internal, thinking processes by the ways in which they can be modified and measured by elements in the external environment. Because of these restrictions and the hesitancy to accept various ways of reporting subjective feelings and awareness as reliable, there is little known about the details of higher levels of mental activity that provide man with this extraordinary ability for learning much more than stereotyped behaviors. Man and many animals are capable of symbolic thinking and behavior; they have the facility to integrate, spontaneously, wide varieties of learning and information in their reasoning processes to evolve solutions and insights.

The unique characteristics of the biofeedback learning process classify it as an awareness or cognitive process. It is, ultimately, awareness of the relationship between subjective activity and the feedback signals operated by physiologic activity which is the behavior that is learned. The majority of biofeedback experiments, whether learning to control heart rate or single muscle units or skin electrical resistance or brain waves, all indicate that complex learning takes place on a pre- or subconscious level, and that this learning is orderly, symbolic, specific and highly discriminating.

The information that the brain uses during biofeedback is an abstraction, a man-made symbol to represent continuously varying body activity. The abstraction contains the synthesis of physiologic, psychologic, conceptual and mechanical information. Moreover, the control to be learned is in itself a complex process of abstraction of the relevant information from both the feedback symbol and elements of past experience as integrated with the information content of the surrounding environment, including attending human attitudes.

In learning to control a selected item of mind-body behavior, the item must first be identified. But the feedback signal is *not* the item to be learned; it serves only to label the item, or response, once it has occurred. It remains neutral and meaningless until some intelligence of the central nervous system identifies it as an abstract label for a complex, dynamic event having certain *temporally* reproducible characteristics. The feedback signal initially becomes activated only accidentally according to the probability for the behavioral event to occur, and only later is its activation intentional. It accrues significance only as a result of continued activity and as the identification of its meaning becomes successful. To add to the complexity, confirmation of the identification of the feedback symbol appears not to be complete until the signal is discontinued by termination of the behavioral event that activates it. In this sense, the behavioral event to be learned is its own detector and its own selector.

The learning in biofeedback evolves from an internal circular process. The behavior to be learned can be learned only by self-analysis of the symbols of its occurrence. In other modes of learning, behavior is either directed or judged by events external to the system, i.e., both the behavior to be learned and the criteria for learning it are indicated and judged externally. In biofeedback, successful learning depends completely upon internal effort by the learner. He must generate both his behavior to be learned and his rewards for learning it. He must even select the qualities of his own rewards. He must select the significant values of his own behavior in order to generate a signal that is his own reward for successful learning, and it must be appropriate or learning does not occur. The circuits of the feedback system are either closed and operating or they are not closed and not operating.

In the feedback system the entire learning process is internally directed. The subjective attributes and influences of motivation, reward, error, anticipation, preparation, expectancy and drive all stem from verification and awareness of an internal event. In biofeedback, learning is entirely dependent upon the consequences of the behavior while it is being learned. The consequences are organized into a flexible scheme that systematically uses the information provided by itself to learn about itself.

One of the major deficiencies of all learning concepts is the failure to define the ways in which information during learning is handled. It is customary to evaluate learning in terms of the information provided, but rarely, if ever, is learning evaluated according to the ways in which the information to be learned is used. This largely accounts for the failure of conventionally used intelligence and performance tests to reveal the rather remarkable efficiency of many minority groups for using the limited amount of information that has been provided to them. Further analysis of biofeedback learning offers a new approach to evaluating differences in *ways* of using information rather than *how much* information is used in learning.

Exploration of EEG Alpha Biofeedback As a Technique to Enhance Rapport

While the establishment of good rapport between therapist and patient is a key element of successful therapy, it is often slow to be achieved and difficult to consolidate and characterize. Past literature indicates a tendency for coincidence of certain physiologic reactions during the development of rapport. It was decided to explore whether learned physiologic correspondence between two individuals might enhance the possibility for rapport and provide physiologic indices when a sympathetic relationship occurred. Preliminary experiments only are being reported. Experiments were conducted in which EEG alpha feedback was provided as a light signal to pairs of subjects only when alpha occurred simultaneously in both subjects. Limits for simultaneity were 3.0, 1.0 and 0.5 seconds. Subjects were informed of the conditions for the feedback signal. Training sessions consisted of 2 periods of 20 minutes each, separated by a 5 minute rest period. During the periods of feedback of the synchronized alpha signals, subject pairs showed a significant increase in the amount of time that alpha occurred simultaneously. Effect of the feedback training was tested by asking each subject to signal when he believed alpha to be occurring in his partner. These tests revealed a striking accuracy in some subjects, usually only one of each pair, to predict the presence of alpha in their partners, but occasionally subjects were completely unable to predict. In those pairs in which one of the pair demonstrated ability to predict the occurrence of EEG alpha in his partner, both members of the pair reported similarities in subjective activities.

Rationale

I am going to describe some preliminary experiments in which the synchronized physiologic feedback of two individuals is used to accelerate the developmental and strengthen rapport or empathic relationships.

The rationale for these experiments is very straightforward. First, with few exceptions the physiologic reactivity to emotional stimuli across populations is strikingly similar. Psychophysiologic responses of the central nervous system, the autonomic nervous system, and even the skeletal muscle system to emotional stimuli are roughly similar in direction of change and often in magnitude. With this kind of commonality of physiologic reactivity, it might be expected that states of empathy or rapport would be characterized by a rough synchronicity of physiologic activity in the individuals involved.

Moreover, since the internal qualifiers of emotional physiologic responses derive from relationships between internal physiologic feedback systems and brain neuronal activity or brain states, it might also be projected that the greater the identity of physiologic response patterns between individuals in an empathic relationship, the greater might be the similarity of their subjective activities.

Fortunately, this is not mere conjecture. Since the mid-50's, reports have appeared in the literature of psychosomatic medicine and psychophysiology that document the similarities of physiologic responses to emotional stimuli and emotional situations during rapport states. In general, the greater the rapport, or the longer the association, the greater are the similarities.

One of the earliest studies was that of Coleman, Greenblatt, and Soloman in 1958, reporting on the physiologic and psychiatric data of 44 interviews for a patient-therapist relationship. Synchronous recording of EKG, respiration, and finger temperature revealed an overall correspondence in physiologic reactivity between the therapist and patient, disrupted only by occasions of preoccupation of the therapist by other thoughts or severe disturbance engendered by the patient's productions. These investigators concluded that a "physiologic relationship" had developed between patient and therapist.

One of the more exciting physiologic studies of empathy was reported by Chessick and Bassan in 1968. Two psychiatrists interviewed 6 patients each for 2 sessions and 1 patient each for 12 sessions. A large variety of indices for scoring empathy was used, and these evaluations were employed as the control variable along the time scale of the interview sessions. Remarkably, there were extraordinary coincidences of heart rate, EKG R wave amplitude, finger temperature, blood pressure, and skin resistance at specific moments of empathy.

Other studies have approached the physiologic basis of empathy on a systematic basis, as, for example, during intentional understanding and intentional non-understanding of a patient's reaction to emotional stimuli. Or as in another example, having psychiatric residents match psychologic indices of empathy for 2 subjects and then comparing the physiologic responses, which were found to show remarkable correspondence.

There are also relevant studies in which vicarious experience has been measured physiologically and studies showing that vicarious conditioning occurs relatively easily. Finally, a report in the EEG journal in 1971 has described evidence that the alpha activity of one person appeared to modify the alpha of other people!!

In the light of this background, the role of biofeedback is obvious. Since the physiologic indices are sensitive monitors of even unconscious responses *not* recognized in conscious awareness and hence not communicable by ordinary means, the potential contribution of biofeedback to the development of empathic states is considerable.

Method

The ultimate objective of our experiments is to devise feedback techniques to accelerate the development of empathic relationships and to reinforce and strengthen the relationship.

For our initial experiments we chose alpha brain waves as the monitor and the parameter with which to observe response synchrony. The reason for choosing alpha activity was that it additionally allows for estimates of brain state, which in turn permits inferences about the consciousness continuum. It was also felt that an "alpha state," while specific in its general physiologic attributes, provided a broad, general subjective state of well known characteristics.

The initial experiments were carried out as follows:

Ten pairs of subjects were used. Half of these reported a strong empathic relationship between the individual pairs; half were strangers to each other. Instrumentation was arranged such that each member of the pair received an alpha feedback signal only when alpha activity was present simultaneously in both members of the pair. The limits for simultaneity were, for different levels of training, within 3, then 1, then one-half second. The difficulty of the criteria for simultaneity was increased as training progressed. EEG recordings from similar electrode placements were obtained for each subject along with recording of eye movement activity.

The synchronized feedback sessions were generally two 20-minute sessions, broken by a 5-minute rest period. The subjects were told about the requirements for a feedback signal. The feedback signal was a blue light that increased in intensity with the amplitude of the alpha signal. All sessions were preceded by a 15-minute period during which each subject experimented with producing alpha activity, and in these pre-training periods, each was provided with his own alpha feedback signal. Subjects could see each other.

The test for successful training was for each subject to detect ("guess") when the other subject of the pair had alpha in his EEG pattern. During the tests, no feedback signals were present, and each subject was provided with a switch which activated a marker signal on the EEG recordings.

As a control for the test for "guessing" when alpha was present in the other person's EEG, similar guessing was done before the pairs received synchronized alpha feedback.

There are numerous problems in experiments of this type, and these make presentation of meaningful values of significance difficult.

Results

One of the control problems is the progressive development of alpha as a result of adaptation and diminishing tension during the experiment. While we can provide values indicating the degree of spontaneous synchrony prior to synchronized alpha feedback training, such control values are less important than control values obtained in pairs of subjects *not* receiving the synchronized feedback. This I confess we have not yet done; however, the results of the effect of synchronized alpha feedback training showing marked improvement in *both* the production of more alpha individually and in relative synchrony, plus the results of the tests to detect the presence of alpha in the other of the pair, are presumptive evidence that a learning to produce alpha synchronously did occur in subject pairs.

The incidence of pre-training synchronous alpha—eyes open condition—was roughly 15 percent and averaged more than 60 percent following training, i.e., within 1 second of each other. The control "guessing rate" was approximately 10 percent correct, going to better than 50 percent following training.

In some cases the bursts of alpha appear to become more discrete as subject pairs become more and more synchronous with each other. In other pairs the duration of alpha bursts increased during the synchrony learning. The rate of learning to produce alpha in synchrony was compared between those pairs who claimed marked rapport with each other and those pairs who were strangers to each other. Using the index of correct guessing for presence of alpha in the other of the pair, essentially no differences between the groups were found.

The rather remarkable ability for the subjects to detect the presence of a specific brain electrical activity in another person after synchrony training is difficult to explain unless one resorts to an explanation involving the two factors of awareness and biological rhythms. Since some biofeedback research indicates that the ability to produce alpha activity at will is a function of awareness of a subjectively characterized feeling state, the present experiments suggest that the synchronized feedback signal has essentially "entrained" both the subjective state and its accompanying EEG parameter, i.e., alpha, to a temporal rhythm peculiar to the two individuals involved. In other words, the synchronized signal acted not only as a feedback signal for the presence of alpha in *each* individual, it also imposed the criterion that the alpha could appear only at specific intervals, and these intervals were dependent upon the occurrence of alpha activity in the second person.

We became interested in determining whether or not a biological rhythm had indeed been entrained in the subject pairs. To check this possibility, we separated the subjects, putting each in a separate room after first establishing they had demonstrated a high level of correct guessing of alpha in partners. We then asked the subjects to repeat the test of guessing the presence of alpha in their partner's EEG. Results showed that the guessing rate was almost the same as if the partners were in the same room.

In view of previously published reports which have demonstrated the tendency for various physiologic parameters such as GSR, heart rate, blood pressure, etc. to change in a specific temporal relationship during empathic relationships between therapist and patient, the present results tend to support the concept that during rapport or empathy, a variable biological rhythm may be established, in which the cyclic period of the physiologic change is contingent upon reinforcement by one of the pair.

Since rapport and empathy are naturally occurring states and can be characterized by relative simultaneity of physiologic reactivity, then the entrainment of these states via synchronized feedback signals appears to be an effective catalyst. We are currently studying the effectiveness of the technique in pairs of psychiatrists and patients, and to date, results appear promising.

Learned Control Of EEG Theta Activity

One of the difficulties in attempting to induce learned control of EEG theta activity is the relative rarity of EEG theta under normal experimental conditions. In the first of a series of experiments designed to clarify factors involved in theta wave biofeedback, a heterogeneous subject population was divided into 4 groups to evaluate techniques believed to affect the process of learned control of EEG components. All subjects were given an explanation of the experimental situation along with instructions to attempt to identify and relate mental events to the feedback signal. Subjects were also asked to try to define subjective states that were associated with the feedback light. Some subjects also received a short series of tests designed to elicit theta (imagery, problem solving, closure, orienting, etc.). The 4 subject groups received varying degrees of added information about the feedback process and/or augmented feedback. After psychological testing and control recordings, subjects were given two 20 minute theta training sessions separated by a five minute rest period. EEG data was analyzed for relative abundance, frequency, amplitude and topographic distribution of major EEG components, and then correlated with findings of the psychological tests, subjective reports and tests to elicit theta. Results indicate that increasing theta production depends upon one or more of the following factors: a predisposing EEG pattern consisting of below average alpha content and a greater variety and irregularity of EEG components, the availability of cognitively useful information about the task and an ability for imagery. (Supported in part by Grant MH 19849-01)

This study involves the first year of a two year project designed to define various characteristics of EEG theta activity such as abundance, amplitude and frequency in terms of various specific feeling or behavioral states which relate to theta activity such as orienting, recall, dreams, imagery, drowsiness, etc. Virtually nothing is known about the relationship between various characteristics or types of theta and the various behavioral states that are accompanied by theta activity in the EEG pattern. For example, it may be found that slow theta frequencies relate to drowsy states while faster frequencies in the theta range may relate to orienting or adaptation.

Methods were as follows.

Eighteen male and 11 female volunteers from the local community were recorded for conventional EEG's bilaterally at temporo-parietal, parieto-occipital and occipital sites. Because of the possible relationship between eye movements and EEG activity reported in some people, eye movements were monitored in all experiments.

After an initial session for control recording with eyes closed and eyes open, subjects received at least 4 feedback sessions of two 20 minute theta feedback periods separated by a five minute rest period. Some subjects also received a short series of perception-recognition tests designed to elicit theta by creating situations requiring imagery, problem solving, closure, orienting, etc.

All subjects were instructed that a portion of their thinking and feeling activity was being mirrored via a column of six small digital lights that monitored both the presence and amplitude of the theta activity. The subjects were asked to uncover the mental events successful in turning on and maintaining the display and to try to define the subjective states when the feedback occurred. Information given to the subjects regarding this specific task as well as the general process of biofeedback was maximized and included, for example, verbal encouragement by the experimenter. Thresholds were determined and adjusted according to the amount of theta present in the individual's EEG.

It is interesting to note an accident which occurred during one of the first experiments. The green plastic cover of the display slipped down, allowing the top light to show as white. Subjects immediately thought this was a great display, suggesting that it reminded them of the "test your strength" attraction at a carnival. You may remember that this game required you to hit the weighted spring with a sledge hammer in order to ring the bell at the top. The top light represented the bell or ultimate goal for the subject and so this display was used throughout the experiments.

The subject was seated in a comfortable chair in a small room with moderate ambient lighting and was isolated from the recording room except for continuous communication via an intercom system. The display was placed behind a diffusion screen approximately 3 1/2 feet in front of the subject.

Criteria for success in producing and controlling theta activity included percent change in theta abundance and amplitude measures as the training progressed. Upon completion of all feedback sessions, further tests were administered to evaluate the subject's ability to recognize the presence of theta in his EEG. For the first test, there was no feedback and the subject was asked to signal via a switch when he felt that theta was present in the EEG pattern. The second test required the subject to guess which of three feedback lights activated by filtered alpha, beta and theta activity was the one being driven by his theta activity. The lights were randomized with respect to color and EEG pairing during three successive trials.

Analysis of the data yielded the following results.

First, analysis of EEG patterns indicates that all subjects who were able to learn to control their theta had relatively similar EEGs. Specifically, this predisposing EEG pattern consists of relatively little alpha activity, faster alpha-beta activity and a wide variety of EEG components. On the other hand, non theta learners exhibited dominant alpha, slower alpha-beta activity, slow and mixed background EEGs with virtually no fast activity or theta and generally high amplitude EEG signals.

Data for the tables and figures below were taken from 14 good theta subjects receiving EEG theta feedback for 4 training sessions. All statistical evaluations were done using the Wilcoxin matched-pairs signed-ranks test.

Table 1 compares intra-session changes of mean theta abundance. As the values indicate, theta activity increases in each session except the control session. Changes between initial and final values during session number III were the only intra-session changes that were statistically significant.

TABLE 1

Means of abundance of theta activity during 1 control and 4 sessions of practicing voluntary control of theta. N = 14

Practice Session	Mean % Theta Activity Present in the EEG		Level of Significance of Intra-Session Changes in Theta Abundance
	Initial %	Final %	
Control	12.9	9.8	NS
I	4.7	8.1	NS
II	6.6	8.9	NS
III	9.1	15.3	.005
IV	16.6	21.9	NS

[1] Significances were determined by the Wilcoxin matched-pairs signed-ranks test.

Table 2 indicates differences in abundance and amplitude of theta for different training sessions. The greatest changes were observed between sessions III and IV, Control and IV, I and III and I and IV. The timing of these changes suggests that significant learned increase of theta production proceeds rather slowly.

Table 3 is more clearly illustrated in the following figure.

Figures 1, 2, and 3 demonstrate the trends which occurred over all sessions for mean values of theta abundance, amplitude and frequency. In figure 1, theta abundance decreases slightly from

TABLE 2

Levels of significance of inter-session changes in theta characteristics during 1 control and 4 sessions of practicing voluntary control of theta.

Theta Characteristics Examined	Practice Session Number								
	C-1	I-II	II-III	III-IV	C-II	C-III	C-IV	I-III	I-IV
Abundance	NS	NS	NS	.025	NS	NS	.025	.01	.005
Amplitude	NS	NS	NS	NS	NS	NS	.025	NS	.005

[1] Significances were determined by the Wilcoxin matched-pairs signed-ranks test.

TABLE 3

Mean values for theta characteristics for 1 control and 4 sessions of practicing voluntary control of theta.

Theta Characteristics Examined	Session Number				
	C	1	2	3	4
Abundance (%)	8.9	6.2	9.7	13.1	20.8
Amplitude (μV)	19.3	10.1	18.2	20.5	32.9
Frequency (Hz)	6.1	5.1	6.0	6.0	5.0

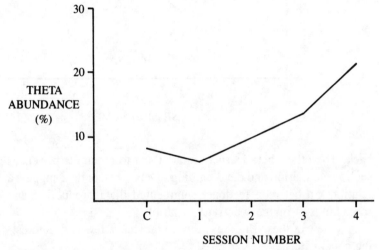

Figure 1.

control session to feedback session 1, after which it increases steadily. Figure 2 shows a similar pattern for theta amplitude. Theta frequency did not vary significantly as can be seen in figure 3.

To continue with results, theta recognition tests showed that subjects averaged 57% correct when predicting the presence of theta in the EEG. 68% of the guesses of which of three lights represented theta were correct.

With regard to subjective reports, it was found that half of the theta producers indicated enhanced imagery during theta biofeed-

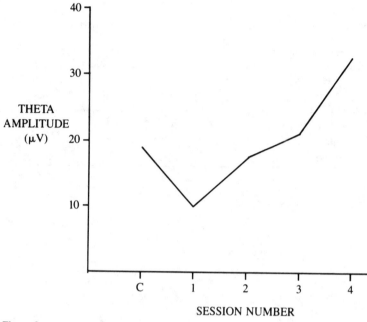

Figure 2.

back. The other theta learners relate theta to mental experiences such as meditation and daydreaming. Thus, present data suggest a relationship between feedback augmented theta production and some kinds of imagery activity or ability.

A review of these findings seem to indicate a few very interesting conclusions.

First, a particular type of EEG pattern seems to be more conducive to production of theta activity. Approximately half of the subjects exhibited this pattern which consisted mainly of a diversified EEG with little alpha activity. The other subjects had a dominant alpha pattern and were not able to learn to produce theta. These results may imply some sort of constitutional, personality or other factor which is associated with or causing the particular EEG pattern. It may also be possible that the subjects who were unable to learn to produce theta could not do so because of the lack of any significant theta in the baseline EEG to serve as a reference. Continuing investigations designed to elicit theta via perception-

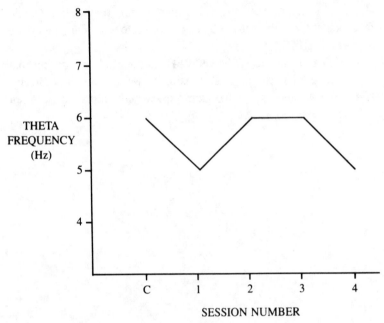

Figure 3.

recognition tests may eventually give these people a reference from which they can begin to increase their theta activity.

Second, on the average, theta learners require at least 4 feedback sessions to produce significant increases in theta abundance. Theta amplitude also tends to increase, but theta frequency does not appear to change to any significant degree.

Third, although only preliminary analysis has been completed on comparisons of elicited theta versus theta appearing during eyes open biofeedback, one particular conclusion seems clear. It appears that faster theta is more often found during intense vivid visual imagery while slower theta relates more to periods of drowsiness. Also, it should be noted that data analysis can be complicated by such differences. For example, unreported unsolicited periods of drowsiness could lead to misinterpretation of frequency data as it relates to normal eyes open theta production

Fourth, as theta training progresses subjects seem to gain an awareness of when theta is present in the EEG. This is probably the result of a set of subjective feelings which they relate to the presence of the light. One subjective correlate which appears to be important is imagery.

And last but not least, I would like to conclude by stating that there is no evidence of any relationship between EEG theta activity and eye movements, as has sometimes been reported between alpha and eye movements.

Part II
Mind and Dis-ease.
The Origins of Stress Ills

A Conceptual Analysis of "The Stress of Life" Phenomenon

An analysis of "the stress of life" is presented in which widely accepted observations about its causes and effects are used syllogistically to deduce the nature of the dynamic processes involved in converting extrinsic psychosocial factors into emotional and physical distress. Four categories of "the stress life" are qualified. The examination defines specific characteristics for the common observation that "stress" is simply the circumstances affecting people in the course of a lifetime that require adjustments of attitudes, feelings, and behavior to achieve states of well-being. Stress management procedures are examined for appropriateness for the different phases of the stress process, emphasizing the generally prolonged incubation period before clinical symptoms occur that suggests modifications of stress management procedures toward controlling the process before debilitating consequences develop.

This paper represents an effort to examine a number of widely held but unconnected notions about "the stress of life" and link them together into a unifying, internally consistent hypothesis accounting for the apparent diversity of causative factors and capable of justifying the dissimilar procedures used for the relief and prevention of its effects. The analysis was undertaken first, because "the stress of life" has not yet been characterized precisely as a cause of human distress independently from direct or imminent physical stress; second, because current concepts of stress mechanisms do not present a congruent account of the processes by which the stress of life results in psychophysiological distress; and third, because stress management procedures have not been systematized around a comprehensive concept of the mechanisms involved in the development of both stress and stress reactions.[1]

The paper illustrates two departures from traditional scientific conjecture about natural phenomena in employing infrequently used processes for examining biopsychological events and also a seldom used method of reporting. It is speculative from the standpoint that it employs syllogistically based reasoning; however, all premises derive from substantially confirmed observations, thus the analysis is analogous to data analysis although not dealing with discrete units of data.

Except for occasional explanatory footnotes, the reporting style adopted duplicates the analytic process as the most parsimonious means for moving through a lengthy analysis, avoiding repetition of established evidence, and allowing the focus of the analysis to be directed toward new deductions and inferences of clarifying previously ambiguous or incompletely formulated concepts.

I. Objectives of the analysis.

1. To develop a system of generic, unifying, defining characteristics of "the stress of life" phenomenon by the systematic organization of consensual observations about its manifestations, responses to treatment, and generally postulated causes and mechanisms.
2. To develop tenable concepts about the dynamics of the stress process from consensual observations and set relationships.
3. To develop principles of stress management appropriate to the dynamics of the stress process derived from the analysis.

[1] When Hans Selye articulated the phrase "the stress of life", it was a disarmingly seminal observation expressing the feelings most people have about untoward circumstances of life. At the same time, the observation crystallized the recognition that life is, indeed, stressful. The importance of recognizing "the stress of life" as a true cause of psychical and physical distress (the diseases of society) lies in also recognizing the prolonged incubation period between cause and effect when overt signs and symptoms are few but when "the stress of life" can nonetheless undermine the energy of body and psyche. While "the stress of life" can cause disturbing emotional and physical consequences, examination of the process suggests they can be largely avoided by directing attention to the events of the process.

4. To develop a consistent terminology definable in terms of the generic characteristics of "the stress of life".

II. *Background of prevailing concepts.*

1. Semantics.

The terms stress, "the stress of life", stress states, stress reactions, and distress are used ambiguously. Lexicographers define stress as a pressure or force causing a response within the system stressed, while in psychology and medicine, stress is frequently used to mean both the influences causing emotional and physiological reactions and the reactions themselves. In the popular idiom, "the stress of life" often refers to external psychosocial influences. Selye defined stress as, "the nonspecific response of the body to any demands made upon it."[2] The nonspecific response is often interpreted as a stress state and distress as the consequence of the response.

2. Principal data bases used in concept development.

    a) Clinical data indicating relationships between varieties of psychosocial influences and the incidence and severity of diagnosed emotional and physical disorders.

    b) Psychophysiological data from correlations of autonomic, endocrine, immune, or subjective responses with experimental, emotional, or physical stressors.

3. Current concepts.

    a) Prevailing clinical concepts.

       1) Psychodynamic theory ascribes stress reactions to psychosocial circumstances causing unconscious conflicts in turn producing inappropriate defenses.

       2) Cognitive theory postulates unspecified cognitive mediators between stressful events and the individual's reactions.

       3) Psychosomatic concepts presume a relationship between psychosocial factors and psychosomatic disorders.

[2] H. Selye. The Stress of Life, McGraw-Hill, 1956.

b) Prevailing psychophysiological concepts of stress mechanisms implicate activation of aspects of the neurophysiological, endocrine, and immune systems.

c) Summary of prevailing opinion about "the stress of life".

1) Psychosocial influences can trigger stress and stress reactions.

2) When human beings perceive stress, some respond by subjective and physical tensions and by homeostatic imbalances.

3) The implementing mechanisms of stress responses involve general and selective activation of the neurophysiologic, autonomic, endocrine, and immune systems.

4. Unresolved issues.

a) Identification of the characteristics of psychosocial influences that define them as "stressors".

b) The nature of the mechanisms that process information contained in psychosocial circumstances and lead to the perception of a conflict.

c) The nature of the mechanisms involved in selecting and elaborating psychological and physiological reactions to perceived "stress of life".

d) The nature of the mechanisms by which psychosocial influences activate physiological systems.

e) Causes of individual susceptibility and system specificity of stress reactions.

f) A comprehensive, unifying concept accounting for the diverse effects of "the stress of life".

III. Analysis of the phenomenon.

A. Stress systems.

1. Set designation for stress phenomena.

A general definition for the stress phenomenon is: stress is an external force or pressure causing a change within a system.

2. Table 1 compares a series of selected, related stress systems according to the characteristics of the essential elements required to satisfy the general definition for the class of stress and according to the characteristics of the primary response and resistance mechanisms.

3. Conclusions from Table 1.
   Two subsets of the stress phenomenon, physical and non-physical (ideational) can be identified from the nature of the elements qualifying the stress set:
   a) Direct or imminent physical force evoking physical responses and resistance.
   b) Nonphysical external forces evoking nonphysical responses and resistance (that may in turn evoke physical responses and resistance).

4. Inferences.
   a) As life systems increase in complexity, the nature of the external force shifts from directly exerted physical force to, first, predominantly imminent, directly exerted external force, and second, predominantly imminent nonphysical forces.
   b) As life systems increase in complexity, the characteristics of responses and resistance to external force change from immediate, direct responses and resistance first to time-delayed, coordinated physical responses and resistance, and second to nonphysical, ideational responses and resistance.
   c) The most complex systems possess capabilities to respond to and resist both physical and nonphysical external forces.

5. Implications.
   a) Physical reactions and resistance to nonphysical external force violate the internal correspondance among elements comprising the stress phenomenon (i.e., primary activation of physical implementing and resisting mechanisms (arousal, alarm) to nonphysical stress is inappropriate and nonadaptive).

TABLE 1

Operational classification of stress systems
(where stress is an external force causing a change within a system)

System	External force	Response	Response mechanisms	Resisting mechanisms
Inorganic	physical (pressure, heat, cold)	strain (change in shape, structure)	molecules/elements	opposite force
Primitive life forms	physical	change in shape, structure, location, direction	ion exchange reflexes	inclusion, secretions, regeneration
Higher animals Primitive man	physical: threats to physical well being; threats to group	local & general arousal; fight-or-flight; aggregation	interacting neural networks; specialized organs; fostering systems	coordinated neural & hormonal systems; primitive control of external force
Socialized man	predominantly nonphysical threats to social well being; intellectual pressure	primarily intellectual, emotional, perceptual; change of consciousness. Secondary physical arousal	integrative brain functions; language; imagery; thought; logic	exploring resources & alternatives; securing relevant information; awareness; social coping; understanding

b) Since nonphysical, external stress forces, nonphysical response and resisting mechanisms are the elements implied in the stress and stress reactions of socialized man, then both the qualities of the stress forces and the mechanisms of response and resistance can be identified in a way that is congruent with the general phenomenon of the stress.

B. Characteristics of nonphysical stress forces.

1. External forces.

   a) Table 2 classified kinds of nonphysical "stress of life" circumstances observed to affect socialized man.

   Information sources are: (1) established correlations between life events and subsequent illness; (2) the kinds of social situations and relationships generally reported to be related to stress reactions; and (3) the kinds of psychological reactions reported to be involved in stress states.

   b) Four subclasses of "the stress of life" phenomenon can be identified, each subclass differing from the others by qualitative differences in characteristics of the external nonphysical forces.

2. Distinguishing characteristics of "the stress of life" subclasses.

   a) Table 3 summarizes some general observations about "the stress of life" in terms of 4 categories. Characteristics common to all "stress of life" forces can be deduced as:

   1) not directly affecting the organism.
   2) not intrinsically stressful.
   3) they involve the integration of events occurring through social time and space.

   b) From Tables 2 and 3, the essential elements of "the stress of life" can be deduced to involve:

   1) human relationships.[3]

---

[3] Human relationships include not only relationships between individuals and groups of individuals but also "people-surrogates" such as the IRS, insurance company, welfare agencies, and all organized groups created and operated by human beings.

TABLE 2

Categories of "the stress of life" (nonphysical stress)

Category	Examples	Major distinguishing features
1. Customary, anticipated life events	marriage, divorce, beginning or ending school, changing residence, children leaving home—any major change in life pattern or life style*	events anticipated by most people events determined in part by decision (capacity to influence consequences) usually single, spaced, unrelated events accumulate stress symptoms only when events accumulate
2. Unexpected life events	unexpected death of a loved one, sudden failure, sudden loss of job, major accidents, sudden loss of home, learning of terminal illness, being victim of serious crime—any major life event occurring suddenly and unexpectedly*	stress symptoms usually sudden and severe events cannot be influenced by individual usually nonaccumulating single events stress usually not chronic
3. Progressive, accumulating situational events	job stress, family problems, love and sex problems, school stress, competition—and continuously recurring problems in life's activities	events centered on human relationships stress source from many dissimilar situations (depends upon many events in social time and space) events concern values, attitudes, beliefs, perceptions, and communications situation control depends on interaction dynamics stress symptoms usually develop slowly
4. Personal trait stress	low self-esteem, insecurity, lack of confidence, fear of failure, guilt feelings, poor decision making, poor communications—any personal trait that creates social problems	stress events related to personality traits events center on single theme stress source pervades all time and space dimensions a perceived failure to influence situations chronic stress symptoms

*Other examples can be found in the "Holmes and Rahe" list of life events in the report by Thomas J. Holmes and M. Masuda, Life change and illness susceptibility. In *Stressful Life Events*, Eds: Barbara Dohrenwend and Bruce Dohrenwend, John Wiley & Sons, 1974.

TABLE 3

Distinguishing characteristics of "the stress of life" categories

Characteristics	Anticipated stress	Unexpected stress	Accumulating situational stress	Personal trait stress
Time-space dimensions	unrelated, spaced, single events	single events	recurring, related events	through all time & personal space
Feelings/emotions	mild to moderate	marked	fluctuating, accumulating	continuous, low grade
Reaction time course	gradual	sudden	gradual	continuous
Symptoms appear	late in process	immediately	late in process	continuously present
Focus of attention	on coping	on loss	on uncertainty	on defects
Expectations*	predictable; reality-oriented	none or vague	modest; variable & intermittent; some fantasy	pessimistic
Perceptions*	accurate; transient	focussed on event	depend upon interpretational set	negatively skewed
Problem solving*	customary mode	"automatic", slow	depends upon situational information directed toward situational control	poor, inhibited
Social adjustment required for relief	conventional, to situations	to rebuilding life, compensating, psychological rehabilitation	to social interactions	personality development

*Elements of "the stress of life" process outlined in Section IV, implied dynamic processes, Phases 1 and 2.

2) uncertainty about future social life.

3) concerns about personal psychological well-being.

c) Implications.

1) Uncertainty and concern about psychosocial well-being develop from processes common to all human interactions. Concerns about personal, social and psychological well-being depend upon interactions between the individual and social situations, with the kinds of concern implied being concerns about the relationships (social performance, social acceptance, meeting social criteria, social survival).

2) Significant differences in characteristics of the 4 subclasses of "the stress of life" imply factors specific to each subclass operational during the development of stress and stress reactions.

C. Stress of life reactions.

1. Table 4 classifies stress reactions according to the nature of the psychophysiological systems affected.

a) Taken as a whole, stress-related problems are estimated to comprise about 75% of all human ills.

TABLE 4

Some psychologic and physiologic disturbances believed to be caused by or related to or aggravated by psychosocial stress

Emotional: anxiety, insomnia, tension headache, aging, sexual impotency, neuroses, phobias, alcoholism, drug abuse, learning problems, general malaise

Psychosomatic: essential hypertension, auricular arrhythmias, ulcers, colitis, asthma, chronic pain, acne, peripheral vascular disease, angina, bruxism and its consequent pathologies

Organic: epilepsy, migraine, herpes, coronary thrombosis, rheumatoid arthritis

Psychological adjustment problems: adapting to life events (family, job, school, loss, success, failure, change); difficulties due to personal traits

Sociologic adjustment problems: adjusting to economic instability, unemployment, peer pressures, legal restraints

The stress of being ill: The aggravated or prolonged distress of being ill, disabled, or mentally, psychically, or physically diminished

b) Evidence indicating the incidence of stress-related ills significantly exceeds the incidence of physical ills:
   1) the limited absolute incidence and types of physical ills (infection, injury, tissue abnormalities (including endocrines), congenital and birth defects).
   2) estimates of stress-related ills are generally based on categories of standard diagnoses, thus do not include numerous psychological and physiological distresses that are (1) chronically lived with, (2) relieved by OTC medication, (3) treated but not diagnosed, and (4) ameliorated by varieties of nonprofessional help.
2. Consensual observations have established each stress-related problem as characterized by (1) association with psychosocial factors and (2) manifest by subjective, muscle, or visceral tension and by homeostatic imbalances.

D. Definitions.

The conclusions and inferences noted to this point suggest the following definitions:
   1. "The stress of life" (nonphysical stress). Any perception of the social environment and its dynamics interpreted as a threat to social and psychological well-being.
   2. Nonphysical stressors. Psychosocial influences perceived as threatening to social and psychological well-being.
   3. Stress states. Conditions in which nonphysical stressors are cognitively, emotionally, or physically appreciated.
   4. Stress reactions. Psychological and physiological disturbances that are: (a) specifically incited or aggravated by psychosocial factors and (b) evidenced by subjective, muscular, or visceral tensions and by homeostatic imbalances.
   5. Distress. Altered states of perceptual, cognitive, emotional, behavioral, or physiological activity during reactions to "the stress of life."

E. Nature of the interface between nonphysical.
   stressors and stress reactions.
   1. The set designation for "the stress of life" specifies that nonphysical stressors evoke concerns abut psychological

and social well-being and the set designation for stress reactions specifies the presence of subjective and physiological changes. The unresolved issues thus are:

a) The nature of the mechanisms converting extrinsic psychosocial influences into concerns about future social and psychological well-being.[4]

b) The nature of the mechanisms mediating the emotional and physiological expression of psychosocial concerns.

2. Implied response components.

The above issues can be examined by organizing various consensual observations about subjective operations implied in expressions of communicated thought, emotion, and behavior during the development of stress states and stress reactions.

a) The following subjective mental activities are generally agreed to be components of all situations involving human interactions:

1) Expectations. The presumption of probable future events results from complex mental activities that depend upon individual history and are modified by individual motives, desires, and how the individual detects the meanings of social behaviors, and by the social consensus.

2) Perceptions. The complex process of attaching meanings to sensed information that depends upon observations of both specific events and series of often tenuously related events, upon interpreting human behavior and its expression, using past knowledge about influences of personality, social customs, body language, and other factors modulating human behavior.

b) The following subjective mental activities are generally

---

[4] While the term psychosocial is often interpreted as implying most nonphysical factors affecting human behavior, it is more frequently interpreted to indicate associations between emotional reactions and social circumstances. The term nonphysical additionally includes ideational reactions to concepts, ideas, and thoughts.

assumed to occur when discrepancies exist between expectations and perceptions of situations involving human interactions:

1) Problem solving. Whenever living organisms detect novelty on the environment (differences from the familiar and anticipated), attempts are made to resolve the differences (exploratory behavior).

   a. Images. It is generally agreed that problem solving in human beings is mediated in large part by the recreation and creation of mental images, i.e., by central or mental representations of things not present or real encompassing various units of associated material, including both abstract and concrete representations and with the process manipulating the image units to produce a coherent, unifying image consonant with some intentional influence.[5]

   b. Outcomes. Problem solving concerned with resolving differences between expectations and perceptions of a social situation can be either:

   1. Productive, maintaining a state of well-being.

   2. Unproductive, leaving the future uncertain.

2) Anxiety. It is generally agreed that anxiety is a major identifying component of the perception of stress.

   Anxiety is a general term applied to various combinations of subjective concern about a psychosocial problem and physiological tensions. It is also qualified according to whether the attention is directed predominantly toward the cause of the perceived stress or toward the sensations accompanying the stress. Thus anxiety can be classified as:

   a) Subjective anxiety identified by concern about future well-being and by the attention and problem

---

[5] Imagery is popularly construed to be visual only. While visual imagery has received the bulk of scientific attention, the average person's imagery is a mixture of visual, auditory, tactile, kinesthetic, emotional, and even abstract and symbolic imagery.

solving activity directed toward resolving the perceived problem.

b) Subjective anxiety accompanied by objectively manifest physical tensions, homeostatic imbalances, and the attention directed toward the subjective sensations.

3) Rumination. The process of continuing subjective-preoccupation with disturbing thoughts is recognized as a major component of severe or prolonged anxiety.

IV. Implied dynamic processes.

1. Since all of the above components have been identified as essential characteristics of the subjective events leading to stress states, any descriptive account of "the stress of life" process is required to:
   a) demonstrate verifiable relationships among the response components:
   b) account for a continuity of events;
   c) relate subjective events to physical events in a way that can be tested.
2. Figure 1 is a schematic account of the dynamic activity of the implied response components. Each subjective event has the capability to produce known consequences leading either to states of well-being or to stress states. Three phases of "the stress of life" process can be distinguished:
   a) Phase 1. Intellectual concern.
      1) Stress is generated when a significant difference between expectations and perceptions about a social situation is perceived.[6]
      2) Taken together, the processes producing intellectual concern indicate a stressor processing phase in the development of stress and stress reactions.
      3) The mechanisms capable of converting extrinsic psychosocial influences into concerns about future social and

[6] The single term perception has two quite different meanings: (1) the sensory detection of the qualities of objects or events, and (2) knowing the meaning of objects of events.

Figure 1

Flow chart of processes leading to states of well-being or states of stress and stress reactions.

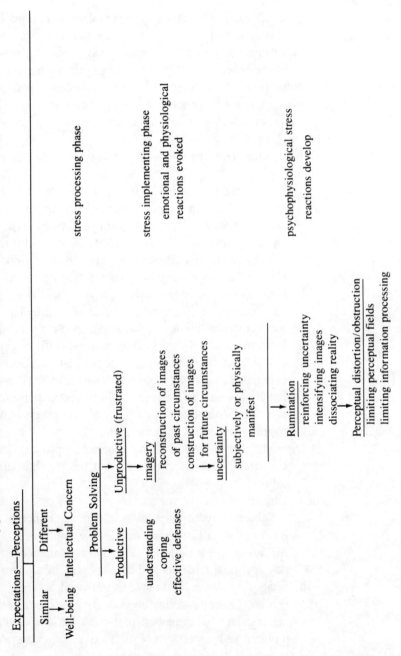

psychological well-being can be postulated to require: (1) information processing systems that select relevant expectations and perceptions appropriate to particular social experiences, and (2) processing systems that detect similarities and differences between the content and implications of the expectations and perceptions and initiate processes to minimize incongruities.

b) Phase 2. Problem Solving.
  1) Intellectual concern (stressor processing) results in either:
    a. Productive problem solving that resolves the differences between expectations and perceptions and favors states of well-being by using reality-based psychosocial information, experience, and mental skills to achieve effective coping (understanding, rationalizations, positive action, ego protecting defenses).
    b. Unproductive problem solving that fails to develop means to maintain or recover states of well-being.
  2) Major factors leading to unproductive problem solving:
    a. Informational deficits. Lack of either specific or general information relevant to stress situation, lack of experience, lack of problem solving skills.
    b. Psychological influences. Beliefs and experience skewing perception, attention, self-awareness, and cognitive information processing.
  3) Unproductive problem solving generates 3 products:
    a. Uncertainty that is concern about the psychosocial future.
    Uncertainty can be manifest.
    i) Subjectively, principally as intellectual concern.
    ii) Physical tensions and homeostatic imbalances.
    iii) Subjective emotional reactions accompanied by physiological tensions and homeostatic imbalances.
    b. Images unfavorable to psychosocial well-being.
    i) Images accompanying unproductive problem solving consist of fragmented past contributions to the problem and projections of ineffective, inappropriate image-solutions into the future.

ii) Mental images evoke measureable physical tensions in those physiological systems involved in the imagery. When imagery is more or less sustained, some physiological adaptation to increased tension levels occurs.

c) Phase 3. Physiological imbalances.

1) Muscular and visceral tensions are responses to:

a. Images. All images involving physiological responses evoke liminal physical activity specific to the image.

b. Uncertainty. Concern about the future initiates preparation of physical defense mechanisms for action to preserve physical well-being.

2) Homeostatic imbalances. Autonomic, endocrine, and immune regulatory functions become disturbed:

a. when untoward images and uncertainty are generalized to apprehension or fear for physical well-being.

b. when rumination reinforces subjective sensations of apprehension and fear, limits perceptual activity, and reinforces the tension-images.

V. *Stress management and therapeutics.*

A. Major considerations.

1. "The stress of life" process is comprised of 3 identifiable phases. Since both the appreciation of stress and stress reactions depend upon cognitive mechanisms processing information about psychosocial interactions and upon central recognition of proprioceptive signals, the two principal factors affecting the process can be assumed to be: (a) the information processing systems and (b) the quality and quantity of both cognitively useful information relevant to perceptions, expectations, and problem solving and relevant proprioceptive information. Since non-stress related information processing is relatively unaffected in stress states, deficits of relevant information can be deduced as the principal factors responsible for the stress process. The 3 phases of

the stress process and their major informational deficits are:
   a) Intellectual concern, in which the primary informational deficit is specific and general cognitively useful information about human behavior, reactions, and psychosocial relationships.
   b) Unproductive problem solving in which the primary informational deficits are information about psychosocial problem solving and information to facilitate cognitive skills.
   c) Physiologial imbalances in which the primary informational deficits are proprioceptive information and information about physiological processes.
2. Considering all phases of the development of the appreciation of stress states, the kinds of information required to resist the stress process include:
   a) the information that information is needed;
   b) information about human behavior, reactions, and interactions;
   c) information about mental processes and their operations;
   d) information about physiological processes and their reactions;
   e) information to apply information.
3. Each phase of the stress process requires orientation of stress management procedures toward providing information relevant to the particular psychological or physiological events of the phase.
4. The nature of the stress process indicates that treatment of stress reactions requires treatment of signs and symptoms while prevention of stress and stress reactions requires management of process events.

B. Procedures.
   1. Reduction of intellectual concern. Phase 1.
      Rationale: This phase represents the incubation period of the stress process in which the problem solving of perceived difficulties is initiated and thus requires primarily cognitively useful information. Since intellectual concern

about psychosocial situations arises from the perception of a discrepancy between expectations and perceptions, the effect of either can be corrected by introducing information providing greater accuracy of expectations and perceptions of the practical social reality and human relationships, i.e., by providing information that reduces the magnitude and scope of the discrepancy.

Procedures: Procedures noted for Phase 2 are appropriate for Phase 1 when achieving cognitive understanding is emphasized.

2. Reduction of the uncertainty and disturbing images of unproductive problem solving, Phase 2.

   Rationale: Since the inciting and continuing pressure of stress is the need to solve problems, ensuring the understanding of how to solve problems is of paramount importance in stress management. Effective problem solving in the psychosocial domain requires information that is relevant, accurate, and realistic. The nature of such information is: (1) information about psychosocial reactions and interactions, (2) the nature of psychosocial problems, (3) information about mental processes and their operations, and (4) strategies for problem solving, including general procedures, procedures for psychosocial problems, and modifications of procedures for specific problems.

   Procedures:

   a) General procedures for problem solving. Problem solving is explained through instruction in the principles of problem solving, using models, examples, and analogies.[7]

---

[7] Problem solving entails only two approaches, either using a known procedure or developing a process, to move from a particular state to a desired goal. There are, however, many strategies and guidelines for successful problem solving that are not generally observed, especially for problems of psychological or social origin. Some of these are, e.g., (1) establishing goals. (2) recruiting information. (3) eliminating unnecessary restraints (unproductive associations, direction of attention, working backwards). (4) eliminating redundancy. (5)establishing a proper attitude. (6) asking questions. (7) detecting patterns. (8) organiz-

b) Techniques for solving psychosocial problems.
All varieties of psychological procedures used for personal growth, psychotherapy, and counselling contain information about either the nature of human behavior, reactions and interactions or about the nature of the mental and emotional self.

c) Examples of appropriate procedures are: discussions about the nature and psychology of human beings, creating and using support systems, the journal process, modified reality-oriented psychotherapy, counseling, group therapy, family therapy, behavioral therapies, marriage encounter, dream analysis, Gestalt therapy, psychosynthesis, transactional analysis, guided imagery, meditation, bioenergetics, assertiveness training, psychodrama, and related techniques.[8,9]

d) Rationale for modifying standard techniques. Since "the stress of life" does not generally result in debilitating disorders, and also because the emotional and physical distress that does result from stress occurs late in the

---

ing the information (observations). (9) discriminating generalizations from specifics. (10) establishing values. (11) identifying interfering influences (emotions, culture, language). (12) permission to doubt. (13) understanding relevant concepts. (14) use of objective evaluation. (15) withholding judgement. and (16) sustaining logic.

8 It should be remembered that many of these procedures were designed to deal with emotional problems that may or may not be stress related. The significant difference between emotional or psychosomatic problems caused by stress and psychopathology is that the bulk of the stress process takes place long before its serious consequences, and even when the consequences appear and require therapeutic attention, the intellectual capacities retain their normally functioning capability. This suggests that regardless of the specific objective of a psychological procedure, the emphasis of the procedure for stress management purposes can be more efficient when it is less on directed concepts of behavior and more on developing intelligent understanding and awareness of both the psychosocial phenomena and the stress phenomenon.

9 The apparent success of imagery techniques in the relief of both stress problems and certain organic illnesses further suggests that imagery processes may play an important and perhaps primary role in the stress process.

stress process, two kinds of modifications of frequently used psychological techniques are specifically indicated:

1. When the reactions to stress do not interfere extensively with social and psychological functioning, appropriate remedial measures are those emphasizing strategies for problem solving, developing effective coping, and eliminating untoward imagery.

2. When symptomatology seriously interferes with participation in life's activities or threatens physiologic functions, appropriate remedial measures are those directed principally toward relief of symptoms, with problem solving assistance secondary.

3. Reduction of physical tensions, Phase 3.
   Rationale: The central appreciation of information signals has been shown to have a finite capacity, i.e., signals compete for processing. Attention to one modality of sensation diminishes attention to other perceptual modalities, thus the sensory perception of tension competes with cognitive perceptual processing and can inhibit cognitive processes. When attention is focused on the subjective sensations of uncertainty and on untoward images, the central appreciation of proprioceptive signals is diminished. When proprioceptive signals of tension are not recognized centrally, the content of the integrative functions (uncertainty and undesirable images) continue to signal muscle and visceral regulatory mechanisms to maintain tension (preparedness) as a defense against perceived impending assaults. Further, the increased muscle and visceral tensions are then appreciated as reinforcement of subjective sensations of uncertainty.

   Relaxation procedures can increase awareness of physical tensions and can increase detection of inappropriate tensions, leading to reinstitution of normalizing processes. Directing the attention to quantitative changes in physical tensions has been found to lead to (1) increased central sensitivity to tension signals, (2) comparisons of tension levels and appraisal of appropriateness of tension, (3) diminished sensations of physical tension, (4) reduced attention to sensations caused by stress problems, and (5) decreased effects of uncertainty and untoward images.

Procedures: Most body awareness techniques provide effective reduction of physical tensions. Examples are: Progressive Relaxation (tense-relax exercises), Autogenic Training, biofeedback, yoga, structural integration, Alexander technique, sex therapy, breath awareness, shiatsu, dance therapy, and similar techniques.

4. Integral, Optimizing stress management.

Rationale: Because the development of stress and stress reactions is a dynamic process of feedback between cognitive and physical functions, optimal treatment and management of stress states require corrective procedures for the dynamics of the interactions as well as for each of the two factors.

Three primary processes are involved in the interaction dynamics between cognitive and physiological functions: (1) attention, awareness, and perception, (2) experiential and cognitive information processing, and (3) use of perceptual, experiential, and cognitive information to restore homeostatic balances.

Cognitively useful information acts to assist the problem solving process that in turn relieves the effects of uncertainty and untoward images. Information augmenting awareness of physiological tensions acts to relieve tensions, to reduce the sensations of tensions, and to shift attention from sensations to problem solving fuctions.

An example of the interactive dynamics between cognitive and physiologic activities is given in Table 5. The material is excerpted from Edmund Jacobson's

TABLE 5
Jacobson's anxiety-relaxation thesis[10]

Major assumptions
1. Anxiety and relaxation states are mutually exclusive
2. Comparing tension to relaxation (tense-relax exercises) develops awareness of feelings of relaxation
3. Anxiety is not caused by a problem "out there," but results from unproductive energy expenditure in trying to solve the problem
4. The imagery during problem solving evokes physiologic activity and expends energy

Anxiety (tension) reducing procedure
1. Identify the tension producing situations
2. Identify the reaction, i.e., the tension-image patterns
3. Use the images during relaxation learning
4. Eliminate the images while maintaining relaxation

---

[10] E. Jacobson. *Progressive Relaxation*, University of Chicago Press, 1958.

analysis of the relationship between anxiety (stress) and relaxation.

Procedures: Combinations of psychologically and physiologically oriented stress management procedures selected for appropriateness to the phase of the stress state and for interactive, synergistic potential (a) on cognitive processes effecting relief of physiological tensions, and (b) physiological processes effecting improved cognitive function.

VI. Conclusions.

1. "The stress of life" is commonly interpreted as the things that can and do happen to people in the course of a lifetime that require adjusting their attitudes, feelings, or behavior. The present report qualifies four categories of such stress and distinguishes the common features that permit definition of "the stress of life".
2. Examination of the principal factors associated with "the stress of life" indicates that the appreciation of stress develops from the cognitive processes involved in unsuccessful attempts to

resolve differences between expectations and perceptions detected in psychosocial situations.

3. Since all expectations and perceptions are not skewed and problem solving processes generally remain logical and consistent, unsuccessful problem solving can be inferred to be caused by lack of information relevant to the psychosocial circumstances and not by a fault in the information processing systems.

4. When psychosocial problem solving is unproductive, the stress process is characterized by uncertainty and images inimical to well-being.
   a) Uncertainty stimulates psychological and physiological tensions.
   b) Images threatening to well-being stimulate physiological activity in those systems involved in the imagery and in systems vulnerable to assault.[11]

5. Stress reactions are reactions to the products of cognitive processes, images and uncertainty, that supervene in homeostatic regulation.

6. The physiological systems activated during unproductive problem solving reinforce both intellectual concern and the subjective sensations of stress, and limit the recognition of information signals contained in perception, proprioception, and mentation.

7. The nonphysical stress ("the stress of life") process appears to be analogous to the physical stress process defined by Selye in that different varieties on nonphysical stress are converted into different varieties of disorders all manifesting nonspecific symptoms of subjective anxiety and signs of physiological tensions. The nonphysical stress process also appears to be mediated by a specific set of cognitive mechanisms in a way

[11] Images may comprise the major contribution accounting for individual susceptibility and the system specificity of reactions to nonphysical, psychosocial stress since (a) psychosocial problem solving is the pivotal stage in the appreciation of nonphysical stress. (b) varieties of mental images are accompaniments of problem solving. and (c) mental images evoke physiologic changes specific to the images.

similar to the mediation of the physical stress process by a specific set of biochemical and endocrine mechanisms.
8. Stress management and therapeutics are examined for appropriateness to the major phases of the stress process and the rationale for modification of existing techniques is noted.

References

1. Holmes, Thomas J. and Masuda, M. (1974): Life change and illness susceptibility, In Barbara Dohrenwend and Bruce Dohrenwend (eds.) Stressful Life Events. New York: John Wiley and Sons.
2. Jacobson, E. (1958): Progressive Relaxation. Chicago: University of Chicago Press.
3. Selye, H. (1956): The Stress of Life. New York: McGraw-Hill.

Understanding Stress: Muscle Tension. The Habits of Stress

One of the most elusive concepts in understanding stress is understanding the involvement of muscles. The reasons there are such vague notions about the role of muscles in both the cause and cure of stress problems lies in the widespread acceptance of some very incomplete and quite thoughtless theorizing about stress.

I will concentrate on the muscle story and try to describe to you exactly why and how the muscles of the body contribute to all kinds of stress disorders, from relatively uncomplicated anxiety to serious physical reactions to stress such as coronaries or epileptic seizures or hypertension and even to social behavioral difficulties. Once we thoroughly understand how the muscles contribute to emotional and physical reactions to stress, I will review the reasons why treating the increased muscle tension of stress can so easily lead to the cure of so many stress problems.

I'll explore with you how it is the mind—actually the human intellect—that is the source of all stress disorders, the cause of all stress reactions, and I'll describe how the mind can both prevent and relieve all stress problems. For, you see, it is really the mind that controls everything that muscles do, good or bad, productive or harmful to well-being.

Although the mind controls what the muscles do, it is the reaction of the muscles that causes most of the problems we observe and feel when we react to stress. So the first thing to do is to understand the role of the muscles, and to do this, we must first put the muscles in their proper perspective.

The Unique Properties of Muscles

There are two extremely important and interesting features about muscles that people rarely consider. The first is that muscles comprise the greatest mass of the body, that is, they are the tissue or organ we have the most of. This is so obvious, it is very curious why muscles have received so little attention for their importance to health and illness. Our new interests in relaxation techniques and in jogging and exercise have been so successful in helping people to stay well and feel good, and these effects are only a sign of the part muscles can play in curing and preventing illness.

The second fascinating feature about muscles is that they cannot live, they cannot perform, they can do absolutely nothing without the nerves that feed them electrical impulses from the brain. Unlike the viscera and the body's vital organs that can function quite nicely without a nerve supply, muscles can do nothing without their nerves. It is the nerves that bring life to the muscle. And for every muscle cell, nerves can be traced to and from the brain. Within the brain there are a score of special areas that work to coordinate muscle activity, and for every such area there are hundreds of other nerve connections with nearly every other part of the brain, including the brain activities that give rise to the mind.

So the brain and the mind are the ultimate masters of all that muscles do and are responsible for everything that happens to muscles. In a cerebral stroke, for example, the damaged blood supply deprives brain areas concerned with muscles of blood and oxygen, and the result is muscle paralysis. On the other hand, when the modern athlete gets ready for competition, he uses the mind to prepare the muscles for a precise kind of performance.

Before we look at how muscles react under stress, we should know something about how muscles react normally. Actually, it's a rather simple story. Muscle functions are carried out by means of feedback systems. A feedback control system is simply a system that performs a function by using information fed back to it about the effects of its performance.

Feedback is Crucial to All Life Functions

I'd like to make a couple of points about things like feedback control systems, the physiology of the body, physics, electronics, medicine, and psychology. What do they all have in common? They are all assumed to be "tough" subjects, difficult to understand and take years of work to become expert in. The point I want to make is that the only reason these subjects are believed to be difficult is because in all the thousands of textbooks and lectures by experts, the explanations are always mired down in minutiae and made unnecessarily complicated. I can illustrate this point by the explanation of feedback control systems. I have some five books on feedback systems, and in absolutely none of them is there any clear explanation of what feedback control systems really are.

Since virtually every function of the body, and in fact every self-regulating system of nature, operates by means of feedback systems, it is important to understand how they work. As I said earlier, a feedback control system is simply a system that performs a function by using information fed back to it about the effects of its performance. Feedback control systems have three main parts: sensors that detect the effects of what the system does, a control center that compares the effects to a pre-set condition about what the effects should be, and third, a switch that turns on when more effects of the system are needed and turns off when the system's effects are O.K. Very simple. Take the electric skillet as an example. Central control can be set for the desired temperature and the system operates, producing heat. The sensor monitors the heat, relaying the information to central control. As long as the heat is not enough, the switch remains open. When the heat reaches the present level, this is recognized by central control which in turn sends a signal to the switch to turn off. And so on.

Body systems work the same way. If I want to raise my hand to a certain point, the brain directs the muscles to move. As the muscles move, sensors within the muscle cells relay information back to the central control in the brain about where the muscles are, how fast they are moving, and other relevant information. Central control compares the information with the information preset about where the hand should be, makes any corrections needed, and turns off the switch when the hand reaches the desired point.

Aha, you say—how did the control center get set? This is the secret hole in feedback theory when it is used to explain body functions. The theory is fine for explaining the body functions that normally run on automatic, such as the digestive tract, but when it comes to body functions we can exert voluntary control over, we have to postulate some higher system that can actually set the controls. And as we all know, we human beings have the ability to set the controls for muscle activity in almost any way we decide to, within physical limitations. And now, with the advent of biofeedback, autogenic training, relaxation and imagery techniques, we have discovered that we can even set the controls for what we used to believe were the body functions that were invariably automatic and beyond voluntary control. We now know that we can exert intention and the will on such body activities as intestinal motility and secretions, on every aspect of the cardiovascular system, and even on the activity of the brain itself.

What this all means is two important features of human activity. First, because of the way feedback systems operate, we can function quite well on automatic mechanical operation of the body . . . provided the controls aren't disturbed too much. And the second important fact is that we have, innately, the ability, the potential, to change and to direct the automatic functions of the body, with, of course, the limits of physical nature.

What has happened in the evolution of man is that we have learned, through our culture, certain ways of using our muscles to perform certain tasks or feats and to communicate. But what our culture through all these centuries has not considered is how to use our innate ability to control body functions for ensuring health and relieving illness.

The reason for this is because in the history of civilized Western man, the religious ethic has believed man to be simply a superior animal, and superior because man was endowed with a mind-spirit given by God. The potential of mind was to purify the spirit. Then when science came along, it excluded the spirit, and with it, excluded any recognition of mind that could not be measured directly by the tools of science. The result was that no one cared about the potential of mind, and certainly not about the potential of mind to care for its own body and being. It is only within the last dozen years that evidence for the ability of mind to control body has crept into the annals of science.

We are, in fact, very unlearned about the behavior of our bodies, and because we know so little, the behavior of our bodies and the behavior of body functions often can react disastrously and in a way harmful to well-being simply because we have never learned how to be aware of internal body functions and how to ensure their well-being.

Let me illustrate what happens in the body that clearly shows how very primitive we are in body behavior.

The Mind and Muscle Tension

The universal reaction of human beings to *any* kind of concern is anxiety—or worry—or fear. Call it what you will, whenever human beings are uncertain about the outcome of future events, they worry and become anxious, and the body reacts immediately. No matter how trivial or urgent the uncertainty is, the body reacts.

If you are cleaning out the basement at home, for example, and reach up to wipe away a cobweb and suddenly see a black spider with a red hour glass on its belly, you react immediately. Whether in apprehension or outright fear, you and your body react the same way. You jerk your hand away, you gasp, you may feel clammy or sweat, your heart will race, and your gut may tie itself in a knot. Most often, for a fleeting second you will freeze.

This is a universal response to direct, immediate, physical threat to well-being. What happens in the body is the fascinating phenomenon of preparing the body to take action. Psychophysiologists call it the arousal response, but most of you have heard about it as the fight-or-flight reaction. It is, in fact, a primitive reflex, and obviously a very useful one. The most important part of the reflex is the arousal of the body's systems. That is, before the body can take action, the systems must be prepared to take action. What happens during the arousal phase before action is that the muscles tense, ready to go, and the cardiovascular system shifts its activity to give the muscles more blood and oxygen, the respiration changes, the gut stops its activities, and other secretions may stop—dry mouth. The body is now prepared to act with its greatest efficiency.

What does this primitive reflex have to do with health and illness? Absolutely everything. It is a reaction that is set in motion *whenever*, in varying degrees, we have a concern about the future, from worrying about the bill coming in today's mail to concern about performing well in a job, to what the spouse will say about changing vacation plans to whether you'll survive an operation. The body reactions are all the same, to lesser or greater degrees. But remember, the muscle tension comes first.

The interesting part about the arousal or fight-or-flight reaction is that man has very stupidly transferred this reaction from very real situations of physical danger to situations of social uncertainty. And this is why understanding the reaction is so important, and why it is important to know how to control it.

There is a big difference between threats to physical well being and threats to social well being. In the first case it is not only appropriate but necessary to react physically and take physical action. But think how foolish it is to react physically by arousal of the body's physiological systems as a reaction to a threat to social well being. But this is exactly what we do—because we don't know better—and it is a reaction that is hazardous to the health.

Let me show you that we really do react quite violently inside to any threat to our social well being . . . and why reacting this way is hazardous to the health, and finally how we can learn not to.

Suppose you heard a friend was going to give a party and for many reasons you wanted to be invited. But you also knew there could be reasons why you wouldn't be invited. You begin to wait for the phone to ring, and as the days pass you become more and more uncertain about being invited. At what you think is the eleventh hour to get an invitation, the phone rings. You jump with a start, you gasp, your heart speeds, you feel nervous, maybe butterflies in the tummy (the gut stops), or dry mouth. Your muscles are tense.

Ridiculous, isn't it? You know it's ridiculous, I know it's ridiculous, but our dear medical and psychology friends never realized how ridiculous this kind of a reaction is until recently, and many theorists still don't know. But what earthly good is a physical reaction in solving a social difficulty? Absolutely none. Social problems are created by faults in mental activities. They come from interactions among human minds, so the appropriate response to a social problem is a mental, and intellectual response, not a physical response.

Yet reacting physically to social situations is what we do every day of our lives. And when there are many social uncertainties, and many social problems to cope with, these physical reactions add to each other and cause real physical and emotional problems.

Yet we know, and we have known for some time, that we can learn to react much more appropriately.

Take the psychological technique called desensitization. This is used to treat phobias and other kinds of excessive reactions we view as pathological. Nonetheless, the same idea can be used to prevent and to relieve any stress reaction.

In a specific phobia, such as the classical fear of snakes, the treatment consists of first having the patient just visualize a series of scenes having to do with snakes while learning to stay relaxed. Nowadays with biofeedback instruments, even the faintest muscle tension can be detected, and patients can readily learn how to stay fairly relaxed first while they are visualizing snakes, then later during real encounters with snakes.

So we can indeed learn *not* to arouse the body unduly, and not to put too much wear and tear on the body. Some concern about the future is necessary, but excessive reactions do do harm to the body. So what we want to learn is *control*, and learn to react in a productive, useful way.

The Need to Relearn Our "Reflex" Responses

We desperately need to learn how to control the body's internal machinery in today's modern society. Most of our emotional and physical problems—some 75 percent of all illness today—stem from worry about social problems.

As I described, in virtually every social difficulty, every social conflict, whether on the job, at home, personal relationships, or even in games, whenever there is any uncertainty at all about what happens next, the body reacts by the arousal reaction and preparing to take some action. But it is not the body that can solve personal and social problems, it is not the body that can resolve social conflicts or cope with social problems. It is the mind that is the appropriate instrument to use in social situations, and the mind cannot function well when the body is overreacting and reacting unnecessarily. Now, how can we learn how to react more appropriately and more productively? Simply by learning how to use our innate, inborn mental capacities to protect the body and keep the mind free for productive thought.

When we react by the arousal response to social problems, the muscle tension that occurs is not enough to move the muscles, so we ordinarily do not feel it. It is *unfelt* muscle tension, the kind of tension we have never learned to become aware of. Nonetheless, when we continue to worry about a social problem, not only does the muscle tension persist, it gradually increases until it can cause pain, such as in tension headache or back pain. But the muscle tension is there even though we don't feel it.

Now that we know the muscle tension is there whenever there is any kind of social distress, there are two questions. First, can we learn how to become aware of muscle tension we normally can't feel, and if we can, can we then learn how to control muscle tension? The answer to the second question should be obvious. All of us can control felt muscle tension, as you know when you control tensing the arms or legs, or typing or playing an instrument or playing tennis. And that should also tell you that you can learn how to become aware of muscle tensions you normally aren't aware of. When you play tennis, for example, the better you get, the more you have learned about your muscle tensions.

We now have a number of new techniques that can help us to become aware of unfelt muscle tension and to learn how to control excessive muscle tensions from developing. The most quantitative method is biofeedback. In muscle biofeedback, the EMG instrument gives you an exact reading of muscle tension levels. When this information is fed back to you, several very interesting things happen. One is that you relate the information about muscle tension to some internal feeling state, as you continue to make associations between the readings of muscle tension levels and some special way of feeling inside. The information about this association is then put into memory so that whenever muscle tension begins to increase, you recall the memory and recognize that tension is beginning. Knowing that the tension is present, you can then practice learned relaxation and prevent any further increase.

The other interesting effect of learning how to detect low levels of muscle tension and the beginning of increased muscle tension is that now you are paying attention to the state of the muscles, you have less time to pay attention to the problem causing the problem. Then because the mind is not as much occupied with its concerns, its call for arousal of the body is diminished. That means that the mind-brain slows down the nerve messages to the muscles to be tense, and so the muscles begin to relax. And with less tension, the mind can function better.

It's really all in what you decide to pay attention to. If you want to learn how to keep muscle tension under control, put your mind on learning how to detect unfelt tensions. Biofeedback is a precise way for learning, but it is not necessary to learn how to cope with many stress problems because many other techniques can be used to achieve similar results. The tense-relax exercises of Progressive Relaxation, or Autogenic Training or guided imagery are all ways to become aware of the state of muscle tension and to learn how to prevent unnecessary body tension reactions. They are all effective techniques because you learn to pay attention to low levels of tension and with that information you exert control over the muscles exactly the same way as when you use the muscles in movement. It is simply learning to use the inborn capabilities of the mind.

Muscle Tension and Relaxation

The Mechanics and Psychogenesis of Muscle Tension

The reality of muscle fibers is that they have a response reper-
toire of one. All they can do is contract and this is the response they
make to the electrochemical stimulation of impulses carried via the
motor nerves. Relaxation is the removal of this stimulation.

There are at least two, or two sets of, muscles to maintain the
balance or posture or set of any particular body part. To produce a
movement some muscles contract while their opposites stretch.
The stretching is both passive and a result of the action of special
nerve-muscle control systems in which inhibitory impulses are
conducted to important junctions where they act to block excitatory nerve impulses. Thus what muscle fibers do is dependent
upon highly complex neural networks which can, upon direction
from the brain that is making constant adjustments, selectively
excite the fibers to contract or actively prevent (inhibit) the excitatory impulses from reaching the muscle fibers.

What is known about tension in muscles has been accumulated
from studies concerned mainly with movement and contraction,
and while tension is the basis of contraction for movement, tension
without movement is a normal body reaction to any stressful
stimulus. What muscles do (contract, tense) is dependent upon the
number of nerve impulses coming down the motor nerves which
innervate them, and the number of nerve impulses in turn is
dependent upon a large complex of muscle control systems in the
brain and spinal cord. What the muscle control systems do in turn

is dependent upon the kinds and amounts of sensory information coming inward from sensory receptors throughout the body.

There are at least five sets of internal nerve-muscle sensing systems, two sets of skin sensing systems, along with auditory, visual and vestibular sensing systems, and it is the central (brain) integration of all of this sensed information that is used by the central muscle control systems as the moment-to-moment monitoring of muscle activity and is the reference from which subsequent muscle activity is projected and initiated. Functionally, all of these neural, sensory information channels provide the information input to the internal muscle feedback control systems of the brain and spinal cord. The control systems then integrate the internally derived information with other sensory information about what the muscle should be doing or what it is projected to do, then activate the appropriate mechanisms (the motor nerves) to alter the muscle activity. The cycle acts continuously in this fashion; hence "feedback control system."

Muscle control systems are exceptionally efficient mechanically, and once muscle behavior is learned, they function almost automatically with no specific conscious direction and only a vague, general conscious concept of the objectives of muscle performance. Muscles attract attention only when they become obstinate in a new muscle learning task, or when they are extremely fatigued, or when tension or bruising knots them up and causes aches and pains. These kinds of minor muscle problems are not considered harmful enough to warrant serious biomedical study, yet over time they can be just as destructive to an individual's well-being as hepatitis or a broken leg. But because such problems primarily affect social rather than physical well-being, their impact upon medicine has been greatly neglected. Although teaching muscles new patterns of activity can be frustrating, and fatigued muscles may recover slowly, it is the insidious toll of stress and emotional tension on the well-being of muscles that can aggravate emotional disturbances, that can cause psychosomatic disorders, and that can magnify the distress of all other illnesses.

Muscle Behavior Under Stress

Exactly how stress, social pressure, and emotional tensions are translated into the tensions of muscles is poorly understood. One reason for this is that it is traditional in medicine and psychology to consider reactions to stressful situations either in terms of the mechanics causing physiologic changes, generally ignoring psychologic causes (as in asthma, colitis, etc.), or in terms of the psychologic mechanics involved in the emotional changes, generally ignoring the contributing physiologic causes. What has *not* been conceptualized about the kind of stress that modern society faces and suffers in response to is that it is not a stress directly affecting the physical organism, but is a cluster of stresses related to social behavior in a social environment. A more detailed discussion of how social stress can cause the whole range of tension reactions from anxiety to ulcers follows this section dealing with the physiologic changes involved in muscle tension.

The most popular current theory of the mechanisms underlying muscle tension posits that the organism is "aroused" or "alerted" by threatening stimuli, and the arousal activates a physiological preparation of the body to take action. It is much the same as the "fight-or-flight" theory formulated more than fifty years ago, and is based upon the observation that when obviously threatening situations occur (you meet a grizzly bear on a narrow mountain path), the body responds by mobilizing its resources. The muscles tense, ready to fight or flee or freeze; the viscera respond in such a way as to ensure emergency functioning, i.e., the heart rate and blood pressure increase to give emergency supplies of oxygen to tissues, the gut stops, the blood pools where it is needed, and so the skin blanches, secretions dry up, etc. All of these physiological responses are dramatic and obvious.

When threatening stimuli are less obvious, such as in socially threatening situations (as competition for jobs, or for affection), many of the same body changes occur. If someone is apprehensive, say about meeting someone new, his heart rate and blood pressure may increase, and his muscles will tense. The physiologic changes can be recorded biomedically although the person himself often may not be aware of the changes.

Most people do respond to social pressure with increased muscle tension. This kind of muscle set is called "bracing," the muscle act of preparing to defend or freeze or to avoid unpleasantness by having the important action muscles ready to move or stand by. Considerable degrees of muscle tension, even "knots," can develop in the muscles. For the most part, such muscle tensing is scarcely recognized consciously, especially during the tension-producing situation or even when recalling it later emotionally. It is only when the conscious attention is not concerned with the emotional situation that the muscle tension becomes significantly appreciated. Even considerable muscle tension may not be felt. This is understandable if we remember that muscles are large masses of muscle fibers, and that an enormous amount of partial tightening of muscle fibers can occur before it is recognized in the form of muscle spasms or knots or as pain.

To understand the consequences of stress on muscle tension, we have to assume either that the social pressure and tension are fairly frequent if not almost constant, or that the responses to it are frequent, if not sustained. Spontaneous relaxation following increased tension occurs very slowly; even sleep is generally not the answer, since subconscious memories can keep the muscles tense during sleep, and dreaming may actually increase the tension further. Since the tension diminishes slowly, it can still be at a high level when the tension-producing situation recurs or a new one comes along. If the situations are frequent, or if the individual continues to think or ruminate and mentally recreate even one such situation, two muscle events occur: muscle tension becomes sustained at higher levels and may continue to increase, and the tightness of the muscles causes them to be hyperreactive. Uptight people usually startle easily and vigorously.

If muscles are not given relief from tension by relaxation or change of activity, the muscle fibers physiologically "adapt" to the states of increased tension. It is as if there were some deficiency in the internal muscle regulating systems. Under normal conditions the special nerve cells in muscle tissue sense when a fiber is contracting, how fast it is tensing, the length of the fiber at any given moment, and other complex aspects of the muscle contraction, sending the information to the central muscle control systems for the appropriate adjustments. But when it comes to sensing *how long* muscle fibers have been tense, the system seems to become inefficient (as if man were not designed to handle so much social stress). With continued stress or rumination about the stress, the muscles have little chance to recover completely from their increased tension, and the tension becomes sustained at higher levels. Even this is not the entire picture since with so much muscle mass being tense, the muscle tension sensors relay an excessive number of tension messages to the brain muscle control areas. These should be enough to attract conscious attention, and sometimes do under acute circumstances, but with conscious attention generally occupied with the emotional situation, tension states are only minimally appreciated in awareness. To account for this relative failure to appreciate increased muscle tension consciously, it has been postulated that cortical inhibitory effects come into play; that is, some active cortical process blocks recognition of the increased tension. At the same time normal muscle control is inhibited, and the cortical effect is to direct the muscles to stay prepared for action, and thus they tend to remain in a tense state until either the tension-provoking situation is removed or until it is recognized and reevaluated and emotional adjustments made.

Mental Processes and Muscle Control

One of the curiosities of medicine, especially psychosomatic medicine, and of psychology, particularly the psychology of emotion, is the long-continuing neglect of the obvious role of muscles in illnesses of both mind and body. It is the custom of Western medicine and psychology to focus on the mechanisms of the physical nature of man, even when that nature is heavily influenced by the mind and emotions.

If we were to look at man whole and afresh, undissected by science, we would see man as mainly muscles. Man can, in fact, do nothing without his muscles. All of his behavior, all of his expressions, are implemented by muscles. If his well-being is implemented and expressed by muscles, it would be eminently logical to believe that disorders of his mind and body would also be implemented and expressed by his muscles.

It has taken biofeedback to change the scientific perspective on muscles. No longer can we talk about muscles solely as the vehicles of our desires, as the mechanical devices that move us about, sit us up, make us tired, help us to see and hear and eat and survive. The extraordinary utility of muscle biofeedback in relieving all varieties of human problems is convincing us of the role of muscles as expressors of a great complex of mind and body activity. Even the most subtle of the mind's machinations, even the most sophisticated of the body's nerve electrical actions, have now been demonstrated to be intimately tied to a maelstrom of unfelt, unseen muscle activity.

Precisely because the complexities and intricacies of the mind's and brain's effects on muscles are unfelt and unseen, science has had difficulty in pinning down the relationship between mind and muscle. Physiology and physical medicine have learned a great deal about muscle mechanics and the remarkably complex nature of the brain's control of muscle activity, but although the neural networks of the motor systems of the brain are known in great detail and they form a dominant mass of the brain with widespread connections, virtually nothing is known about how they relate to the higher brain systems that mediate emotion, feeling, mood, attitude, cognition, motivation, curiosity, or desire.

If man can do nothing without his muscles, his muscles can do nothing without the central nervous system and its nerves. People, even medical people, tend to think simplistically about muscles, as if it were the muscles themselves that can be trained to perform fine movements, or that they can be rested by simply not using them. But it is anatomically and physiologically true that the muscles themselves can do very little without the activation and direction and modulation that come from the highest, the most cerebral, of the brain's activities. It is, in fact, the complicated and still obscure operations of higher mental activities that coordinate and direct, plan and project, every muscle movement we make, consciously *and* subconsciously.

The potency of higher mental control becomes clear in biofeedback learning. For example, in most kinds of anxiety the physical expression of anxiety, if not a good share of the anxiety itself, is in the unfelt, unseen muscle tension that braces the body against fearful situations without consciousness being much aware that tension exists, generally not until long after the cause for anxiety has been removed. With the biofeedback signal monitoring the actual muscle tension, and with the desire to relieve that tension, the feedback signal responds to decreasing tension effected by nerve impulses initiated by some indefinable and inexpressible cerebral appreciation of the problem at hand and its ability to set in motion the nerve networks needed to remove the tension.

Studies using various relaxation or meditation techniques to achieve states of tranquility and relaxation show significant reductions in muscle tension. Here also, as with biofeedback, there are no externally controlled interventions that force muscle activities into other modes, such as drugs, or deep massage or electric shocks; the relaxation and meditation techniques deal with *mental* aspects that intuitively and cognitively, yet passively and subconsciously, affect the cerebral mechanisms that are tied to those that make the muscles respond.

Little is known about the subtleties of such cerebral control, or of the psychophysiological aspects of muscle activity. The problem is further complicated by the fact that neither language nor biologic measures can define the effect of most influences of mental activities, particularly as they relate to their role in changing physiologic activities. It is largely for such reasons that the practice of biofeedback can sometimes remind one of the shotgun approach to therapeutics, or the laying on of hands. As described below, both clinical research and practice surround and supplement biofeedback by many different, but related, techniques, all of which elicit the influence of cerebral control for effects.

Those mental activities which subtly but surely affect muscles are influenced in turn quite specifically by various orders of information which are perceived. These can be illustrated easily in examples from everyday life. Take, for example, driving a car. First, there is the physiological information directly from the muscles about the degree and status of muscle activity that is relayed to the cortical integration areas of the brain. This is chiefly various kinds of information about muscle tension sensed by special nerve cells in the muscles and by pressure sensors in the skin; it gives a measure of how much muscle pressure is on the accelerator. How *much* pressure to put on the accelerator is also guided by other information, visual and auditory. All of this physiological information is directed by and toward the goals of driving, but achieving the goals is implemented by a judicious use of a variety of *other* kinds of information that are used cerebrally: cognitively useful information (some knowledge of the mechanics of the car), strategy information (how and when to get in the right lane), and experiential information (e.g., knowing how to move with the flow of traffic).

In the world of biology and medicine, in psychology and physiology, academic attention has concentrated on the mechanical control of muscles, and by and large our culture has been conditioned to accept the concept that muscles respond to the demands of environment, with relatively minimal or tangential interference by complex cognitive processes. It is the politics of science, quite literally, that has shaped the behavior of our muscles:[1] the physics and chemistry of nerves and muscles account for the nature of muscle activity, but they do not account for the *reasons* muscles do what they do. Nonetheless, despite their inability to account for mental activity, it is the physical sciences which dominate theories about the physiology of the body, and from their position of power, they have ignored volumes of research evidence that implicate, with equal data, the superiority of mental processes over physical ones in the control of the body's physiology. It is a situation similar to the one N.F. Dixon, the famous British authority on subliminal

[1]For centuries and predominantly even today, we sit bolt upright for hours in badly built chairs (built for the "average" body) expending vast unproductive quantities of muscle and cerebral body control energy while we listen to lectures with the half-mind not occupied by struggling with an unnatural position.

perception, commented on, noting that there are more research papers on subliminal perception than for any other aspect of psychology, yet less space (if any at all) devoted to the subject in any college or graduate text.

Subliminal Cognition and Muscle Control

So it is little wonder that Westerners, including the biomedical scientists themselves, find the biofeedback process perplexing. It is only when we begin to think through the biofeedback phenomenon that we are forced to face all of those compartments of complex mental activity that have been kept in scientific obscurity. For there are, in truth, only two observable events in the biofeedback process: the intake of information (what the muscle is doing; what should be done about it; perhaps a clue about how to change it), and the result, a specific change in muscle activity compatible with the intention to change it. At the very least one must acknowledge that the information taken in somehow got associated properly, in some way got matched up with intention, and by some exquisitely precise mechanism, exactly the right physical and chemical processes were activated to produce the desired change.

It is an elegant process, and one that far exceeds the capacity of modern science to dissect and catalogue. If, however, we analyze what may be going on in the mind as we carry out voluntary acts, we can recognize and label distinctive steps in the process, as in the example of driving a car. These steps are perceiving, associating, and integrating perceptual data with experiential memory data, using logic patterns, evaluating the significance of past and present experience, making judgments, etc.

It is likely that much the same thing happens in the biofeedback process. Here most of the physiological information is provided by the feedback monitor. Used alone, without other, supplementary information, the feedback signal information may be enough to allow the patient to change muscle activity, although often it may be a small change. Most experimental work has found that the other categories of information are almost equally important. Paralleling the example of driving a car, there is the cognitively useful information, such as descriptions of what the physiologic process is about, what the instrument does, and what the relationship of these is to therapeutic effectiveness. There is also the strategy information, such as the more formalized relaxation procedures or modifications which emphasize visualization, passive volition, directing attention internally, capturing awarenesses, etc. And there is the kind of information that provides clues about how the physiologic change may occur, clues both to dissociate conscious effort and to learn how simply to feel or become aware of internal states.

Finally there is experiential, supportive information, the kind of information that is conveyed by concept and attitude and surroundings. Whether this information is conveyed simply by an understanding and pleasant demeanor, or by set and setting, or whether the therapist discusses the biofeedback process in terms of the patient's ultimate ability to control internal states, the significance of the information lies in its capacity to encourage, impart confidence, motivate, and consolidate the biofeedback learning experience.

What the patient experiences during biofeedback training and his awareness of the physiologic changes are chiefly subjectively appreciated events only, and can be referred to and described vaguely at best. Our communications about internal events are solely by agreed upon analogies to experiences which have been previously analogized over the centuries. For example, in temperature feedback training in Raynaud's syndrome, the patient may say, "My hand feels as if it were alive again," or, "It feels the way I thought it would feel if my hand were in a basin of warm water, except without the wetness of water."

Such fumbling attempts to describe new sensations typify the difficulties in communicating the biofeedback experience as well as the difficulties involved in guiding the patient toward a goal of self-control of his own biological activities. The idea of control itself also can be communicated only by referring to vague analogies, such as, "It's much like the feeling, the knowing, you have when you are hitting a golf ball exactly right, or when you are braking your car for a perfect stop." Even though these kinds of communication are rough and indirect, they supply the information that the patient does indeed have the capability for control and that he is on the right track. The effect of information couched in these terms also contributes to an awareness that the idea in successful biofeedback is to deemphasize the idea of conscious effort.

Because biofeedback learning deals with completely internal processes, it is important for the therapist to recognize that it is indeed a different kind of learning experience, and that it is dependent upon mental activity and not upon external events designed and controlled to elicit responses. What is important is the kind and quality of the information supplied to the mental processes. Given adequate and accurate information, the mental activity can effect quite remarkable changes in the body's physiology. The difficulty in understanding the process is that it takes place without conscious awareness. All learning, in fact, takes place via subconscious mechanisms, a fact that we rarely acknowledge. In biofeedback learning, the role of subconscious mental activity is not only readily apparent, but it can easily be demonstrated that conscious awareness and attention interfere with biofeedback learning.

Cognitive Influences in Tension and Relaxation

The mind-brain mechanisms that mediate the physical effects of *social stress* have received scant scientific attention, presumably because of the considerable difficulty in documenting the elusive, poorly expressed, and often unaware subjective state for use in correlating subjective changes with physiological changes. Nonetheless, the chain of events occurring between perception of social dynamics and the physiological responses to social stress can be readily deduced.

Social stress becomes distress because of uncertainty about future social relationships. Shifting social relationships are often immediately traumatic, but their persistent effects are sustained to a large degree by mental manipulation of the emotions. Imagery, interpretations, expectations, and assumptions about how future events will be affected by the directly disturbing experience are all used to extrapolate the significance of social events. Other social stress derives from observations and interpretations about one's social environment, colored by inferences, suspicions, hopes and fears, and other mental activities recruited in an apparent attempt to maintain a relatively stable state of emotional well-being. When changes in the social environment and social dynamics become stressful, it is largely because the information needed to adjust or resolve problems is incomplete, and thus mental projections about the social future continue to be uncertain. It is the uncertainty that keeps both the mind and body alerted and prepared to take action against seemingly impending threats to well-being and security and survival. In other words, social stress is not stress until the mind-brain interprets perceptions as indicating stress or disharmony or threats in the social environment and relationships. Only then is the body alerted, and only then does the body react.

There are a number of subjective mechanisms that can be inferred to operate to maintain stress reactions of the body's physiological systems. One is the process of rumination (not necessarily obsessive), that conscious or subconscious activity of recall of social events, mental regurgitation, preoccupations, pondering and speculation about the social stress that amplifies and intensifies the social stress complex. The effect of rumination is to occupy a good deal of the associational mental circuitry with the stress idea, focussing attention on the stress problem and so concomitantly less attention and awareness are available for perceptions *not* related to the stress problem. Equally as important is the fact that rumination is a series of mental images, and the images themselves can and do produce profound effects on the body's physiology (for details, see section on Progressive Relaxation). Second, the process of perceptual modulation tends to become concentrated on the stress because of the persistence and force of rumination, and so the narrowing of perceptual interpretations over time modulates perceptions such that elements in the social environment not originally concerned in the stress projection gradually become encompassed in the mental stress construction and projection. Cultural influences and belief systems also tend to become concentrated toward the social stress problem and intensify the perceptual modulation effect.

Another mechanism which sustains the stress reaction is the internal feedback of information about the status of the physiological systems reacting to the stress. Proprioceptive and visceral afferent information about the uptight muscles and viscera is relayed to the central nervous system where it is available for association with interpretive mechanisms and reinforces both the emotional sensations and the cognitive reactions to stress.

To relieve the effects of social stress one of these mechanisms must be reversed. Aside from drugs, the chief device which can interfere in the mental construction of the stress is to redirect the attention and rupture the fixed, self-reinforcing circular mental activities of perception interpretation, rumination, perceptual modulation, and the effect of these mental activities on physiologic activities. Distracting the attention is effective but transient. More effective devices are to provide information that can rechannel the information-processing activity and intervene in the perceptual-conceptual-physiological information loops that have become fixed in their activities.

There are two major routes by which information can be introduced into the information-processing systems of the mind-brain, which is then used to modify and resolve the imbalances among social realities, the perceptual interpretation of the events in the social environment, and the body's reactions to the interpretations. One technique for introducing remedial information into these systems is to supply conceptually useful information that leads to interpreting the stress situation differently and expands perspectives on stress-coping mechanisms, and this, of course, is psychotherapy and counselling.

The second technique for introducing therapeutic information is by supplying information about the physiologic state, i.e., information about the degree of tension of the muscles and viscera. And this, of course, is biofeedback.

Muscle Responses to Social Stress

Although the skeletal muscle control system is effective for muscle movements, it is strangely inefficient in handling the effects of social pressure or emotional tensions. Not only do the muscle fibers themselves adapt to higher levels of tension, there is also an effect in the cortex that works to maintain muscle tension and prevents recognizing the tension. The cortical effect suggests that much of the inefficiency in handling tensions occurs within the higher cerebral systems, quite possibly at the interfaces of information input and information output of the mind-brain mechanisms. It is often forgotten that the muscle feedback control systems have multiple information inputs, and very powerful inputs are perceptual, cognitive, and memory. Much like Jacobson's demonstration that imagination activates muscles, it is known that rumination, that insidious process of mentally rehashing an annoying or disturbing incident over and over, also increases and sustains muscle tension, often quite dramatically.

In essence this circular mental activity is part of a closed feedback loop between muscles and the mind, i.e., the mental activity is also a feedback loop, operating between sensory mechanisms subserving perceptions and brain mechanisms concerned with the integration and synthesis of information. Since these cerebral mechanisms also process the information about muscle activity and the cerebral-muscle system can operate automatically as a feedback control system, the integrative brain mechanisms can be viewed as providing two interfaces, interacting on the one side with muscle control activity and on the other side with perceptual recognition processes. Within the integrative brain, information is exchanged between the two feedback loops. Thus, as the cerebral processes are engaged in rumination, there is a stream of emotional stimuli impinging upon the muscle control systems, activating and tensing the muscles. The tense muscles in turn send streams of information about the tension to the cortical appreciation areas which simply continue the stimulation to ruminate about the tension.

On the other hand, because the system consists of a perceptual-cerebral feedback loop and a muscle-cerebral feedback loop which dynamically interact with each other to sustain both the subjective and muscle states of tension, the effect of excessive tensions can be relieved by relieving either the muscle or the cerebral tension.

When muscle tension is relieved by relaxation procedures, tension information from the muscles being sent to the central nervous system becomes less and less, and its stimulating effect on the cortex is diminished. There is a good bit of research evidence to indicate that the stimulating effect of increased muscle tension on the cortex activates muscle control mechanisms preventing relaxation. That is, the neural pathways from the cortical muscle control areas to lower brain muscle control areas are activated and the downstream neural message is to maintain the tension. The effect is to prevent relaxation, keeping the muscles uptight and ready to move or defend. As the alerting effect on the cortex is relieved by relaxation training, there is then a relief of the cortical tension-activating effect and the muscles begin to return to normal activity.

This explanation has been derived from neurophysiologic studies which measure effects of muscle contraction (not tension) on the muscle-activating mechanisms of the cortex only. Effects on subjective cerebral activities have not been measured. Nonetheless, psychologic and psychiatric therapeutic techniques are used effectively to induce changes in the mental and emotional (the perceptual-cerebral) feedback loop, decreasing its activity and resulting in less internal cerebral activation of muscle tension.

In light of EMG biofeedback research, which involves the effects of perceptual and cognitive information on muscle activity, it would seem logical to assume that there may be changes in the higher cerebral activities that parallel changes occurring in the more reflex regulation of muscle activity (the muscle-cerebral feedback control system).

Since the cortex reacts to alerting by relaying excitation causing inhibition of other brain neuronal activities, it is likely that the cortical alertness may also inhibit cerebral appreciation of the incoming neuronal messages about the increased muscle tension.

That is, since muscle control systems receive information both from peripheral muscles and from higher cerebral activities, tension information from the muscles may communicate as well with those cerebral mechanisms contributing to the subjective appreciation of body activities. The effect would be to inhibit cerebral functions that evaluate the significance of perceptions of social and emotional stimuli and of internal states of tension. When alerting of the cortex decreases, whether from relaxed muscles or diminished cortical tension effected by psychotherapy or drugs, so does this effect of cortical inhibition, and muscle tension levels can then be appreciated, either consciously or subconsciously.

This explanation may account for the differences in correlations between muscle and subjective changes resulting from the different relaxation techniques, including EMG biofeedback-assisted relaxation, when used under different therapeutic conditions. Because the concept seems somewhat involved at first glance, it is restated as follows:

Research and clinical evidence suggest that the central nervous system mechanisms relating to control of muscle activity are comprised of two dynamically interacting aspects: the muscle mechanisms and the cerebral mechanisms. Of these two subsystems, the cerebral system has the more dominant and extensive capabilities. Every purposeful muscle activity, including unfelt muscle tension, is initiated and guided or modulated by integrated cortical or higher cerebral actions and these actions include such complex influences as the meaningfulness of perceptions, consideration of consequences, projection of intention, etc. The fact that muscle activity can quickly become automatic means that the muscle control systems can function automatically with a minimum of cerebral intervention, and thus the system can rely upon feedback control systems. That is, in the oversimplified concept of the muscle feedback control systems, information from the muscle fibers is relayed to central control areas where it is compared to what the control is set for in any given situation of muscle activity, and appropriate adjustments are activated. This is the muscle-cerebral feedback control loop. In this automatic mode of operation, the effect of alerting or stressful stimuli activates primarily the more mechanically involved cortical mechanisms which affect movement and preparation for movement, and this, of course, changes muscle tension levels toward a defense mode.

Obviously, at the same time the alerting or threatening stimuli have activated the perceptual-cerebral mechanisms which judge stimuli to be threatening and set in motion the muscle reactions. At the same time the response of the cortex may parallel the changes going on in the direct muscle control system, i.e., the occupation of the cortex with the emotion-producing stimuli continues to activate its focus on the emotional problem and raises its threshold for recognizing or appreciating the increased muscle tension. This would mean that while the cerebral mechanisms are concerned with the perception (and rumination) of the alerting situation, the stimuli would continue to convey the alerting signals to the muscle control systems, aggravating the tension, increasing or sustaining it, as actually happens. Only when a cerebral or psychologic change occurs to affect the *significance* of the alerting information would the cerebral aspect begin to appreciate and be aware of the increased muscle tension, which would then in turn release the inhibitory effect on the muscles sustaining the tension and restore normal control functioning. This sequence could account for the effectiveness of psychotherapeutic effects in relieving muscle tension.

In parallel fashion, inducing relaxation by focussing awareness on muscle effect (such as Jacobson's tense-relax exercises) results in fewer muscle tension impulses being sent to the central nervous system, and so there are fewer stimuli to affect the cortex, keeping it alerted, and this in turn decreases the cortical action on the lower-brain areas which have been maintaining the muscle tension. At the same time there are fewer stimuli reminding the cortex about the reasons for the tension, and this relieves the inhibition of awareness by the cortex. Continuing in this dual circular fashion, the increased awareness of muscle tension causes a decrease in the cortical action on the muscle control systems, augmenting the peripheral relaxation effect.

In the Jacobson type of learned relaxation, a cognition or awareness of the differences between tension and relaxation is developed, and the cerebral effect is to attend to relaxation, which signals the muscles to relax. As this occurs, fewer tension impulses are sent to the cerebral association areas, and this in turn diminishes the stimulation of perceptual-memory associations related to the tension, diminishing both cortical inhibition of muscle relaxation and the calling forth of emotional significances, hence mental tension diminishes as well.

The concept of a perceptual-cerebral system at least equipotent with the more mechanical muscle control system fits well with the research findings of Hefferline. From his studies, Hefferline concluded that people learn to block the recognition of muscle tension at the brain level, a process he called conditioned inhibition. Part of the evidence for this conclusion was that when people could learn to become aware of their muscle tensions, they would recover the memories of what had caused them to tense their muscles in the first place. This has been reported in biofeedback-assisted relaxation, and it seems possible that as relaxation proceeds, and awareness of tension occurs, the cerebral associations of the need to defend would lead to recovery of memories of why there was a need to defend, and so both muscle and mental tension are relieved.

The same series of events occurs without any "conditioning" at all. The following anecdote illustrates the significance of the two factors, muscle and cerebral, that are concerned in developing and relieving muscle patterns of tension or action. I became aware that I was having difficulties remembering friends' telephone numbers during times I was in my office. I then recalled that the office phone is a dial phone whereas my home phone is a touch-tone telephone. I often ring up my friends from home and rarely do so from the office, and when I do, I find that my fingers hover over the dial uncertain of the numbers to dial, and the actual numbers refuse to jump into consciousness. On the other hand, at home the fingers touch the right numbers without any conscious thought at all of the number I am calling. The numbers have become muscle action patterns, much like Jacobson's muscle tension-image patterns, to be used just as the action-image patterns for my leg muscles can be called upon for walking action patterns.

The concept of a perceptual-cerebral muscle control system at least equipotent with the more mechanical muscle-cerebral control system has important implications for the way in which biofeedback therapy is implemented. If reversing a physiologic change that has caused both physical and emotional symptoms, and only the medical aspect is considered, then the usefulness of the treatment may suffer. Consideration of the importance of the cerebral aspects can contribute both to optimizing the therapeutic procedures and to capitalizing on the effects produced by relaxation. The former is discussed under the heading of strategy information such as the use of visualization, inwardly directed attention, distinguishing passive from active concentration, and other subjective factors. As biofeedback training continues and awareness of internal states develops, the changing awarenesses bring forth associated memories, changing perspectives on the status of internal activities, and the significance of external stimuli on the body's reactions. These new insights then can be understood and used to maintain the improvement.

Relaxation Techniques Used with EMG Biofeedback

The use of learned relaxation for the treatment of emotional and psychosomatic disorders is not new. Two quite different techniques. Autogenic Training and Progressive Relaxation, have been used successfully as medical therapeutic techniques for more than fifty years. The former is popular in Europe and in various medical centers around the world; Progressive Relaxation is practiced mainly in the United States. Both entail months, sometimes years, of relaxation practice.

The popularity of EMG biofeedback-assisted relaxation seems to be the result of its adding efficiency to proven therapeutic procedures. While EMG biofeedback improves the efficiency and effectiveness of demonstrated relaxation procedures, in actual clinical practice, EMG biofeedback relaxation is almost invariably combined with elements of the other relaxation techniques. The following discussion reviews the concepts and principles of those techniques most commonly used with EMG biofeedback.

Autogenic training (A.T.) was borrowed from hypnotic techniques, and is a combination of self-suggestion about relaxation and more advanced self-suggestion phrases for learning to control consciousness, as in meditation. The emphasis is on the subjective aspects of relaxation or nontension, and experimental evidence suggests that there is not always a correlation between muscle relaxation and relief from mental tension. Progressive Relaxation (P.R.) relies largely upon sensations of muscle activity, using the differences between the feelings of muscle contraction and relaxation to develop an understanding and awareness of deep relaxation. In P.R. relative muscle relaxation is first induced, and is compared to muscle tension to develop the feeling of relaxation. Both A.T. and P.R. are selective in that only those patients with considerable persistence follow the training procedures long enough to enjoy their benefits. Both techniques also have the same disadvantage: the lack of specific information about the level of existing muscle tension. Learning to control muscle activity depends on a variety of sensory information, including visual information from watching muscle activity and pressure information from the skin when muscle masses move, as well as upon the internal information about muscle tension sensed by special nerve endings that send the information to the central nervous system. During relaxation training, only the latter is available.

The obvious and critical new element that biofeedback brings to relaxation training is the technology to detect and provide precise information about muscle activity that is otherwise unfelt. In a sense, it replaces much of the internally derived information people usually use to learn to control muscles, and precisely because it does supply direct and accurate information EMG biofeedback should be, and is, extremely efficient in achieving the goals of relaxation procedures. The goal of relaxation procedures is not simply relaxation; the goal is the voluntary control of the tension-relaxation dimension of muscles, and the inexpressible but subjectively known awareness that gives one the ability for control.

Progressive Relaxation

The prime expert, perhaps the sole expert, in the psychosomatic specialty of muscles has been Edmund Jacobson, who, since 1908 through the present, has supplied both the fundamental and applied researches of mind-muscle relationships to medicine. Through some delightfully creative research, Jacobson has forged decisive, convincing evidence for the mutual interdependency of mind and muscles upon each other for their well-being. While other medical researchers have accumulated evidence to support one or another psychophysiologic theory of emotion, particularly arousal theory, by studying reactions of the autonomic nervous system, Jacobson has systematically documented the powerful effects on muscles of such higher mental activities as imagination, attention, and awareness.

In the medical world of therapeutics, Jacobson's contribution rests upon his major thesis that anxiety and relaxation are mutually exclusive. That is, anxiety does not, cannot, exist when the muscles are truly relaxed. And while the physiologic details to support this idea have not been worked out with the precision that particulate neurophysiology demands, the clinical successes of Jacobson's relaxation techniques give the concept a good bit of merit.

Jacobson's Progressive Relaxation is based upon the very simple procedure of comparing tension against relaxation. Since a person generally has very little awareness of the *sensation* of relaxation, he is asked first to tense a set of muscles as hard as he can until he can feel real tension, even tenderness and pain in the muscles. Then he allows those muscles to relax, and tries to become aware of, to feel internally, the difference between tension and relaxation. For example, in some of the first exercises in Progressive Relaxation the patient is asked to hyperextend the wrist, i.e., to bend the hand so the back of the hand is aiming toward the top of the forearm. The muscles contracting the hand backward are tensed as much as the patient can, and are held until he feels the sensations of tension and even tenderness in the muscles of the upper side and about the middle of the forearm. Then the hand is flopped down to a lose, relaxed position. As a single exercise, this alternation between tensing and relaxing is practiced no more than about three times in a fifteen-minute period. A good share of the time is spent in trying to discriminate the feelings of tension and relaxation, i.e., the absence of tension. As practicing continues, the patient begins to discriminate more and more finely different degrees of tension and relaxation. The procedure is not hurried; each exercise with *each* set of muscles is practiced for perhaps two weeks, and only then does work begin with another set of muscles. Since the procedure goes progressively through all of the muscles in the body (hence its name), to accomplish the entire procedure requires considerable time, let alone persistence.

As used first in desensitization techniques and then in conjunction with biofeedback training, Jacobson's relaxation technique has been modified. In current practice, all time periods for the different exercises have been shortened, and some practitioners run through the entire progression within an hour or even less time.

Jacobson's work has contributed much more to understanding the effect of tension and anxiety on the health of human beings than just the development of a relaxation technique. He demonstrated, for example, that learned relaxation of the muscles can generalize to smooth (involuntary) muscles and can cause relaxation of muscles of the gastrointestinal and cardiovascular systems.

A major contribution stems from his work with imagination. Jacobson conducted a number of fascinating experiments which recorded the physiologic effects of imagination. For example, when people were asked to pretend they were operating an old-fashioned telegraph key with a middle finger, but not to move a muscle, as they imagined pressing the key there were bursts of muscle activity only in those muscles involved in moving that middle finger to tap a key. From such kinds of experiments, Jacobson was able to demonstrate that there is an energy expenditure during imagination. Actually, the objective of the experiments was to identify various influences on the awareness of internal states. Jacobson incorporated the concept of energy waste in his Progressive Relaxation therapy, particularly in the treatment of anxiety and tension.

Jacobson pointed out that while most people believe anxiety and tension are caused by the existence of a problem, that is, by external influences, his experimental and clinical evidence indicates that anxiety is caused by the effort-tension to solve problems, and that anxiety is really *muscle tension-image patterns*. In other words, the mental review of tension-producing situations, even the subconscious image or sensation of the experience, sets the muscles into particular patterns of tension, such as bracing for a blow. Since many of these tension-image muscle patterns are lost to memory, Jacobson conceded that imagery could be used to elicit an accurate identification of the muscle tension-image pattern. After one could relate the image causing the tension to the muscle tension, the idea would then be to practice relaxation and gradually eliminate the image which in itself caused tension.

In clinical practice, Jacobson's technique, combining psychologic with physiologic awareness, constitutes a psychobiologic therapeutic procedure for the treatment of anxiety and stress-related problems. The procedure consists of three stages: (1) identification of the difficulties, i.e., the situations which cause tension; (2) identification of the muscle tension-image patterns (e.g., the businessman in a conference must concentrate on listening, analyzing information, etc., and so tenses the face, around the eyes, even the ears, tenses the shoulders, etc.), then (3) practicing the relaxation procedures. Identifying the tension-image patterns is similar to visualizing or recreating the feelings accompanying the difficult events that cause tension, as for example, the businessman imagining the tension-producing situation of the conference can become aware of the eye tension, and this activates the muscles making them tense. Once the tension-image is identified, the patient is asked to relax that image, or as Jacobson directs, "go negative," and repeat this exercise along with the relaxation exercises until the tension-images no longer produce muscle tension. This aspect of the technique is similar to desensitization, where the procedure is to imagine as vividly as possible anxiety-producing situations while learning how to maintain low muscle tension.

It should be pointed out that Jacobson consistently documented the reductions in muscle activity that occurred as a result of following his relaxation procedure, and his results are supported by the consistent reduction currently being reported in studies comparing Progressive Relaxation with other relaxation techniques.

Hypnotic Suggestion and Autogenic Training

Research and clinical application of biofeedback-assisted relaxation has also brought three other relaxation techniques into prominence: Schultz's Autogenic Training, meditation, and hypnotic suggestion.

Like Jacobson's technique, these techniques are also exclusively concerned with manipulations of the still mysterious activities of the human mind that continue to elude definition by the physical biomedical sciences.

Hypnotic suggestion is not used extensively in either medical or psychological therapy for the purpose of inducing and sustaining relaxation although it is used occasionally in a form of systematic desensitization and in research studies.

Autogenic training did, however, develop directly from the therapeutic practice of hypnosis for relaxation as a countermeasure for anxiety and related problems. The complete training program is divided into three categories of exercises: autosuggestion about relaxation, single-focus mental concentration (as in yogic meditation), and finally meditation on abstract qualities of universal consciousness, much as in yogic or Zen meditation. It is principally the first series of exercises, and only occasionally the second, that are used practically in medical or psychologic treatment.

The first series of exercises used with EMG biofeedback are simple self-suggestion phrases designed to mimic the hypnotically induced relaxed state. The phrases range from "my arm is heavy," "my arm is warm," through all parts of the body. In the original, the phrases began with the concept of heaviness, which was serially applied first to the whole body, then to each of the major parts. The sequence was then repeated using the idea of warmth, going on to the concept of deep relaxation. Allowing sufficient time for the autosuggestions to take effect in the mind and in the muscles required somewhat excessively long periods of time, both for each practice session and for the entire course. In modern practice the amount of time has been considerably shortened, so that a whole "round" can be practiced in an hour's time.

As used with biofeedback muscle signals, the autogenic training phrases are focussed primarily on the physiologic aspect (muscle tension or skin temperature) used in the training, interspersed with general suggestions for relaxing. Each phrase is said slowly, allowing time for the patient to begin to feel some awareness of the effect of the suggestion. Often the therapist, at the beginning of treatment, speaks the phrases at the proper pacing and in a soothing voice, similar to hypnotic induction. Some therapists further encourage the use of imagery of situations or memories accompanying states of heaviness, warmth and relaxation.

Transcendental Meditation

Almost concurrently with the development of biofeedback, certain philosophies of the Maharishi Mahesh Yogi became popular in the United States. His simplified formula for meditation, called Transcendental Meditation, has been studied extensively in psychophysiology laboratories and it is claimed that the procedure, calling for two 15-minute meditation periods a day, produces profound physiologic changes characteristic of tranquillity, when practiced faithfully.

The use of Transcendental Meditation to normalize body functions may be more a matter of changing lifestyle than its having any specific effects on physiology. It occupies a peculiar position in the new categories of psychophilosophic healing arts, being a meditation practice adapted to Western concepts and philosophic backgrounds. T.M. consists of two essentials: the twice-daily meditation practice, each of 15 minutes duration, in which no particular direction of thought may or may not be attempted, but instead, a mantra is constantly repeated to oneself, and second, belief that the practice will bring order to the mind and body.

Research studies demonstrating the dramatic changes in physiologic activity occurring with T.M. practice have been widely advertised by rather professional promotional techniques, with the result that the general population at least has been impressed by the scientific data.

Most serious psychophysiologic and biomedical researchers, however, point out the failure of all research on the physiologic effects of T.M. to date to compare to the effectiveness of simple rest. Their criticism suggests that similar, possibly identical, physiological changes may occur if individuals would simply rest quietly twice daily for fifteen minutes at a time. It is unfortunate that no one has taken the time to gather the data to support this criticism; nevertheless, it is a crucial issue, and most medical professionals hesitate to accept the available data.

The criticism does not, however, deny the usefulness of T.M. practice as an adjunct to therapeutic relaxation techniques, including EMG biofeedback. Nonetheless, as I often remark, practicing Transcendental Meditation twice daily is the first time Americans have ever sat still and focussed on their minds, and one easily could expect to see physiologic changes resulting from this voluntary regime of inactivity. Most responsible people try to meet the fast pace of today's world, and siestas, naps or simply sitting quietly are not part of the average American's routine. There is also the element of belief in T.M. practice that is common to the practice of any other therapeutic exercise. Westerners believe in medical authority by and large, and it is often this belief that produces the beneficial results along with the actual effect of the relaxation exercises or tranquillizers or psychotherapy or even biofeedback.

Of the very few research studies conducted by researchers not within the T.M. fold are two studies, confirming each other, which provide physiologic data indicating that transcendental meditators spend most of their meditation time in sleep stages 1, 2, 3, or 4. One investigator suggests, somewhat catishly, that T.M. teaches people how to cat-nap; the other researcher interprets his data as failing to support the concept of T.M. researchers that meditation produces a single, unique state of consciousness, refuting Wallace's claim.

A third study compared effects of T.M. practice in experienced T.M. meditators with the effects of subjects simply being instructed to relax. Measurements of heart rate, muscle tension, and brain wave alpha activity revealed that the only significant changes occurred in the relaxed not the T.M. subjects.

It may seem unconscionable for investigators to quibble over a T.M. conclusion that cannot be completely confirmed by present-day psychophysiologic techniques or data analyses. The psychophysiologist who desires to deny the therapeutic significance of learning to control states of consciousness that (1) resemble certain sleep stages electroencephalographically but cannot be proved to be exclusively those sleep stages, and (2) give rise to consensus of subjective reporting of improved physical and mental health, would seem to be more interested in quibbling than in the true objectives of research. It certainly is an important step if T.M. can teach people how to cat-nap, a technique universally agreed upon as a helpful preventive medical procedure, regardless of whether the context of the control is religious, philosophic, mystical, or medical.

Relaxation Is an Awareness Process

It is a particularly interesting observation to note that three of the four major relaxation techniques used in combination with EMG biofeedback stem directly from Hindu yogic meditation. I have not mentioned yogic exercises which are used by Patel and by Datey and by biofeedback researchers in India since these are discussed in the sections on biofeedback and essential hypertension. Information on yogic exercises is readily available and there is no need to discuss them here except to note that both Patel and Datey use Hatha yoga exercises which require both physical manipulation and concentration on awareness of the body activities.

All of the relaxation procedures described above have been used in conjunction with biofeedback; in fact it is rare that one reads a scientific report on EMG biofeedback without their reported use as supplementary procedures. Although the use of combined techniques for relaxation has been justified on a scientific level, there are interesting social reasons why the combinations are so successful. In addition to the direct accessibility of important information, as noted above, most Westerners have been educated and reconciled to the scientific dictum that what one cannot see or feel about the body cannot be controlled voluntarily. All supplementary relaxation techniques focus upon awareness of internal states, i.e., attention is directed inwardly instead of the usual outwardly directed attention. This change in the normal person's perspective entails a learning process, and the aids supplied by autosuggestive phrases, comparing relaxation with tensing, and sitting quietly becoming aware of the self, act as self-teaching devices to explore personal territory that has been so long screened from awareness.

The Second Illness

The Stress of Being Ill

The academic, intellectual, and therapeutic schisms between psychology and medicine have made the problem of being sick—from any cause—a hundredfold worse than it has any right to be.

The very sectarianism of these two therapeutic disciplines may be why neither of them has seen one of the most fundamental problems of being sick. The fact is that *any* disturbance of body or mind spawns still another, a second, very real disease. There is, I have ventured, for every illness or mental distress, a "second illness" that is the distress of just being sick, or, for that matter, the distress that comes from being out of any part of life's normal course for any reason at all.

The "second illness" is the mental and emotional reaction to being sick, to having a problem, and it is a very real illness with very real and important effects on mind and body. Almost inexplicably, both medical and psychological therapists treat illness as either a problem of the emotions or a problem of the body. Rarely, very rarely, do they treat mind and body as the inseparable whole that they are. Even exclusively emotional illnesses are often treated as if they are solely of physical, physiological origin, and just as curiously, psychotherapy itself concentrates its attention much more on the roots of raw, primitive emotions (suppressed anger, hostility, hate, fear) than on the mental apparatus of the literate, ingenious, inventive human mind that is the well-spring for emotional distress.

As we begin to understand more about the interrelationships between mind and body in health and illness, it becomes clear that problems of the mind (and emotions) can seriously affect the functioning of the body, as in psychosomatic illnesses, and in the same way the mental, emotional problems caused simply by being sick can aggravate existing problems, emotional or physical, and interfere with recovery.

The prevailing tendency of the professional therapists for dividing sick people into two parts has profound consequences for the welfare of society. For when we neglect the Second Illness, we quite literally create two kinds of outcasts: the psychological outcast who becomes either neglected or is regressed to a state of pseudo-infancy by family and friends, and the social outcast who is rejected by society as a whole because his illness has removed him from the activities of a normal social life.

Even the Least Unwellness Distresses the Emotions

To appreciate the surprising scope and true virulence of the second illness, let's look at different kinds of illness in a very general way. First there are the illnesses or distresses of life that cause moderate discomfort and diminished ability to participate in life's activities. The almost infinite varieties of health problems, from recurring headaches, ulcers, or bouts of hay fever to bereavement or high blood pressure, no matter how mild or severe, all impose restrictions on both an individual's performance and on his participation in social activities. The physical distress or the emotional discomfort pushes the individual to the side of the mainstream of his normal life, often with annoying, sometimes intense psychological reactions to the strange circumstance of his inability to perform up to potential, and to being different in a society that prizes normalcy and effort and achievement.

The second main category of illness is the disabling illness, such as paralysis, loss of a critical body part, cancer, other debilitating, chronic illnesses, and even severe mental illness. Victims of these illnesses become social outcasts, set aside as permanently impaired and beyond rescue. Even with partial rehabilitation, any deficiency in ability to perform is generally considered to be a total inability to perform. The person is the eternal patient, consigned to the back corridors of life with the meagre gift of custodial care.

Both categories of illness, mild and severe, share the powerful effects of illness on emotions, mind, and spirit. As long as the mind survives, it perceives and responds; it perceives its wholeness diminished, it perceives its deprivation from social wholeness, and the mind reacts with the force of any perceiving mind, understanding the problem but none of the answers because, for the most part, our society has not been concerned with answers to the psychological and social effects and needs of the Second Illness.

Consider the psychological impact of *any* illness. Whether the illness is distress of mind or body, emotional or physical, the mind and its intellect perceive the slightest loss in capacity to perform, to participate, to behave as a normal human being. The housewife with a headache is not just uncomfortable, she is also aware that the performance of her family role falls short of what she desires. For the double amputee, the *nature* of the emotional reaction to illness is basically not much different, even thought the emotions are much more seriously disturbed and for much longer times. The emotional reaction to not being able to perform up to expectations, personal or public, involves a tangle of nearly every emotion known to psychology: anxiety, depression, frustration, anger. And the anxiety is multiple because of the fear of the unknown, the not-knowing if the signs of sickness herald something even more serious, the not knowing how to get by until one can perform again, the not knowing where to get help or what kind of help to get, the not knowing about how long the illness may last.

The anxiety about a diminished ability to perform is compounded by the sheer frustration of not being able to perform. The secretary with a headache, under pressure to produce work, also suffers the distress of not being able to keep up, and the very real implications of any flagging for job security. The pains and aches and physical discomforts of illness are modest troubles compared to the distresses of mind that illness brings. Whether it is high blood pressure that diminishes activity or a crippling arthritis, the emotional impact goes far beyond the anxieties and frustrations, social relationships, and outlook for the future. There is as well the uncomfortable feeling of suddenly losing one's independence and becoming dependent upon the experts and family or friends, and suffering the companion of dependence, the loss of self-esteem.

Being ill, in short, is stressful—seriously, interferingly stressful. The stress of being ill is a surprisingly large component of illness to be so neglected in the treatment of it. Typically, when the emotional symptoms are obvious or disturbing, they are treated by tranquilizers or sedatives; but while tranquilizers and sedatives are necessary to relieve obvious or acute anxiety, they are not helpful over the long haul. They have, in fact, helped medicine and psychology to create a drug society, and the second illness that accompanies drug abuse.

The Treatment Gap

When the second illness, the "stress of being ill" is not treated, the first illness becomes more debilitating than need be, and recovery from the illness takes longer than it should. Even the seemingly most benign physical problem, the tension headache, has distressing emotional overtones. To lose a day to headache, and over time to lose many days to headache, is a serious disruption of life's activities, performance, social relationships, earning money, and ensuring the security of job and finances. But the headache is the symptom that receives the medical attention, and often not too successfully at that, while the patient endures the emotional problems and mental distress as best he can.

The emotional distress of the chronically ill or the handicapped bears a similar hallmark. The problems that such illnesses cause are much the same as for the less severe problems. But because the disability is obvious, these kinds of illnesses often attract enough understanding, concern, and affection to provide some measure of the needed psychological support, although official, medically sanctioned treatment is a long way away from dealing with any effectiveness with the disturbances to mind and of mind to body that engulf the handicapped.

Slowly, bit by bit, emotion by emotion, the mental and emotional torture of being ill is being recognized as part and parcel of all illness. There is no unified attack yet on the "stress of being ill" by medicine or psychology, but there is a growing awareness by professional healers that the psyche, the core of modern man, exerts a profound effect on the course of all illness. More and more the need to treat mind and emotions during illness and physical problems is being recognized. The need of the handicapped for improved self-esteem has become a part of therapy, the need of the dying for understanding and love has produced the new science of thanatology, while at the other end of the spectrum, self-help and awareness techniques are proving to be equal to drugs in the management of distresses caused by the stress of life.

The mind, it turns out, can be a master healer. The problem now is to learn more about the resources of the mind to heal its own being.

The Dis-ease Immune System, A Creation of the Psyche

New Thoughts on the Nature and Origins of the Psyche

No doubt because we are only now reaching the frontiers of learning about the mind-body interface, the words we use to describe intangible, abstract mind states and feelings tend to be more confusing and ambiguous than truly informative. The word "consciousness," for example, is abused as much by the mind-brain scientists as by anyone, and scientists routinely fail to specify whether they are discussing conscious awareness or unconscious mental activity (as in unconscious conflicts). I have described a number of examples of the operations of the unconscious (subliminal) intellect, and to be consistent, we really should talk about unconscious awarenesses as well as conscious awareness.

When, for example, we feel a deep commitment to someone or have a strong rapport or feel empathetic, we really have two kinds of awarenesses—a conscious awareness of the *fact* of a particular state of mind and thought and feeling, and second, we have an *all over* awareness, an all-pervading sensation through the entire being that is almost impossible to describe. I suspect the latter reflects a subliminally constructed consciousness about the total, *whole* state of one's being. I suspect, too, that awarenesses that seem to involve the entire being in a way that cannot be described in words are complex awarenesses of the whole being, known to the unconscious mind and poorly communicated to the conscious mind because *conscious* awareness can focus on only a limited number of events at any one time. Consciousness has some "in-kling" of the inner knowledge or feeling the unconscious mind is aware of, but consciousness (as conscious awareness) cannot artic-ulate the sensations except in vague analogies. Whole being awarenesses perhaps should be called psychic awarenesses (be-longing to the psyche) since it is the psyche that holds the whole network of mind and body and feeling sensations together.

Elsewhere I present some new concepts about the human psyche. In essence, the research and analyses support Jung's description of the psyche as the innate, inner organizing center and guiding force of the self and of the growth of Self during life, the ground substance of self-realization. The new study of the psyche also supports the dictionary definition of the psyche as, "the mind functioning as the center of thought, feelings, and behavior, and consciously or unconsciously adjusting and relating the body to its social and physical environment" (*American Heritage Dictionary,* 1976).

As the concept of the psyche is expanded and updated in the light of the new psychologies and changing psychosocial influ-ences of the late twentieth century, it becomes clear *that the psyche determines states of human well-beingness.* Because the psyche is the bridge, the link joining mind and body and spirit, and because it is the unifying principle that establishes mind-body harmony in beingness, behavior, and feeling, it responds to all insults to mind and body and spirit.

Stress Is Assaults on the Psyche

Mind, body, and spirit never react separately; whatever assaults one diminishes the wholeness and health and well-being of their core-link, the psyche, and when the psyche is affected, mind, body, and spirit all respond. A physical ailment may be not only physically painful, its implications for secondary effects on job security or economic well-being create both anxiety and depres-sion of the spirit as well. Stress assaults to the mind's beliefs and opinions or to its values or hopes and dreams such as rejection, ridicule, being ignored or forgotten, lead to deeply troubled emotions, usually with equally troubled functions of the physical body. Similarly, an insult to your moral integrity can make you both physically sick and emotionally disturbed, while a disappointment or failure to reach goals nearly always upsets the body and saps the spirit. Physical, emotional, mental, or spiritual hurts, they are all psychic blows and they are all stress.

It is clear that stress affects first and most deeply the psyche. Because stress involves human relationships and causes uncertainty about life's future social relationships and concern about psychological well being, it strikes at the most vital of the foundations of human life—the center where mind and spirit work for fulfillment and self-realization. Stress jeopardizes the integrity and wholeness and harmony of the psyche.

Now, to complete our circle of thought from the notion of psychic awareness to the notion that stress is first and foremost psychic toxicity (assaults to the psyche; psychic bruises), still another very new concept emerges. Our evidence strongly suggests that the psyche contains and sustains an immune (defense) system that functions to prevent and relieve the effects of assaults to the psyche (stress). The immune system that defends against psychic assaults and psychic bruises looks to be a very specially evolved set of awarenesses and potential awarenesses.

It is well known that the body possesses an immune system that acts to defend the body against *physical* assaults. Tissue biochemicals, for example, tend to resist effects of injury and the body also possesses the capacity to manufacture antibodies that fight off invading infectious organisms. I suggest that the intangible nature of human beings also possesses its own immune system, a line of defense the psyche can develop to resist the effects of psychic assaults and psychic bruises (stress).

Awareness and consciousness and understanding are *not* the same notions regardless of how careless we have become in our language. Awareness and awarenesses are *mental sensations*—special, higher order, evolved sensations created by mind senses that recognize the products of higher mental activity such as beliefs, attitudes, thoughts, and feelings, the dozens of mental sensations that are usually just lumped together and called self-consciousness. Self-consciousness is not simply an awareness that one's mental activities exist and an awareness that one's self is unique. Self-consciousness is a *collection* of awarenesses (the sensations accompanying understanding) of the self *as the whole participates in different qualities of the self.* They are like the gods in the Hindu pantheon where each whole deity is a manifestation of a different quality of the Supreme Being, and each special quality reveals the whole. *Psychic awarenesses belong only to the whole being,* and not to any one mind or body part (such as an awareness of fatigue or awareness of a problem or an awareness of being scared).

Psychical Awareness Is Awareness of the Whole Being

Awarenesses are the natural antidotes to stress. These extended senses of the psyche are the *mental sensations* of our beliefs and ideas and thought-sensations that encompass the whole being. The sense of your own name is one example. When people in the distance are talking and you can catch only a word here and there, you may suddenly be brought up short—did they say my name? You check. They did. You heard it, of course, with the subliminal mind, not the conscious mind.

The subliminal awareness of recognizing your own name in a very unlooked-for circumstance is very different from the primary sensing of a smell or touch. It is really an all-over feeling. You can feel the name recognition down to your toes. And note that your respiration halts for a second, you stand at attention if only for half a second, and some inner remote whisper says, "that's me!" But awarenesses are also awarenesses of exactly how something relates to you—to *all* of you. Awareness of your own very special identity is one of the self's most important protective, defense devices. It is not only essential to growth and maturity, but becoming aware of the wholeness and harmony of the self is profoundly therapeutic.

A striking, heartwarming example of the healing power of awareness is a simple self-suggestion. One cannot measure the enormous relief of so much psychic hurt in blacks as when the Rev. Jesse Jackson encourages them to repeat the phrase, *"I am somebody."* Thousands of people have come to *feel* being somebody, being someone special, having their own identity, being their own person, and feel the sensation *all over.* You can't pick "being somebody" apart to identify its causes the way you can, say, the feeling of Spring because of the sights and sounds and smells. Psychic awarenesses are created only when meanings for the whole being are understood by the whole. Awarenesses of the psyche's remarkable qualities that work for wholeness and harmony and for growth and individuation resist assaults to the psyche.

This, my friends, is what I believe to be the psyche's defense against psychic hurts: the special awarenesses of special qualities of *the whole being,* the awarenesses taught by the psychic senses, by the mind senses that belong to the psyche. These are *not* simply intellectual appraisals or isolated, specific feelings about special properties of the self; they are *sensations of the wholeness* of the self as the self participates in each quality of the self.

Part III
The Hidden Intellect and Beyond

Biofeedback and the Deeper Levels of the Mind

To the Limits of Mind

For most people, the explorations into the deeper levels of the mind are guided by knowledge gleaned from religion, philosophy, and psychology. To ourselves we dream dreams about the mind as if it were spirit, an entity of self somehow liberated from material constraints. We tend to acknowledge the rigid boundaries of life support systems with reluctance, if indeed we acknowledge the substantive world at all, except perhaps when we claim those precious moments of breaking through our molecular prisons. We tend to focus our desires on magical flights of pure mind, when mind is unencumbered by reminders of its dependence upon physical elements.

The experience of pure mind is, of course, ineffable. But its mood can sometimes be captured, as in a poem Millay wrote long ago:

Euclid alone has looked on Beauty bare.
Let all who prate of beauty hold their peace
And lay them prone upon the earth and cease
To ponder on themselves, the while they stare
At nothing, intricately drawn nowhere
In shapes of shifting lineage; let geese
Gabble and hiss, but heros seek release
From dusty bondage into luminous air.
O blinding hour, O holy terrible day,
When first the shaft into his vision shone

Of light anatomized! Euclid alone
Has looked on beauty bare. Fortunate they
Who, though once only and then but far away
Have heard her massive sandal set on stone.

No one who has truly experienced the sudden ethereal essence of pure knowledge, no one who has known such immateriality of thought and being, who has known identity with a distant but commanding unifying pull of the universe can ever welcome his return to steel and glass and blood and tears.

But the reality of our existence is that we *are* tied to bodies, bodies brimming with blood and muscles and nerves and brains. Yet more often than we care to admit, we lunge with great intuitive surges to free the mind from the body. Probably for as long as man can remember, he has resisted the idea that his mental self is merely the product of his physical self. He consistently and persistently disparages the role of body in the realms of mind; he seems to loathe the tricks of distraction the body plays upon the mind, and, except for the yogi, he has ignored the idea that there may be roles of body to help the mind explore itself and find its liberation.

Our attitudes about mind and body are, of course, paradoxical. It takes little more than ordinary experience with life to understand the eminence of mind; insights into realms of pure mind are shared, exalted, and reverenced. Parallel to accomplishments of mind, biological and medical authority accumulates compelling evidence that the essence of mind is mechanized, a stereotyped subatomic shuttle system, and with all of the discrimination that education so deftly employs in teaching evolution or history or religion, so has biology and medicine exerted its bias to persuade human beings to accept the dominion of the physical self over their destiny and to look to chemistry and physics to explain the mind.

We have come to believe in the identity of mind with body, yet with this dictum from science, science treats only of the physical body. The experiential, however, treats of feeling, of knowing, of beingness. Both experiential and scientific authority are limited; neither is a security for belief, neither equips us suitably to explore and know and use the continuity of brain and being.

The physical science, behavioristically oriented perspectives of the Western hemisphere often fail to recognize that all civilizations from the beginning of time have sought to search the limits of the mind. Yet from the frenetic rush to physical excellence, to material awareness, to crediting physical foundations for the behavior of society, there has evolved the social revolution and the social consciousness of the past few years. And the sudden awareness of consciousness and conscience in the social change has touched a number of biological scientists. There is a hint that the mind will now be explored for its uniqueness, free from its dependence upon yet interacting with the hustling shadows of potassium and sodium, RNA or serotonin. Indeed, these new explorations may not only bring balance to the disparate certainties about the puzzling parts of being, but may uncover untapped resources of mind.

Our more recent experience with states of consciousness has not only discovered more mind space, but fairly safe ways of achieving specific degrees of altered consciousness, as by using meditation or small doses of hallucinogens. But even these are incomplete; their concentration is on mind alone, neglecting the contribution of the body or the mind and body as a unit.

The Biological Mind Guides

I have set my task to explain the biological approach to equipping and guiding the mind to new horizons of inner space. For seeking knowledge of the mind, besides the unpredictable, spontaneous changes of consciousness or intentional manipulations of mind, or drug induced changes, there is yet another way. It is, of course, biofeedback.

The word biofeedback is no longer new. In 1969, when I created the word in a burst of enthusiasm about the apparent fundamental similarity of different researches, I had no idea that the concept of biofeedback would be explored and exploited so widely in such a short period of time. It seems to me that it is precisely because there is a universal truth in the biofeedback concept that it has been exploited so rapidly, but I also feel that it is going to be a very long time before we understand the biofeedback phenomenon well enough to use it to its fullest capacity.

There are really two parts to the explanation of biofeedback. The first covers the psychobiologic priniciples and the technology, and the second deals with the use of the technique.

Biofeedback simply means the feedback of biological information to the individual who generates that biological information. The information fed back may be about any body system, organ function, or even cellular activity. Most of you are probably familiar with the type of biofeedback that uses alpha brain waves as the feedback information. But any biological information can be used, such as breathing rate or heart rate or blood pressure, muscle cells, other brain waves, or even skin electrical activity.

Now, how is this done? Well, by some fortunate circumstance, every physiologic activity of the body is carried out by chemical reactions which produce electrical energy. The electrical activity that occurs in the course of the vital functioning of the body's cells is extremely small, often in the neighborhood of a few millionths of a volt, but with today's electronics, these small electrical changes can be sensed and amplified and used to operate *external* signals. That is, with suitable amplification and electronic manipulation, the smallest electrical change can be used to manipulate the *external* environment, such as lights or tone generators. For example, the electrical activity of the heart beat can be used to activate a sound system so that when the heart speeds up the tones become higher in pitch, and when the heart slows, the tones become lower in pitch.

As biofeedback is generally employed, body signals are converted into lights or tones. This is an electronics job, often requiring a high degree of electronic sophistication. The reason for this is because each body system is enormously complex, and the systems and their cells are in constant dynamic interaction with other systems and other cells. You know, for example, that when you become apprehensive, your heart rate accelerates. That is an obvious and marked change. But what you may not know, is that your heart rate is constantly reflecting a myriad of body and mind changes. It is responsive to changes in the blood's oxygen content, to the rate of breathing, to muscle activity, to many chemical changes, and it is responsive to every small emotion and thought. These changes in normal body functioning are quite small, but it is these small changes, particularly as they reflect emotions and attitudes and mental processes that are important to an understanding of the relationship between mind and body and ultimately to understanding the self. And these small changes require considerable electronic expertise to decode and to be used to feed back to you this important information with any degree of fidelity.

The other aspect of biofeedback is practice or training. If you are provided with some signals that are reflecting a certain body activity, whether it is a selected brain wave or a few muscle cells or blood pressure, and if you have any curiosity at all, you can soon learn to control what the signals are doing. And or course that means that you are controlling a specific body activity.

How does this happen? There are no sure answers, but there are some interesting conjectures. I will give you my thoughts on the precess as we go along and indicate what biofeedback has to do with deeper levels of the mind.

Never Give the Guy a Nickel

Some of you, I am sure, know that biofeedback also developed in part out of the concept of operant conditioning. If not, let me explain for a moment. In operant conditioning, some naturally occurring behavioral activity of the animal or individual is rewarded—or in conditioning terminology, that activity is reinforced. The classical example of the Skinner box is that a rat is put into a cage with nothing in it except a lever, and when the lever is moved, a food reward is delivered to the rat. At some time when the rat is exploring his cage, he will accidentally move the lever and receive some food. Since this happens every time, the rat gradually associates his moving the lever with the delivery of food. In a relatively primitive sense, he has "learned." Exactly the same kind of procedures have been used with human beings. Substitute a human being, substitute the heart rate, and give the guy a nickel every time he increases his rate so many beats, and you've got operant conditioning.

So the guy learns to increase his heart rate to get nickels. So what? How much money can he make running around saying, "Hey, for a nickel, my heart rate will go up?" Suppose another fellow says, "O.K., if you're so good, make your heart rate go down or I'll give you a clout to the chin." And the nickel-happy guy, whose heart is by now racing with anxiety, makes a mad dash back to the psychologist's laboratory and says, "Hey, you guys, what's with this nickel biz? I almost got scalped. Teach my heart to go down when someone says I'll give you a clout on the chin."

And that's the basic difference between conditioning and biofeedback. With biofeedback techniques *you* learn how to control your own heart rate. Or brain waves. Or whatever. It is your head that is in charge. You become the master of your body, not someone else with funny little laboratory quirks about how to make *your* body behave (God forbid, not theirs).

One of the interesting things that has come out of the application of the psychologists' conditioning learning theory, however, is that while it seems to work great in animals (at least under certain conditions), it is an effective technique in human beings only when it is supplemented or augmented by supporting techniques. That is, to coax someone into changing his behavior or body activities to the desires and commands of someone else, such as a therapist, requires, for significant effectiveness, supplementary procedures *that involve the mind.*

Biofeedback is More Than Nickels

And when that happens we are into biofeedback. In the broadest view, there is nothing that concerns human behavior that does not depend upon biofeedback. Every movement, every breath, every emotion functions by way of feedback circuits, and because they involve the use of biological information, it is biofeedback. And in the broadest sense every biofeedback operation involves some influence from brain processes, from mind. Take the simple knee jerk, the jerking of the leg when the knee cap tendon is tapped. It is a classic example of the primitive reflex arc, the sensory nerve carrying the stimulation of tapping into the spinal cord, connecting with another spinal cord cell or two and exciting filaments of the motor nerve that makes the leg muscles contract. Cut off the head and the reflex still works. But with the head on, the brain can concentrate attention in a certain way and presto, no knee jerk when the tendon is tapped. The mind has the last word, or almost the last word.

The mind, that is, mental processes, has the option for active influence on all body processes; it *can* influence every process of the body. Whether the option is taken up appears to depend upon how aware the mind is of itself.

What I am saying, literally, is that the mind possesses the capability not only to influence the major, operational functions of the body, but it has the potential to direct and control the activities of single cells, perhaps even the movement of molecules within cells.

Now that is a pretty powerful statement, a statement that any respectable biologist or neurophysiologist probably would not be caught dead saying. The reason biological or biomedical scientists generally refuse to acknowledge this enormous potency of mind is principally because they lack information. They lack information about the many-sided philosophers' problem of the mind-body relationship and we all lack information about relationships between mind and body.

Physiologists, both biological and medical, research brain and body mechanisms, isolating systems and cells, but fail to inspect behavior except for the obvious, ignoring the complex hierarchies of higher mental functions that provide for shades of awareness, evaluating significances, making judgments, producing insights. In contrast, psychologists and psychiatrists research behavior, principally the external indicators of behavior, and particularly how organisms respond to *external* changes. Rarely do they study body functions except for an isolated monitor such as heart rate, and they are generally unconcerned or uneducated about biology.

To both physiologists and psychologists the mind is represented by emotions. This scientific tradition and bias is a curiously dichotomized emblem for the human species that functions best in a mind-body harmony. Even the world-wide acknowledgment that psychologic problems can incite physiologic problems, i.e., psychosomatic medicine, has not evolved any institutions where the fundamentals of psychosomatic medicine are taught.

So, it is very difficult to accrue intimate knowledge about the cooperation between mind and body processes. Certainly we can practice meditation and contemplation which give us information about the mind-self as it explores itself in splendid isolation from its physical nature. But such tehcniques often ignore or reject the great contribution that intentional control and understanding of mental or brain processes can afford to explorations of the interior man. Yoga of course attempts to exercise and expand the mind's resources more holistically. The yoga practitioner educates himself to the nuances of the body's experiential. By concentrating his mind energy, he can bring into consciousness the functioning of different body activities, and with this information and understanding, he can direct his body's activities with remarkable accuracy.

Experiencing the Deep Within

But yogic practice takes almost forever. With typical Western efficiency, the West has developed technologic yoga: Biofeedback. The important and remarkable thing about biofeedback is that it provides information about mind-body units.

Suppose that you have a monitor, a signal of one of your body's activities. Take the pulse, for example. You can press the medial aspect of the inner wrist until you feel the pulse. Now you have biofeedback. You are sensing, tactily, some information about your heart beat. The next step is to become aware of that pulse as fully as possible, and as you become more aware of the pulse, you become aware that it is much more than just a succession of pressure changes beating gently against the finger tips. You begin to feel its rhythm, its comforting regularity, and over time you become used to its particular rhythm and regularity and rate and the sameness of the pressure changes. Until suddenly you become aware that some heart beats seem different somehow; the interval between two beats may be different, the vigor of the beat may shift slightly, the rhythm seem to change.

This is a new experience, isn't it? You thought that someone else owned your heart, didn't you? Somehow you've been led to believe that only the doctor had the right to know how your heart, and its pulse, are behaving. Well, file an anti-trust action, and get back your body—it's yours to know.

One of the first things that biofeedback has to offer is a way to experience the within, the interior self, the vast community of mind-brain connections that you have let operate on automatic, and a pretty low grade automatic, at that. But since we have lived our lives reacting with the exterior world, the new experiences we may have with the interior world are new indeed. It takes some thought and searching to understand them, to organize them, to appreciate and use them to lead to other experiences of the deep within.

Suppose now that you have become sensitive to even the most subtle changes of your pulse, and you now decide to explore whether or not you really can control your heart rate. What do you do? Well, there is certainly not much you can do from the outside to force your heart's rate of beating to change. But on the inside you can experiment with imagery, or mental tasks or suggestion. Leaving imagery and mental tricks aside for the moment, let us assume you simply direct yourself to slow your pulse. No mental tricks, now, just say to yourself, slow down, pulse. Of course, if you're in a hurry, you can say, slow down, dammit, slow down, but it probably won't be necessary.

Remember, you have had your fingers on your pulse, and you've become acquainted with its smooth operation, have become intimate with it. Just wait, it will slow down. It may take a while and a fair amount of practice, or it might not take long at all. After this you can ask your pulse to speed up, and it will respond. Here again are new experiences.

How is it that the automatic body can mind the mind? Before we consider how this mental magic is accomplished, let us look at some more examples of biofeedback.

I've talked about learning to control the heart rate using the feedback of information from the pulse. That was using the tactile, the touch sense. We can improve the probability for receiving biological information if we use signals that can be perceived by the senses we are more used to using. If we convert the biological signals into visual or auditory signals, then we can use these senses to discriminate more finely the biological information.

Now, if heart rate is good, then brain waves are better, especially if you think in terms of using biological feedback signals to explore the mind. Brain electrical activity is simply amplified and converted into biofeedback signals, and although brain electrical activity is a complex pattern of many kinds of activity, there are certain brain wave components that can be selected and these, for example, alpha brain waves, relate to certain classes of behaviors and mind activities.

Closer, My Mind, to Thee?

Unfortunately brain waves never stand still so that you can capture them. Just as your thoughts are moving so fast you can scarcely remember them, so are brain waves moving, even faster. Different types of brain waves and brain wave patterns are constantly appearing and disappearing and in different areas of the brain. What happens in the feedback of alpha waves is that the individual learns to produce more abundant alpha activity. If he learns well, he can produce alpha at will, upon his own mental command, and more important, he can keep alpha present in his EEG.

Let me just note a few interesting features about alpha. First, there is a fairly well-defined subjective state that accompanies the presence of alpha—the rather general state of relaxed wakefulness—that is somewhat the same on each occasion and in most people, although the exact subjective feeling or thought state can differ under different circumstances. Second, intentionally flooding one's own EEG with alpha means that for the first time that particular brain electrical activity, alpha, is present long enough to examine it from within. Normally we have no way of knowing when it is present, yet it is one of the most prominent features of our brain's activity. With biofeedback we now have the opportunity to become acquainted with our own minds and brains and learn with more precision the operations and capacities of the mind. The underlying neurophysiologic mechanisms involved in learning to control one's own alpha activity are enormously complex. How is it that an individual can select out those brain processes that will produce alpha activity, and then control when it will occur and when it won't? I'm asking many questions and will attempt the answer after we've explored a bit more of mind-body interactions.

Another very dramatic example of biofeedback is that called motor unit control. A motor unit is a family of muscle cells all innervated by a single final filament of a motor nerve coming down from the spinal cord. Motor nerves are more or less under constant stimulation, mainly just to keep our muscle masses ready to move. For smooth muscle activity, families of muscle cells are activated just slightly out-of-step from each other, else muscles would be quivering masses. Now, each motor unit family can be traced to a single motor nerve cell in the spinal cord. That is, if you were to stimulate that single cell in the spinal cord, one and one only motor unit family in the muscle would become active and discharge an electrical impulse signal.

It is relatively simple to convert the electrical activity of a motor unit into a feedback signal. And then comes what I call the greatest drama of all. When an individual sees (or hears) the activity of this motor unit, excited by a single cell in the spinal cord, he can learn to control that activity within 15 minutes. Imagine, learning to control a single cell in 15 minutes. The process is enormously complex, because when a person activates one single cell, he must also be controlling others so that they won't interfere with the one he is controlling to become active.

Although biofeedback has received a great deal of attention during its relatively short life, there are a good many reasons why it is difficult to obtain any kind of comprehensive understanding of it. There are a multitude of applications that can be made with biofeedback, ranging from an aid to meditation to control of high blood pressure to the treatment of nerve-muscle injuries, and so on. And because there are so many sides to biofeedback, there are many people studying the phenomenon, each with something quite different to say about it. Communications is a factor, as is the tendency for the psychobiological scientist to be a specialist in one or another area of psychology or biology. Yet despite the lack of well developed concepts about the mechanisms of biofeedback, it is now being taught in virtually every university and college in the United States.

Inseparability of Mind-Body

One of the major drawbacks of the undue haste to exploit biofeedback is in the lack of appropriate background information necessary to understand it. For the essence of biofeedback is its unique use of the inseparability of mind and body. Before you conclude that I am espousing the idea of an *absolute* inseparableness of mind and body, let me define this a little further. I do believe that there are units of mind activity and units of body activity that are constantly closely associated with each other, and I call these mind-body units. They *may* be able to exist independently of each other, but I have as yet no evidence to indicate whether they can or they can't operate independently.

So before talking about how biofeedback works and what it can do for the mind, let me give an example or two to illustrate the intimacy of the mind and body, illustrations to demonstrate the reciprocal influences between mind and body.

Hidden away in the scientific literature of psychology and physiology are multitudes of studies that have not yet found their way into evidence for new ways of thinking about the mind, or mind-body units. One cluster of little research gems illustrates the endless feedback loop between the heart and subjective emotion. It is common knowledge, and psychology has given us statistics for it, that when a person becomes apprehensive and anxious or fearful, his heart rate speeds up. Then when biofeedback came along, and some experimental subjects learned to push their heart rates to quite high limits, someone thought to ask how did it feel when you *intentionally* speeded up the heart. Guess . . . anxious, scared, very apprehensive. Now here were calm, unexcited people who intentionally increased their heart rates, and they felt the same thing as the person who became anxious because of interacting with something external that caused them worry. This is an example of an internal biofeedback loop. Apprehension and anxiety cause the heart rate to increase and increasing the heart rate causes apprehension and anxiety. The important thing is that *control* over this loop is wherever you happen to enter the loop, that is, at which point you interfere with the circular action. Control could be exerted in the head or at the heart. This is an example of a mind-body unit.

Now most of such activity takes place without conscious awareness. It is only when anxiety or the beating heart exceeds certain limits that we attend, and even then we may not relate the two activities to each other. But let's see what else goes on without conscious awareness. Experimental psychologists adore playing games with people, and with the advent of biofeedback there are many more games to play. One game is creating a situation where experimental subjects become very apprehensive and anxious. In one such study the experimenter said he would let the subjects hear their own heart beats. He really didn't, he used a machine that produced nice, slow and regular heart beats. The subject *believed* the slow heart rate was his, and so his mind said, well, well, my reliable source of information says my heart rate is slow, so I must be calm. And that is exactly what happened. The subjects promptly lost their anxiety, and moreover their *real* heart rates became slow.

Along the same line, it has been previously found that the heart rate increased whenever an interesting picture was shown, so some researchers gave subjects a dose of false heart rates, some very fast heart rates for some rather uninteresting pictures. Some weeks later the subjects were called into the laboratory and were told that they could keep copies of the pictures they found to be the most interesting. You guessed it. They selected the pictures where heart rates were fastest, either their own or an artificial heart. Their heart-mind unit remembered.

Communication Systems of Mind-to-Skin-to-Mind

Let's look a little more closely at this so little known, remarkable interior universe. This time we will look at skin electrical activity. The skin is a remarkable communications medium. Ashley Montague has written a book called "Touching" about the extraordinary amount of information the skin conveys to the brain. For the present illustration I will talk about the skin's ability to convey information *from* the brain. It does this by changing its electrical characteristics, and this change is brought about chiefly, but not exclusively, by the nervous excitement of sweat glands commanding them to become alert, get ready to sweat. This condition is reflected by the change in electrical activity of the skin and this can be easily recorded and observed. Now suppose that you do something to a person that causes his skin electrical activity to respond, such as touching him with the weak charge of an electric wand. Do that a few times; then tell him that you want him to do the same thing whenever you ask him to. After a period of learning, he will make his skin respond just when you ask him to. How? He has never "seen" the response, and he certainly can't feel it. The only information he had was that you told him when he made the right response. The rest was in his head. Somehow he was able to sort out exactly those nerves which would produce the response and then activate them only on cue. Remarkable.

The skin also appears to have a unique ability to express highly realistic judgments of perceptions with greater accuracy and often with greater perspicacity than made by conscious judgments. For example, while their skin electrical responses were being recorded, subjects were asked to rate verbally the intensity of a noxious stimulus that was continuously increased in intensity. The subjects reported the most noxious stimuli as the least noxious, but the skin's responses increased one to one with increasing intensity.

This curious result was interpreted as indicating the effect of expectancy on verbalizable subjective feelings; that is, subjectively the more noxious stimuli weren't as bad as were expected and the conscious brain processes related to a conscious reality compared the expected bad with the real not-so-bad-as-expected. The mental processes directing the body's responses, however, responded in a direct relationship to a physical reality. One is tempted to conclude that conscious mental evaluations really bollix up our relationships with physical reality.

Another, similar experiment also suggests that the subconscious is more in touch with physical reality than is conscious awareness. Subjects were given shocks being told that the shocks would vary in intensity, and they were asked to rate the intensity level of each shock. Actually all the shocks were of exactly the same intensity. Over time the subjects reported that the intensity of shock became less and less; that is, *subjectively* they adapted to the shock, but the skin responses were the exact same to each and every shock.

A much more complex subconscious evaluative process was found when this experiment was repeated using noise instead of shock as the noxious stimulus. With noise stimuli it was the skin that adapted, responding to each noise stimulus of equal intensity by smaller and smaller responses. At the same time the subjects were reporting that the noise was becoming louder and louder. Here again expectancy and a mental process of comparison may be involved. The subjects expected louder and more disturbing noises, and the subjective appraisal was then the noises were becoming louder. The skin's appraisal, however, was that the noise signals weren't very threatening, in which case they could be ignored. In essence the skin turned out a non-threatening stimulus just as we tune out everyday sounds that we find have no real significance.

Another important property of the skin's communication system is its ability to signal a perception either long before it reaches conscious awareness or even when the stimulus is so weak that the perception never comes to consciousness. The skin, along with a number of other body parameters, responds to subliminal signals. If, for example, a picture is flashed on a screen too briefly to be consciously appreciated, the skin electrical activity nonetheless signals the percept *if* the picture has an emotional meaning to the individual.

We had a bad scare years ago when advertisers decided to use this technique called subliminal perception, by flashing ads on movie or TV screens, flashing so briefly the words couldn't be consciously recognized. The ad might say "Buy Coca Cola"— and although you couldn't recognize the words, somehow they got put into memory so that later when you were thirsty you might inexplicably order Coca Cola when you really preferred iced tea.

The Sophistication of the Subconscious Operations of Mind

Even though the conscious mind does not recognize such subliminal signals, the body responds *as if* the mind had comprehended. This must mean, then, that some mental processes have *recognized, associated, evaluated* and *acted upon* the significance of the signals, all in the absence of conscious awareness.

Such experiments reveal the wisdom of the subconscious—a state of consciousness that we scarcely know. In that state all kinds of magical things can happen. For example, there is another form of biofeedback that may prove useful in the future in explorations of mind. This is using biofeedback signals to identify different and quite specific brain waves or different brain wave patterns. I did a study of this sort some years ago. Neurophysiologists had been aware for some time that certain behaviors or states of consciousness occurred when certain brain waves were present in the brain waves pattern. They knew that alpha was most often related to a state of relaxed wakefulness, that the faster beta waves were related to states of alertness and attention, and that theta waves *could* be related to goal-oriented behavior. All of these relationships have been inferred from using techniques that either stimulated the organism or removed parts of the brain, and then observing the behavior.

I thought it would be of interest to see whether people could identify the particular subjective states that related to these different brain waves. I displayed the 3 best defined brain waves as 3 different colored lights, mixing the colors that represented different brain waves for different experiments in the same person and also in different people. I also did a control study that established relationships between subjective states and color. Then the subjects simply watched their own brain waves, represented as different colors, for about an hour. Then I determined how they related the colors they had seen to their subjective states during the feedback. The results were quite surprising even though they confirmed much of what had already been known. I'll give an example. In most people the feelings they relate to the color red are feelings of anger, anxiety, irritation, annoyance, frustration, etc. After watching their brain waves when their alpha activity was represented by a red light, they subsequently associated the color red with feelings of calmness, peace, tranquillity, etc. Similarly, most people feel that blue is a color of peace, calmness and tranquillity, but if the subject had seen his alpha brain waves represented by a red light, they related the color red to feelings of peace, calmness, and tranquillity. Obviously, during the watching of their brain waves as colored lights, they had come to identify the feelings related to the brain waves rather than the feelings they would normally relate to color.

This kind of technique may be useful to become aware of many different types of brain processes, those processes which underlie the life of the mind. It may be possible someday to use feedback of certain brain wave components to, for example, direct memory searches, to blank out unwanted distractions, to concentrate more effectively on learning, to cause instant relaxation.

Operations of the Biological Mind

How is this all done? I view the feedback learning process as one in which for the first time the human organism can perceive the continuous on-going functioning of his internal physical self. It is simply new information that gets put into memory stores. But before the information can be stored in a meaningful way for subsequent recall, it must become associated with something, information that does make it meaningful, and that other information is from the subjective world where experiential and judgmental information is stored. So in biofeedback associations come to be made between what one's biology is doing and what the mind is doing.

In both the popular and scientific understanding of biofeedback the role of the highest mental processes has been grossly underestimated. There is much evidence to indicate how important high mental function is to fulfilling the potential of biofeedback. There are a number of research studies that have demonstrated that the more information you give a person undergoing feedback training, the more rapid and more dramatic are the results. If, for example, instead of just sitting a person in front of a machine displaying one of his biologic activities, and rewarding him with a nickel when he performs the way you asked him to, you supply him with as much information about the situation as you can, such as what the machine does, what he can possibly do mentally to be successful, and just as important, how his body works for that particular function—when the information is maximized this way, the results are excellent and rapid.

The neurophysiologist's explanations of how the brain is capable of such vast subconscious intelligence relies heavily upon neuronal pathways in the brain—pathways of neurons connecting in long, direct lines. But there are trillions of non-linear neuronal networks in the brain and while their function in mental processes are unknown, it seems quite possible that these non-linear networks speed the association of perceptual data associations with memory and experiential information, and that when situations require it, the linear, direct communications systems are used to bring selected bits of data to conscious awareness.

There are a few more elements of the biofeedback process that fascinate me. Think for a moment what we do in feedback—we give you a monitor, a signal to indicate changes in physiologic function. And the signal is nothing more than a man-made abstraction . . . a symbol. It is not even a very good representation of the biologic function. If your alpha brain waves are fed back to you as a light or a tone, what really does that mean? All it is, is a symbol that someone devised to signal change in an electrical circuit.

The fact that man can utilize this artificial symbol of some hidden, internal, dynamic function, use it to learn to control that body function certainly must mean that the higher mental activities are involved in establishing the relationship between signal and body action.

Then of course there is the puzzle about the will, or intention. Although biofeedback has not yet become sufficiently refined to detect nuances of mental activity, such as the recall of subtle emotional states, we do know merely announcing the intention to one's self that a bit of biology will be changed in a specific way can do the trick. In this respect biofeedback has the same element of mystery in its mechanism as does hypnosis.

So it can be fairly well established that the learned control over body functions by feedback techniques involves complex mental activity. It is also obvious that this complex mental activity does not take place on the conscious level, at least generally not until there has been considerable practice. We are, in fact, forced to conclude that subconscious mental processes may be infinitely more sophisticated than conscious mental processes. There is abundant information from psychophysiologic studies and other studies to indicate that this is so, and I wonder why we have relied so heavily upon conscious mental activity?

I have tried to give you evidence about the great capacity of the mental life that thrives and grows in the absence of conscious awareness. We now possess technical aids to facilitate the further exploration of this universe. We can use these explorations to isolate specific subsets of the subconscious, and just as we have consciously entered into a biofeedback practice to reach other areas of consciousness, so we can use the new and as yet unknown areas of the subconscious to explore another. Every experience along the way adds to our understanding of self.

There is probably not one of us who doesn't hope to achieve complete freedom of mind, and the ability to utilize the many aspects of consciousness to understand the mysteries of self and the universe. We have all had experiences that have told us that it is indeed possible to experience other states of consciousness. What we need now is to use and refine all of our tools to gain access to these states and see what else is there.

Biofeedback: Implications for Concepts of Mind and Consciousness

Analysis of varieties and characteristics of biofeedback learning process and of a storm of evidence suggesting the ubiquitousness of its role in the processes of health and illness is stirring many a researcher-philosopher to a reexamination of concepts of the mind-body problem and of concepts of mind and consciousness. I have had the extraordinary opportunity to be immersed in the analysis of biofeedback research since its emergence, and have reviewed and analyzed more than 2000 scientific reports and more than another 2000 scientific reports on related psychophysiologic, neurophysiologic, and psychosomatic studies. My own scientific background is particularly appropriate to the study of the multiple facets of the biofeedback phenomenon. I have spent my life in research in a wide variety of biomedical specialties, and have published original studies in such diverse fields as biochemistry, immunology, pharmacology, neurophysiology as well as psychophysiology. I have long been disturbed by the bioscientific isolationism which separates medicine and psychology that is a barrier to developing comprehensive, unitarian concepts about human behavior and mind-body processes. My background and interests seem to have been serendipitous to the biofeedback discovery in view of the rapidly accumulating evidence suggesting that the biofeedback phenomenon represents a missing link in our information bank about relationships between mind and body.

The essence of my discussion here is directed toward citing the evidence and logic supporting several notions concerning mind and consciousness. These concepts are: (1) that the biofeedback process of learning to control and to normalize both automatic, reflex, and complex physiologic functions is mediated by mental activities; (2) that mental events not only affect, but control, neurophysiologic events; (3) that the capability of cognitive activity, as in biofeedback, to supervene in the activities of physiologic systems represents an expression of the sophistication and complexity, the orderliness and reality-oriented nature of subconscious mental processes; (4) that the mechanism of biofeedback lies in the ability of higher cerebral mechanisms—the mind and subjective experience—to supervene in all physiologic processes of the body, including those of the brain; and finally, that such energies or capabilities of the mind are dominant over all physiologic activities of the body, including those of the brain.

Differing Concepts of the Biofeedback Process

Since the primary basis for my arguments lies in the biofeedback phenomenon, let me briefly sketch the most salient points of the process. First, and most important, is to clarify, albeit briefly, certain differences in experimental and theoretical and practical approaches to the biofeedback phenomenon that have led to differences in interpretation of the more critical issues in biofeedback. There are two principal procedures now classed under the rubric of biofeedback. One is that of conditioning procedure in which a change in physiologic function in a desired direction is reinforced, primarily by providing information about the physiologic performance to the performer, and is secondarily reinforced by other conventional reinforcements such as verbal encouragement or monetary or other rewards. In general, this type of procedure leads to small although conveniently significant changes statistically, although I take issue with the kinds of statistical analyses employed since they rarely consider individual and temporal aspects of physiologic variation. With the conditioning technique, control over a function is assumed to be demonstrated when the organism can discriminate stimuli and make a differential response of the selected physiologic activity. The results accumulated from use of this technique can be neatly fitted into conditioned learning theory, largely by virtue of the methodology employed.

The second type of biofeedback procedure is that in which information about a selected physiologic function is provided to the organism in a close to real-time, ongoing, continuous form, and supplementary information pertinent to the biological information, some of which is reinforcing, is additionally provided. Since this represents a significant departure from traditional methodologies, I will illustrate the procedure shortly, and will then catalog what I believe to be the informational requirements for successful biofeedback learning. In general, the informational technique leads to obvious changes in physiologic function of the selected activity to be controlled, large enough that statistics are necessary only for scientific communication. Moreover, with this technique the concept of control over a physiologic activity is that the control can, once learned, be evoked by decision and intentions by the individual in the absence of the biofeedback information.

One other difference is that in conditioning, performance is rewarded or reinforced. This means that the reinforcing signal is largely confirmatory and thus occurs post-facto, i.e., after performance has been completed. Whatever information the organism receives suffers an additional processing, that of relating current information to past performance. In the informational biofeedback technique, information is continuously or almost continuously processed while the individual is performing or attempting to perform, and thus the information so specifically relevant to the learning can be both integrated directly and be used as a guide to effective performance. The temporal aspect of availability of relevant information is an important difference between these two techniques.

Because the informational technique, as used in the laboratory, lacks the precision of elements (variables) quantifiable in terms of the physical factors involved, at first glance it would appear to be sloppy science. On the contrary, the procedure can be reduced, upon analysis and practice, to easily quantifiable elements; the difficulty lies in the fact that the results, i.e., the performance of control, is often so dramatic and of such magnitude that it defies explanation in terms of the "independent variable" known with considerable precision.

The Significance of Motor Unit Biofeedback for Understanding the Concept-to-Muscle Effector Conversion Process

I would like to cite the motor unit studies of Basmajian as examples of the second type of procedure. The essentials of this learning situation are the oscilloscopic display of motor unit potentials, usually along with click sounds activated by the firing of each of the motor units. There is thus both auditory and visual biofeedback information available to the individual generating the motor unit activity. In the experimental situation there may or may not be instructions that the individual should try to affect the motor unit activity. It is not necessary to provide instructions, and in such a situation, since apparently there is nothing better to do, many individuals begin an exploration of their situation, their relationship to the motor unit potentials, make observations and deductions, initiate a process of selection and finally, control of their own motor unit activity. Such learning occurs frequently, as I can attest from experiments in my laboratory. In this situation, the only observable variable is the biofeedback information.

Where instructions are given to the subject or patient, the instructions may contain minimal or considerable information. Instructions may be like a command, as "That potential has an interesting configuration, make it reappear every second," or the instruction may add, "Try to control a potential of your choice through some mental means." There is a significant difference in the information contained in these two simple types of instructions. Take the first, that of a command to control. Implicit in the situation to change the electrical signals is the information that it is possible to change them. Moreover, implicit in that information is the information that the individual may well have the capability to change the potentials. There is also the implication that changing the potentials can occur within a certain time period. Whatever information is contained in the instructions, and also from the set and setting of the situation, including attitudes, unexpressed and expressed, taken together constitutes a category of information that can be classified as cognitively useful. Here we begin to run into problems of definition; for the present purpose I use the term tentatively to indicate those kinds of information requiring processing by intellectual capacities, at least reasoning, and equate it with what we popularly consider to be mental activity.

Whether with instructions or not, individuals can learn rapidly to control motor units in a rather dazzling display of voluntary control. Motor units can be controlled singly, in pairs, in large numbers or unrelated units, which constitutes spatial patterns neurophysiologically, or can learn to control specific sequences of motor unit firings, which is control of temporal patterns. One must deduce that since functionally related motor units normally fire in close sequences, the activation of single units or many diverse units entails both selective activation and near-simultaneous, asynchronous suppression of functionally related units.

Information for Conceptualizing As the Key Factor in Biofeedback Learning

When motor unit control is used to facilitate muscle rehabilitation, as in muscle paralysis, and has been used since the 1950's, the basic procedure is augmented by providing the patient with varieties of information which enable him to use the biofeedback information more productively.

Essentially the same kind of procedure is widely used in successful clinical biofeedback. I stress the word successful, meaning that the patient achieves useful control over his problem physiologic function, and the control persists for a significant period of time. The most obvious illustration of the clinical use of this informational procedure is in the biofeedback treatment of stress-related illnesses, emotional or physical.

Let me review briefly a clinical procedure used in the treatment of Reynaud's syndrome. I personally have a collection of some ten cases treated successfully by this technique, and know of many more treated by approximately the same technique. The patient can use either a blood flow meter or a thermometer as a monitoring device for the level of hand vasomotor activity. The biofeedback information is generally continuously available to the patient, but the major effort of the treatment procedure is concentrated on support of the patient's internal processing of the biofeedback information. To this end, he is given instruction not only about what he is to try to do, but about how the instrument works, how his physiologic activity relates to the instrument, what the information means, something about the physiology of his condition, and then he is given clues about how to change the physiologic activity. The clues are generally in the form of relaxation techniques but also include information about dissociating active from passive effort and concentration, self-suggestion, imagery, or that individual mental techniques may be helpful. And the patient further receives encouragement, reinforcement, and is assisted with his insights into awareness of internal states.

Generally, similar procedures are increasingly found to produce beneficial clinical results; in fact, the horizontal evidence is extremely impressive, and I have recently collated all clinical results in a book on the art of biofeedback. I naturally have a bias in favor of this informational technique since my first experiments used the technique. I simply presented a blue light to subjects and asked them whether they could keep the light on as long as possible, and that the light was operated by a certain kind of brain wave which I did not name. In those days EEG alpha was completely unknown to the average volunteer. In fact, learning to control alpha activity was far from the objective of my experiments, and the control ability emerged from an unrelated experimental objective, just as did motor unit control emerge unexpectedly from the original Harrison and Mortenson experiments with motor unit control.

Nonetheless, in assessing the meaning of these experiments and the success of the informational technique on the clinical level, I have approached my analysis from a descriptive standpoint, i.e., on the basis of observations and legitimate deductions of what might be occurring in biofeedback learning.

Essential Components in Biofeedback Learning

Let me return to the Basmajian experiment as an illustration with the fewest essential components. It is difficult to label the components operative in this situation in terms of conventional methodologies which identify independent and dependent stimuli or responses; on the other hand, the situation is more one of observation and description of natural behavior, in which the experimenter may act to create a situation but does little to control it. It is preferable to identify rather than label the observable phenomena. There are three components of this learning situation: the perceptual biofeedback information, instructions with implications for conceptually useful information, and the performance, i.e., the result of a learning process. Only the two, the perceptual information specifically relevant to the objective, and the conceptually useful information, are sufficient for learning, and only the biofeedback information is necessary to the learning. Moreover, an effort to control the biofeedback information runs the risk of directly intervening with response and response possibilities. Whatever alters the biological activity, whether by external interference and regulation or by internal processes also alters the value of the biofeedback information. Moreover, some part of the biological information must always be a part of the learned performance.

It is not my purpose here to adjust this learning situation into terms of conventional scientific methodology since that is not relevant to the analysis of the events as they occur. The plain fact is that the mere availability of biological information can lead to control of the selected or monitored function. Even under such a minimal condition, many striking characteristics of the learning process can be either described or deduced. The first is that the biofeedback information itself constitutes more a concept than it does a condition or physical structure such as a stimulus or excitant for a response, and it certainly does not reflect any change in the external environment. The biofeedback information is actually an arbitrary representation or abstraction of what is happening in both time and space in the central nervous system. The visual motor unit potential is a pictograph of complex spatiotemporal biologic activity, and while it is an element of muscle activity that can be subjectively appreciated when numbers of motor units work together, the activity of a single or even a few motor units occurs without any prior subjective appreciation. From this standpoint the biofeedback information is abstract information which must be processed before a relationship between the representation of the biological activity and the processes which are concerned with the regulation of that activity can be established. This kind of mental information processing is that of forming concepts, and so biofeedback information should be more accurately considered as conceptually useful information.

Properties of Biofeedback Information

What is surprising about the biofeedback information is that it is used as information substituting for the internally derived biological information normally used in the regulation of motor unit activity. Sensory substitution, i.e., using information about a physiologic activity perceived via a secondary sensory route is integral to biofeedback learning. The phenomenon of sensory substitution is explored in a book by Paul Bach-y-Rita from his work on tactile impressions of objects as visual substitution for the blind; however, the significance of sensory substitution in learning and physical performance has been little explored. It should be noted, however, that Taub, in differentiation experiments, has demonstrated muscle regulatory capabilities in the absence of proprioceptive information suggesting either that central regulatory mechanisms of voluntary control are sufficient unto themselves and do not require input about what they are to control, which seems unlikely, or that the central control mechanisms have the capability to associate relevant although not primary information in a precise way toward a specific functional objective.

The instructions given concerning the learning situation, even when minimal, supply considerable implicit information as noted earlier. In this type of biofeedback procedure there are thus several sets of concepts presented to the conscious mind. The information contained in the two concepts, the biological representation and the instructions, is considerable and complex. The information stands in relative isolation from any overt signs of previous experience, and in itself is related to the individual only by a wire (which has its own implications) and the voice of authority.

Since there is nothing between these arrays of concepts and the end result of manipulating motor units, which in turn has been demonstrated to be the manipulation of individual motoneuron cells in the spinal cord, we assume that the individual uses the information, most of which is implicit, to accomplish the objective of control. There is little, if any, evidence that physiologic structures outside of the brain processes conceptual information, so we assume that the mind-brain uses the information—the idea, the symbols, the decision, the ambience—to accomplish a predetermined goal, i.e., the goal of carrying out the decision. The mind-brain has to project what the result should be. And that is what voluntariness or intention is: a very complex operation of mind that uses information to produce effectively and efficiently, an *ordered* alteration of biological activity. The cells, the chemistry, the electrical traffic of the central nervous system are all directed to proceed orderly and efficiently to accomplish a predetermined objective that is still in the mind's eye. The result of this action is control, a voluntary control that changes physiologic activity in such a way that the changes in activity are not only compatible with what the instructions and decision call for, but the changes are also compatible with the maximum precision the biological system is capable of, the finest possible discrimination of biological activity, the changing of the activity of a single cell.

There seems to be little doubt now that concepts alone can move the human organism to alter its biologic function in quite specific and predetermined ways. This bears upon a point I will make later that the optimal functioning of the human being may depend largely upon the quality and accuracy of his information input *about* human physiologic functioning.

The Need to Deduce an "Unconscious" (Biological) Awareness

The demonstration that human beings can rapidly learn to control motor units with extraordinary precision has many other implications for defining components of complex mental activities and states of consciousness. There is, for example, that state of consciousness I call biological awareness. The type of awareness that develops in the biofeedback process is generally described by the individual by, "I know I am doing this" (controlling a selected physiologic function), "but I don't know how I'm doing it." This appears to represent an internally derived, nonverbalizable awareness of biologic states having the distinctive properties that the biological awareness is neither communicable by ordinary means nor is predominantly influenced by consensual consciousness. It is a state of consciousness that is subjectively appreciated only. It may be a system for the internal recognition of the state of any and all physiologic functions at any moment in time. Biological awareness is implied by the ability of complex mental events to isolate perceptual and cognitive information to specific systems and subsystems. Since there is no conscious awareness of the voluntary control process, it is assumed that the association between information about biological activity, the biological awareness, and the perceptual and cognitive information is mediated via subconscious processes. These I tentatively call the integrative subconscious processes which facilitate the associations and integrations among the various informational inputs. It is the integrative subconscious that assesses the significance of biological awareness relevant to the perceptual and cognitive information and selects the appropriate biological expression.

The inaccessibility of the voluntary control process to conscious appreciation may have a mechanism analogous to the Heisenberg principle of indeterminancy. In quantuum mechanics the Heisenberg principle of indeterminancy states that if we know the momentum (of a particle), we can't know the exact location of the particle in space; if we know the energy of a particle, we can't know its exact location in time. Because this discussion is an exercise in trying to formulate new perspectives on the nature of mind and consciousness, for my own amusement I've called the situation of inability to objectify awareness of the voluntary mechanism "The Brownenberg Principle." The Brownenberg principle simply states that if you are processing information in your brain, you can't know that you *are* processing that information, since the information being processed is occupying the same neuronal space.

Biological awareness also manifests the results of experience. In motor unit control the learning is not readily forgotten. Another indication is the ability to control heart rate without a biofeedback signal. At least three experiments have demonstrated that simply asking an individual to change his heart rate can result in large magnitude changes. This suggests that the individual is using his experience with subjectively appreciated events about his heart rate, and can thus call upon a base of experience in the absence of other forms of information about heart rate. As an aside, the considerable differences in magnitude of heart rate change between non-biofeedback-assisted voluntary control and varieties of biofeedback procedures suggests that the internal awareness and mechanisms are more efficient than when external devices or interventions are employed. The relative inefficiency of external intervention thus may suggest it has a component of action inhibitory to the learning of voluntary control. This observation also relates to the concept that the optimal functioning of human beings may depend largely upon the quality and accuracy of his information input *about* human physiologic functioning.

Some individuals can learn to control a motor unit in less than five minutes. I have also read a few reports in which significant "control" of a physiologic activity occurred almost simultaneously with the onset of a biofeedback experiment. In my first biofeedback paper, I noted that alpha frequency decreased a full cycle per second immediately upon beginning the experiment. In my own mind I have questioned whether this type of effect can be attributed to errors in instrument design, yet such rapidity of apparent learning occurs frequently. The impressiveness of many biofeedback responses, as in motor unit control, is truly extraordinary if we take time to realize the precision and rapidity with which the ordered alteration of physiologic activity takes place. There are two implications here: that the physiologic processes are ordered chemically and electrically with exquisite specificity, and that something gave the order.

The Need to Postulate an Ordering Mechanism for Biological Processes

This brings us to another implied activity of subconscious mental processes, the activity we might ascribe to a sense of order. Neurophysiologists and philosophers have described a sense of continuity and most of us recognize in us a sense of harmony. Orderliness of the physiologic entity is established through the substances of genes and chromosomes, and it seems likely that there is recognition of this order by our biological awareness. But a sense of order appears to be a fundamental component of the subconscious mechanisms which implement biofeedback learning. Certainly, the selection of the exact pathways and neurones and motoneurones to activate and suppress in motor unit learning is a matchless application of the ordering process. In its operation in the human body, this may well be the most authentic and sophisticated as well as germinal application of the sense of order.

If we invoke any concept of psychoneural parallelism or correspondence, it is easy to postulate a sense of order on the basis of both genetically determined and learned physiologic activities. It is also relatively easy to infer a sense of order from the disorder that occurs in conscious processes. Dr. Orne, for example, has conceptualized the curious logic of dreams, and psychiatry relies heavily upon the concept of subconscious conflicts, and the disorder of perception and subjective appreciations under the hallucinogens are well known. There is, in contrast, little information about how organisms, particularly human ones, order the vast quantities of information they continuously absorb. If we speak of subconscious conflicts, then we are implying that when conflicts do not exist, the subconscious mechanisms are behaving in an orderly fashion, and that the order is appropriate to optimal functioning.

The exquisite ordering of physiologic processes that occurs in motor unit and other types of biofeedback learned control can easily be discovered to be accompanied by a sense of order. I and many other researchers have tried to fool people who have learned to control, for example, alpha or theta wave activity by giving them a signal of a different brain wave, or even an artificial one. Invariably the individual will exclaim, usually quite vigorously, "That's not my alpha, something's wrong with your equipment." Some people can recognize patterns of their EEG activity, and if presented with a display of someone else's EEG activity, shortly recognize a difference and comment on it.

The Will

Another characteristic of the biofeedback phenomenon is the requisite of intention. It is not necessary to support the concept of intentionality as a mental event, and the neurologist Basmajian has called the control process an act of will power, as have other prominent biofeedback researchers. The decision, or the intention, to perform is integral to biofeedback, and biofeedback learned control is a dramatic example of the effect of the will on physiologic activities. Although decisions to perform may be appreciated in conscious awareness or unconsciously, the implementation of intention occurs via subconscious mental processes. Moreover, the will, or intention, is a specific determining influence but capable of an independence of function. As a mental function it can be applied to any of the major and quite diverse body systems which differ in their chemical and cellular constitution.

If, however, we accept the concept of will as a specific element of mental activity, it is necessary to postulate another specific and independently operating mental function, that of direction. If the will is independent of any body system, then so also is the factor or mental element of direction. Will power can be exercised or suppressed, and it can be identified separately from direction of intention which directs intention and relevant information to produce a change in body function. For example, if I want to smoke a cigarette and am distracted at the moment of implementing my intention, I might end up with a pencil in my mouth. The intention was present but direction was absent from the voluntary process. Intention takes action based on a consideration not only of the value of goals, but upon estimates of the effectiveness of the action and consideration of what the consequences of the action will be. It anticipates the goals and it is direction which selects the correct channels consistent with inappropriate action. In the motor unit example it is the function of direction that guides the selection of exactly which family of muscle cells to activate and exactly when to do it.

These are some of the mental functions and states which can be assumed to be involved in voluntary behavior. The biofeedback process can and does lead to voluntary control both of body activities and mind states, much as various yogic techniques do. The problem now is to begin to confront the complexities of mental activity with systematic study, and biofeedback provides an extraordinarily convenient tool for such study. In addition to the facility with which the biofeedback learning process deals with conceptual information, it is the aspect of voluntariness that when further explored may lead to a better understanding of the mind and consciousness. For more than a century we have neglected the implications of voluntary control and now biofeedback suggests that we should begin to deal with understanding it. A voluntary process is a process of using mind-brain activity to affect physiologic activity in a predetermined way based on establishing goals, making appropriate decisions, and having an idea of what the consequences of the voluntary act will be. This is the basis of much of our behavior. the processing of information, associating it, integrating it, structuring it, and using it to make fine discriminations and to make rapid decisions. It is a very complex process turning volition into action.

The problem is that we have little, if any, awareness of implementing volition. The awareness of the process is either that we intend to do something or that we have already done it. All of the complicated mechanisms subserving volition proceed without conscious awareness of them. Similarly, the learning of voluntary control occurs via subconscious mental processes. The striking insight that biofeedback provides is into the sophistication and orderliness and cognitive nature of the process.

Mental Events in the Regulation of Physiological Functions

Another major contribution of biofeedback to the understanding of mental activity is that it offers a new model, a model in which mental events affect neurophysiologic processes. In the informational biofeedback procedure, the precise and intentional change in physiologic activity is attributable only to mental events. Since there are existing control or feedback regulating systems available for all physiologic systems which are more or less continuously operating, this indicates that mental events supervene in the automatic regulating systems. It is interesting that cybernetic concepts applied to the behavior of human systems recognize feedback as the important element, but more exactly, for a function to operate smoothly, such as for muscle movements to be smooth and effective, each move must be accompanied by awareness of where the muscles have moved and how much more they must go to reach a target, and this awareness relies on the feedback information. It is the factor of awareness that is usually omitted from discussions of physiologic feedback control systems. Further, the cybernetics concept also rests upon assuming an ability to project how much more activity is needed to reach the target. And this in turn implies other mental activity aspects of the voluntary process, those of establishing the objective or target and of making a decision or intention to reach it.

This complex of mental events is that which determines the activity of the physiologic systems. This conclusion is virtually identical to that arrived at by Sperry from his studies of the commisurectomized brain, by Eccles from studies of brain neuronal activity, and by Penfield from his neurophysiologic and epilepsy studies. Each of these neurophysiologists has concluded that mental events control neurophysiology, and of course conversely, that neurophysiology controls mental events.

A review of factors in the biofeedback process that are quite new, and are different from the way in which internal and mental activities have been previously approached in either study or practice may serve to underscore the other evidence for the dominant role of cognitive activity in the regulation and normalization of physiologic activities. There are at least eight new basic elements of the biofeedback process not found in other situations involving mind-body relationships.

First, selected biological information is fed back to the individual generating that activity. Not until biofeedback was there any consistent practice of making an individual's own biologic function available to him. And second, the information is made available in a form that can be readily perceived, that is, the displays or signals of the biologic activity. Third, the physiologic activity is available continuously or almost continuously which also discloses variations and rhythms of biological activity. This display of internal information allows the individual to interact with and experience something about internal states. This leads to evoking complex mental processes to effect control over physiologic processes and the result is learned voluntary control over automatically regulated body activities. The result of this learning is that there is a shift in the identity and control of self from external to internal dependence. And finally, the learned control is a means of communicating an otherwise inexpressible mental activity.

With these characteristics in mind, considering biofeedback as a process that depends mainly upon the mental action of the learner, the therapeutic procedures of biofeedback can be constructed for optimal effects. For the informational biofeedback approach, I have categorized the varieties of information currently important for a favorable outcome, i.e., for learning voluntary control and hence normalizing physiologic activities. These are first, the biological information, that is, the biofeedback information.

Second is that type of information which can be called conceptually or cognitively useful. This is the kind of information which provides a structure into which the biofeedback information can be used, and is represented essentially by educating the individual with respect to his physiology or pathology, the instrument, the procedure, and the objectives. Most individuals have been disadvantaged about physiology and psychology and medicine and technology. The cognitively useful information simply expedites use of the other information by giving it some organization and structure. Next there is what I call strategy information. Even with background information, the individual generally has no idea about how to change his physiology. Strategy information is clues about how to proceed, and currently in biofeedback practice all varieties of relaxation exercises are used, or imagery, or explanations about passive concentration and volition, or exploring one's own consciousness. Then there is the supporting, psychological information, which can be motivating, encouraging, reinforcing, and even directing, and finally there is the experiential information which, when it emerges, is consolidated by sharing the experiential or confirming it. Consolidation of experiential information is also achieved by home practice, record keeping, and record checking.

Successful biofeedback practice generally incorporates all of these categories of information. Clinically effective biofeedback thus consists almost exclusively of information useful to the formation of concepts, and it is these which are used to attain voluntary control of physiologic activities and to normalize them. My favorite saying these days is, "The patient no longer is the object of the treatment, the patient *is* the treatment."

Why Biofeedback is Appropriate to the Treatment of Stress Ailments

A large share of biofeedback clinical success occurs in the treatment of stress-related illnesses. It is well known that stress stimuli activate neural structures such as the hypothalamus, the pituitary, and the autonomic nervous system. The most generally accepted theory about stress reactions begins at this point, and characterizations of stress reactions confirm the involvement of hypothalamus and the other neural structures. The curious disparity is that the sympathetic and endocrine activation that occurs is the same mechanism (although of lower order) as the popularly known flight or fight response of preparation of the body's physical defenses. The utility of this reaction relates to physical survival of the organism, and further, the reaction ultimately relates to mechanisms for survival of the species. The disparity is that man's environment, as well as that of domestic animals, contains relatively few threats to physical survival in proportion to almost a saturation of threats to social and individual survival. In the complex society that man has evolved, environmental elements that are stressful are chiefly those of social stress. In view of the general order of the universe, and particularly the evolutionary order that we describe as survival of the fittest by which species survive because they develop adapting mechanism and structures, it seems particularly incongruous that man's principle stress is social, yet in his reactions to stress his defenses evoke the entire range of physiologic activities used for physical defense. As a matter of fact, these physical defense mechanisms are shared by all mammals, rodents, and even many lower species, as from this standpoint are primitive defenses in a complex society that threatens the individual.

There are other discrepancies in our concepts about stress and stress reactions. There is the phylogenetic discrepancy. Although the defense mechanisms, i.e., the reacting mechanisms, are relatively unchanged physiologically, man is susceptible to remarkably more illness and more kinds of illnesses than is his closest species relative. Even with the reduction in number and kinds of threats to physical survival and functioning, the number of ways man can be threatened has not only increased over the number for his animal relatives, but assaults to his effective existence have increased way out of proportion to his ability to protect and defend the health of mind and body.

A more curious fact is the high degree of selectivity of response to stress seen in man. Generally one body system is dominant in its reaction, and most often only specific subsystems react as in the varieties of psychosomatic illness.

Science has been so occupied with the physical manifestations and underpinnings of stress reactions that it paid little attention to the role of complex mental activities despite an abundance of evidence implicating cognitive factors as possibly not only dominant but primary mechanisms in reactions to stress. It is here that information obtained from biofeedback studies contributes considerably.

If one examines the flood of clinical experimental report and reviews physicians' case reports, which unfortunately are rarely published, there is little doubt that the treatment procedure which I have described is strikingly effective across a wide variety of stress-related disorders. And since the evidence points to cognitive awareness or conceptual activities playing the dominant role in relief from stress reactions, it can be deduced that stress reactions are generated through mental activities. There has always been the question of what happens to perceived stress before it activates neural structures. And it is well known that stress reactions are more related to coping mechanisms than to the amount or severity of the stress; further there is considerable evidence that mental events modulate and modify perceptual information.

When we treat stress reactions, we do so either with drugs or psychotherapy. In psychotherapy the major element is making information more available to the patient, either by discussion or self-inspection; either way the patient has more information accessible, either by adding it, or reorganizing or recalling or by altering the effect of mental events on perception. The additional information and its cognitive manipulation can both prevent and relieve the effects of stress.

The biofeedback process, as I have outlined it, is primarily a procedure for supplying information and activating internal informational sources specifically relevant to the stress reaction process. The effectiveness of biofeedback in the broad spectrum of stress problems further supports the concept that mental events affect neurophysiology.

Biological Awareness as a State of Consciousness

The past few years have seen a dynamic transition in the think-ing of scientists concerned with mind and consciousness. Exciting, innovative approaches to the mind-body mystery have sprung up in every mind science discipline, and the analysis of new data about interactions between mental and biological processes is stimulating new perspectives on that unique property of human beings called consciousness.

Subconscious processes,[1] generally interpreted as all activity of mind not recognized in conscious awareness, have been docu-mented to possess extraordinary complexity, depth of informa-tional resources, associative and integrative mechanisms, mechanisms for evaluation and judgment of integrated data, and a remarkable facility for direction and efficiency of action. The broad scope of these activities and the effective but parsimonious execution of subconscious functions strongly imply a systematic arrangement with discriminable levels of organization. This essay is based on a concept of consciousness that considers three levels: conscious awareness, and subconscious processes having at least two aspects (one confirmed to the subjective appreciation of bio-

---

[1]Although "unconscious" is traditionally preferable in psychoanalytic theory, the prefix "un" connotes absence of consciousness whereas the prefix "sub" connotes below or beneath. Perhaps "para" would be a more apt descriptor, but would be even more confusing to introduce at this time. This essay will therefore use subconscious activity as synonomous with the unconscious.

logical information and the second concerned with the association, integration and evaluation of information).

What follows is an argument to support the concept of independent "subjectively appreciated" mental processes, and particularly the identification and characterization of those subjectively appreciated mental processes perceiving and expressing biological information that is otherwise inexpressible. It is the product of this latter activity that may represent an independent state of consciousness that I will call *biological awareness*. I will describe evidence indicating that this state—although the mental processes which mediate it do not directly communicate with conscious awareness—performs a vital role in the internal communication between physiologic and other subconscious processes concerned with the association, evaluation and intergration of information. I propose that the latter be termed the *integrative subconscious*.

In this discussion the qualifier "subjectively appreciated" is employed in its most fundamental sense, i.e., referring to information perceivable exclusively to the individual. These internally generated perceptions are considered as distinct from "objectively appreciated" perceptions which become characterized in mutual agreement by approximating apparent correspondences of internal events to events external to individual consciousness. By this definition, "subjectively appreciated" consciousness is comprised of all internally derived sensations and percepts, as well as subjective mental activity which process perceptual and cognitive data independently of conscious awareness and direction.

Thus the concept of the biological awareness aspect of subjectively appreciated consciousness may be described as an internal recognition and awareness of the entire range of biological events in the body by mental processes capable of communicating the information so recognized to "integrative subconscious" processes which facilitate association, integration and evaluation of biological awareness with other perceptual and cognitive information. It is the integrative subconscious processes that assess the significance of biological awareness relevant to other perceptual and cognitive information and select appropriate biological expression. The integrative subconscious processes also communicate a synthesis of the information to conscious awareness.

The Definition Dilemma

Probably more than for any other subject, there is a lack of consensus about the substance and mechanisms of consciousness. This is a disadvantage to critical analysis of the subject and particularly when attempting to define a previously undescribed state of consciousness. The disparity of information and concepts about consciousness and the mind (brain) make it difficult to organize the material and logic needed to support new concepts. The effect of this is that the kinetic energy of unavoidably incomplete organization of ideas and data outweighs the potential energy of new concepts, and consequently obscures what might be significant new information and the development of ideas. One part of this predicament is a reflection, a datum, which expresses the absence of unifying concepts of consciousness and the mind and brain.

Because there are many diverse concepts of consciousness, there is a need for meaningful qualifiers of the consciousness set. The need to qualify consciousness descriptively does not appear to have a high priority in discussions of either the characteristics or mechanisms of consciousness. From this one might conclude that there is either broad consensus of the meaning of the concept or that bases for concepts of consciousness are so elusive and disparate that qualifiers about different states of consciousness are more confusing than helpful. A review of concepts reveals that they derive from bodies of knowledge that are essentially separately organized and documented, with little if any concurrence. One may find reasonably acceptable hypotheses from physical, experiential, sociologic or philosophic points of view, yet none of these defines nor qualifies consciousness satisfactorily for all points of view. This suggests either information voids or inadequate communication among bodies of information.

One of the information voids is that of experiential information. Except for certain philosophic considerations, usable (i.e., consensual) information about the experiential is generally inferred from objectively perceived[2] information (that which can be communicated), not from subjectively appreciated perceptions (essentially inexpressible). The present discussion attempts to examine the characteristics of a subset of consciousness that is primarily *subjectively* perceived and to cite the implications which can be deduced from this process of silent perception.

The first difficulty for a discussion of this kind is the virtual absence of definitions, or indeed for any real consensus about levels, states, mechanisms or the nature of consciousness. A second complication for a discussion of subjectively appreciated consciousness is that nowhere has background information from human psychophysiologic studies been consolidated or synthesized for consideration about the mind-body relationship. And finally, many of the supporting data are of such recent origin that they have not yet been incorporated into more structured hypotheses of the consciousness-brain relationship.

For the past several years I have been reviewing new data on the psychophysiology of consciousness and have become aware of a perspective on consciousness and the mind-body problem which as yet eludes interpretation by the classical approaches, i.e., from the standpoint of either the observer or the observed. My thoughts and conclusions are in process—somewhat analogous to a process that would occur following the opening of a Pandora's box of biological events that put to question certain fundamental considerations of the mind-body problem. These events, whose implications may bring a new perspective to concepts of consciousness, are those which can be deducted from the biofeedback phenomenon.

Although the explosive publicity about biofeedback has engendered unqualified enthusiasm among many psychologists, it has been received with somewhat less enthusiasm by physiologists. This may be due chiefly to the failure of psychology to attend to the

[2]Regardless of whether the perception arises from external or internal sources, the objectivity occurs through a communicated agreement about the characterization and significance of the perception.

physiologic implications of both the methodology and interpretations of psychophysiologic research. Therefore, I will review some of the compelling biologic support to establish the role of higher mental processes in the biofeedback phenomenon and how these considerations lead to the idea of purely subjectively appreciated brain processes.

Although evidence for the independence of a subjectively appreciated consciousness and its aspect of a biological subconscious is most striking in the biofeedback process, there is a wealth of unorganized evidence from both earlier and concurrent research. Evidence deduced from a variety of unrelated studies will be cited first, concluding with an analysis of the biofeedback phenomenon as experimental evidence for a subjectively appreciated set of brain processes having the capability to affect or direct itself and its own biologic mechanisms without external physical intervention, which thus may be considered to function with some degree of apparent independence of its substrate.[3]

The Effect of Cognitive Information on Biologic Activity

While it is well-known and there is reasonable scientific evidence that cognitive information (words, ideas, attitudes) affects

[3]This concept of subjective activity is not unlike that expressed by Sperry [1], that "subjective experiences in the form of emergent phenomena actively govern the flow pattern of neural excitation." Additional quotations from the same paper clarify Sperry's concept: "describing consciousness as a dynamic property of cerebral excitation that is inseparately tied to, and a direct property of, the brain process, and not a disembodied or supernatural agent;" "there has been general agreement that subjective epiphenomena do not act back upon, or in any way influence, the brain's physical activity. The present view contends, in contradiction, that the conscious phenomena as direct emergent properties of the cerebral activity do interact with and casually determine the brain process." "The present view differs (from the identity theory) in postulating that the phenomena of subjective experience as pattern properties are distinct, different from, and more than the neural activities of which they are composed. It may be noted further that the same conscious effect in the present view can be produced by different neural events on different occasions in different neural contexts provided the critical operational result at the holistic functional level is the same."

underlying physiologic activities, much prevailing scientific opinion tends to attribute such physiologic effects more to autonomic responses than to non-aware but reasoning mental activity. The present examples from bio-psychologic research are cited to indicate the alternative explanation: that complex high level mental activity operates efficiently and effectively via subconscious mechanisms.

One of the first intriguing studies of the human potential to direct nonconsciously his own quite specific biological activity was reported more than 35 years ago [2]. The significance of this study remained unrecognized for several decades while experimental psychologists were in the throes of conditioning theory and behaviorism which asserted that behavior consisted mainly of responses to external stimuli. In the study noted, normal individuals were trained to produce a change in skin electrical activity in response to the words "electric shock" by giving a mild electric shock to the fingers a few seconds later. The experiment then proceeded to substitute the *words* "electric shock" for the real electric shock, and further, to precede these words by the words "green light." The subjects quickly transferred the skin electrical change to the mere words "green light" when said a few seconds before the words "electric shock." The subjects received no information about their skin electrical activity other than being advised *when* they produced a change satisfactory to the researchers. When the words "electric shock" were omitted after the words "green light," the subjects quickly failed to produce a skin electrical change. Moreover, when a real green light and a real electric shock were used in a duplicate experiment, the learning to transfer the skin response was much less than when verbal stimuli were used.

The situation of the experiment was essentially a "cognitive" one, i.e., the subjects were given minimal information and they were expected not only to deduce the significance or application of the information, but also to provide a specific and appropriate body response to that information. The cognitive information consisted of (a) being told that they had made a body response recorded through electrodes on their hand, and (b) instructions to make the same body response when they heard certain words. One can deduce that the subjects were, in some way, able to first recognize and then associate a particular biological state with the information that they had biologically responded satisfactorily, and then were further able to transfer this particular state of biologic activity to the words used by the researchers precisely when instructed to do so. Since the subjects were not informed either that they were *expected* to transfer the body response to the words "green light" or that they were successful in this, it can only be assumed that they interpreted the highly limited circumstances of the situation, consciously or subconsciously, and performed via a body change which could be recorded through the finger electrodes. At no time was there information available for conscious recognition, thus there appears to be implicated a process of logical subconscious processing of information, presumably stemming from private assessment of differences in specific body activities during different conditions of the experiment. This assessment suggests that mental processes are capable of interpreting differences in specific body activities under quite specific sets of circumstances and it is for this reason that I propose that the basis of this capability be called "biological awareness."

The hypothesis is that there are mind-brain processes which are capable of discriminating specific attributes of biological activity, and that these constitute a form of consciousness capable of independent operation with respect to organizing relationships between mind and body. In the case of the experiment above, this biological awareness appears to have been internally communicated to and associated with the mental activity which assessed the conditions and instructions of the experiment. Over time this association of information became isolated to the specific circumstances of the experiment such that the information derived from biological awareness was used to initiate a change in body activity.

To summarize, the specific "cognitive" situation was that there was an implicit command to do something, and that "something" was limited to changing some body process. The critical part of the process was the transfer of information contained in the events of the experiment (including the prior implicit affirmation—but no explicit information—of what comprised a successful response) to the brain mechanisms which direct changes in body activities. The process implies biologically appreciated, non-consciously aware mental associations capable of directly and effectively discriminating and directing physiologic activity.

Evidential Indications from Various Unrelated Psychophysiologic Phenomena

Experiments with subliminal perception directly support the above conclusion. Numerous studies have been conducted which contrast body responses to words having emotional content and those without emotional significance. Heart rate, skin electrical activity, blood pressure and brain waves all change significantly when emotion producing words are presented to subjects at a level of stimulus intensity below that which allows conscious recognition of the words or symbols. The *significance* of the words therefore has been recognized, associated, evaluated and acted upon, all on a level below (or parallel to) that of conscious awareness. While this phenomenon has been generally interpreted as indicating an activity of subconscious processes, I propose that the actual mechanism is biological awareness operating via the rich non-linear neuronal networks of the brain to monitor the relative state of each physiologic system. Information is thus available for communication with other networks which transmit information both from memory stores and sensory perception as well as available for communication with the linear neuronal systems, i.e., the primary nervous pathways used to convey information to organs to effect appropriate responses.

Other evidence lies in universal observations. In hypnosis, for example, when a subject is deeply hypnotized and is instructed not to bleed to a pin prick or during surgery, he does not bleed [5]. Whatever the mechanism, it is apparent that it is a mental rather than a physical process. It is mental activity that directs physiologic processes to mobilize "automatic," "involuntary" activity in a way that is contrary to normal biologic responses (i.e., normally one bleeds after vascular injury). While suggestions to perform a specific physiologic function are received via the mechanisms of consciousness, the accomplishment of the feat is *not* recognized in conscious awareness, nor is the *mode* of execution of the feat recognized despite the obvious intentionality and voluntariness of the act. These events imply the existence of mental processes capable of mobilizing, integrating and directing informational forces with remarkable specificity operating efficiently and effectively on levels below (or parallel to) conscious awareness. From these processes one might deduce that one portion of non-conscious activity functions to appraise the biological situation, e.g., the vascular activity at the wound site, whereas a different function of the non-conscious mental activity integrates the biological information with the cognitive appraisal of the hypnotic suggestions. It would seem parsimonious for biological information to be monitored and assessed for qualities of dynamics, status and location *prior* to a central integrative action which organizes and discriminates the significance of data from other sources (other perceptual data and other subjective information such as intent, instructions, motivation, etc.).

Alternative perspectives or reinterpretations of other types of experimental observations can also provide support for an independently functioning subjectively appreciated biological subconscious.

There is, for example, a criticism that biofeedback may not differ from the essentials of conditioned learning because the process can be effected in lower animals via conditioning techniques. One answer to this is that it has never been demonstrated that animals are not subjectively aware, just as human beings may be, and animals may accomplish learning by similar mechanisms. One has only to take a leaf from the natural scientist's notebook to conclude that animals display a keen awareness of internal body processes, much more than do human beings. For example, many of the so-called instinctual actions of animals, such as eating grasses for an upset stomach, or kitty's insisting upon a clean toilet, may also represent a keen awareness of internal melieu. There are also the experiments of DiCara and Miller in conditioning rats to change heart rate under curare [6]. Their success in training rats to change heart rate could as well indicate the influence of internal awareness as it does effectiveness of rewards (intrinsic to operant conditioning); not enough experiments have been done to conclude one way or the other. Parenthetically, though, prejudice favors the opinion that animals have no such internal awareness.

Further, in the DiCara and Miller experiments, the direction of learned heart rate changes under curare exerted a profound influence on the animals' subsequent behavior and ability to learn other tasks [7]. Rats who learned to slow their hearts became more tranquil and relaxed and also learned subsequent tasks more efficiently; while rats who had learned to increase heart rates learned subsequent tasks poorly and moreover many became frantic, exhausted and died. While there are several neurophysiologic answers possible, it is also possible that disruption of a normal internal awareness and organized subjective information in the adverse direction may account for the deterioration in both mental and physical health.

Evidence from newer, sophisticated studies can be found in a recent publication by Fetz and Finnochio [8]. Monkeys were trained by a combination of conditioning and biofeedback techniques to effect a series of sophisticated patterned, coordinated muscle actions, including isometric contractions of single muscles among those required for the pattern. It was found, by monitoring selected cortical cells, that a single cortical cell may relate to both the production of a learned coordinated muscle movement and to each of the muscles involved when insolated from the pattern, and furthermore that the *same* cortical cell apparently could selectively abstain its involvement in the action of selected muscles of the coordinated effort while still being critical to the action of another muscle of that pattern.

If the temporarily related responses of cortex and muscle could imply a causal relationship, then the implications of this study are enormous. They suggest that a single cortical cell may have the capability to determine its output for several options selectively. This in turn may indicate how subjectively appreciated information (gained from proprioception and from associations during training) in some way influences cellular discriminations. The study suggests that a single cortical cell may selectively be involved in the actions of one or many effectors, and can control its own excitant and inhibitory effects, possibly by feedback mechanisms.

The Evidence from Biofeedback

Since the vast amount of information about the biofeedback phenomenon has not yet been pulled together into any unifying concept, a brief discussion of both some observable characteristics of the process and some deductions which can be made about events occurring within the process are necessary in order to discuss implications of the process. Certain characteristics of the system appear to constitute "new" (or rediscovered) information and warrant consideration in formulations about the mind-body problem. Some of the "new" knowledge may be simply new perspectives or old phenomena which examination of the "newly discovered" phenomenon has crystallized. In general, the new information accumulating from biofeedback studies appears to support and to extend the concept of a biologic consciousness as an entity derived from and functionally tied to physiologic activity, but with capabilities distinct from the direct products of that activity, and which feed back as part of a self-regulatory system.

Briefly, in the biofeedback process, psychobiologic information, in symbolic form, is fed back to the generator of the concrete forms and logic of that same psychobiologic information. The mechanics and significance of biologic feedback control systems are considered elsewhere. In this discussion emphasis is on the unique nature of the process and the implications about consciousness which stem from observations of the phenomenon.

An important element of biofeedback has been a recognition that intention (the will) appears to possess the capability for functioning as an activity of brain function that can organize, integrate and direct the physical processes of the body with molecular specificity. And, more often than not, intention operates in the absence of conscious awareness. These conclusions are based upon the synthesis of results from hundreds of studies on biofeedback and related phenomena. I will give several examples from the recent scientific literature on biofeedback which illustrate the ability of mental processes to direct the activity of specific biological functions, often when there is minimal possibility for conscious appreciation of cognitive information.

There is some misunderstandings about various aspects of the biofeedback process because the phenomenon evolved partially via conditioning theory. In reality the biofeedback process is more effective and efficient in the absence of these constraints. Moreover, in retrospect, much of the experimental base for conditioning theory can be viewed as essentially a biofeedback process (e.g., influence of information contained in set and setting, in the conditioning stimulus, in the absence of signal, etc.).

In the conditioning-free biofeedback process, a representation of a simple monitor of a complex physiologic function provides information to the individual about the functioning of a system. By means of either direct or indirect instructions, direction of the effect is specified and accomplished without conscious awareness. A non-aware cognitive process appears to recognize both the significance of the abstraction of a physiologic activity and the mechanism by which selective alteration of the biologic process can be directed. The role of information is crucial to the biofeedback process. The more information, whether conceptual, environmental or biological, the more efficient is the process, presumably because communication about internal events is facilitated below the level of conscious awareness. Moreover, in the biofeedback process, the way in which biologic information is perceived is shifted to a fuller representation of the time dimension of physiologic processes, hence it simultaneously utilizes temporarily distributed information as events occur within the spaces of the body.

In biofeedback the biological information can be represented as a mechanical symbol of the information or, in fact, *any* kind of information that is linked, however indirectly, to a biological activity.

In some experiments biofeedback information is in the form of a perceptually recognizable symbol (such as visual or auditory signals) of the biologic activity. An experiment of this type is that in which EEG alpha activity was fed back to the subjects in the form of a blue light signal [9]. Subjects were informed only that this indicated some kind of brain wave activity, and their instructions were to find some mental means to keep the light on for periods as long as possible. Subjects learn this task with remarkable rapidity (this type of experiment has been repeated ad nauseum). Again, the individual is provided only with an artificial symbol of his biologic activity.

The sequence of events deduced to occur in this experiment has a striking similarity to those which may be deduced from numerous experiments in which experimental subjects are simply requested to change a specific biologic activity voluntarily [10]. The events are also similar to those deduced to occur in the non biofeedback augmented learning or "conditioning" of skin electrical activity by verbal stimuli.

Completely Internalized Voluntary Control Over Internal Biologic Activity

Although for many practical purposes and in the laboratory the biofeedback process appears to rely on an element external to the internal circuitry, there is support for the contention that the process is fundamentally a completely internal process. First, the phenomenon may be equally well demonstrated using instructions only [11]. Also, normally, the process rapidly becomes independent of the external conditions when these are used. Moreover, many individuals have developed auto-control over internal physiologic events in the absence of external assistance (heart rate, temperature, pain, resorption of urine, etc.), and some individuals in other cultures regularly develop such auto-control without external aids. The essential difference between biofeedback-augmented and non-augmented voluntary control over internal events is that with biofeedback the process is not only highly efficient, but proceeds without conscious awareness.

In some visceral learning experiments a minimum amount of cognitive information is given in the form of a feedback symbol while in other experiments the subjects are deliberately misinformed about the meaning of the signal which is actually feeding back biological information. Learned control occurs, but less efficiently, less rapidly and less satisfactorily than when cognitive information about the process is supplied.

Recent heart rate biofeedback experiments further reveal the ability of non-aware mental function to process information efficiently and effectively and with definitive focus [12]. For example, in several experiments subjects were confronted with red and green lights which were associated with the sounding of high and low tones, and were told that when the different colors appeared to try by "mental means" to produce high or low tones. They were not told that the tones were their actual heart rates. The subjects learned quite rapidly to shift their heart rates between fast and slow to make high or low tone appropriate to the light signals. In this case, in order to perform correctly, the subjects had to have made some association between heart rate and pitch of the tones, and then to discriminate quickly and precisely between two physiologic states.

Presently several investigators have either maximized the amount of information given to their subjects about what physiologic task they wanted them to do, or others simply have given verbal instructions to change a certain physiologic activity [10, 11]. Many researchers have now reported that simply asking subjects to increase or decrease heart rate resulted in quite large changes—more than in many biofeedback studies. Of course, it should be remembered that heart rate is one physiologic activity with a fairly obvious ability to be appreciated as a subjective feeling. Nonetheless, the question has simply not been asked before: please change your heart rate. The remarkable results have several implications: first, that given a chance, human beings can develop a body of subjectively appreciated information specifically related to a particular physiologic activity; and second, they can then employ the information to direct that activity in a specific manner and accomplish an effect on a nonaware level of mental function.

Many other examples of internally generated alterations of physiologic processes via mental activity are accumulating. Although these rely chiefly on normally operating physiologic feedback systems, current emphasis is on the cognitive (subjectively or objectively appreciated) direction of biologic activity. The central mechanisms are illustrated in these examples: when filaments of the nerve to the trapezius muscle of the shoulder were sutured to remnants of the facial nerve distal to where it had been severed, feedback procedures resulted in recovery of completely normal facial muscle activity [13]. The implication is that voluntary control can be dissociated and redirected with remarkable specificity by intention only. In another example, learned control over EEG alpha activity has revealed dissociation between the usual accompaniments of different brain wave conditions, i.e., problem solving and memory search could occur during a steady alpha state of relaxed wakefulness previously believed to preclude the simultaneous processes of intellection and relaxation [14].

Consciousness and the Biofeedback Process

The last example is a striking one of the existence of an inexpressible intelligence. Basmajian and others have demonstrated that the visual or auditory display of motor unit activity to the generator of such activity, along with instructions to alter the symbol of that activity, results in rapid accomplishment of the instructions to isolate and to control voluntarily one or several such motor units [15-17]. The process occurs in the absence of conscious awareness and, indeed, may be inhibited by conscious influences. Finally, the process becomes stable and can be reproduced in the absence of the external monitors.

This example of the biofeedback process can be rephrased in terms of the conditions and events which comprise the process. First, sets of concepts are presented to the conscious mind; abstract symbols of complex, spatiotemporal biologic activity; instructions; and surrounding attitudes. Second, the conceptual information appears to be utilized to produce an effective and ordered alteration of biological function compatible with projections of the concepts (i.e., one might deduce that the conceptual information contained in the symbols, instructions, and attitudes and that information derived from subjectively identified and perceived mind-body relationships is integrated, evaluated and productively directed to discriminate more and more finely the direction of the intent to alter body function). Third, implementation of the intent is not conceptualized in terms of conscious awareness of mental activity. Fourth, signs of the mental activity are communicated via alterations of physiologic activity.

One very basic and obvious question that the biofeedback process raises concerns the mechanism by which individuals accomplish sophisticated and skilled actions not previously known or experienced, i.e., how individuals use symbolic and abstract information about interior processes not only to mobilize, direct and control a single neuronal pathway, normally functioning cooperatively with many other similar neuronal routes, but also to suppress the others simultaneously and selectively. Basmajian has called it will power, as have others when referring to voluntary control over atrial fibrillation.

The type of awareness which develops in the biofeedback process is one generally described by, "I know that I am doing this, but I do not know how I am doing it." This appears to represent an internally derived, non-verbalizable awareness of biologic states having the distinctive properties that the *biologic awareness* is neither communicable by ordinary means nor predominantly influenced by consensual consciousness. Thus the two subsets of consciousness may be distinguishable: subjectively appreciated and objectively appreciated.

As noted earlier, one concept of brain function which may apply to this situation suggests that sequential, *linear* neuronal transmission of information may account for conscious thought since conscious thought processes are essentially linear, and that the vast paralleling networks of *non-linear* connections provide a rich network of information transfer possibilities since these are essentially incapable of linear output to the normal outputs of conscious thought, and thus may subserve mental activity in a way which is subjectively appreciated only.

The most important result of the process is that for the first time we have reached a point where we are able to manipulate non-consciously perceived mental activity.

Summary

Events in the biofeedback process can be summarized as: (1) Abstract, symbolic information is directly and intentionally used by a form of consciousness to direct alterations in mind-body function. (2) The process takes place in the absence of conscious awareness of the biologic functioning. (3) Specific relationships between subjectively appreciated mental and body functions are manipulated. (4) An integration of conceptual information and non-aware recognition of internal events results in alteration of physiologic processes on all levels of physical activity. (5) The expression of the phenomenon constitutes a formerly unrecognized mode of communication.

Some deductions from these characteristic events may be: (1) The process defines subsets of the mind-body relationship. (2) A "specific" mind-body relationship is identified and isolated. (3) The process defines a distinctive subset of consciousness: subjectively appreciated mental activity which is not incompatible with objectively appreciated mental activity. (4) The integration process is efficient to the concept and directs its own result via a complex organization of spatio-temporally distributed information (i.e., there is correspondence between the concept and the integration of it with non-aware recognition). (5) The concept of auto-control of internal states allows implementation of that control. (6) The observer *is* the observed.

Speculations: The complex interplay of a rapidly accelerating exchange of information and shifting attitudes also provides the base for both expanding concepts of consciousness and penetrating the boundaries of convention physical-world relationships. The apparent dependence of the biofeedback phenomenon upon the subjective appreciation of mental activity stimulates a wide range of speculations. For example: (1) To what degree do objectively and subjectively derived mental activities differ? (2) What are the effects of one type of consciousness on the other? Do they have mutually excitant and/or inhibitory properties? (3) Do the two types of mental activity differ in their mode of operation? (4) Can the events in the biofeedback process unify objective and subjective characterizations of consciousness? (5) Does the isolation of a subjectively perceived consciousness reflect a new or undiscovered, or evolving process of mind? (6) Does the intentional aspect identify a set of consciousness or an independent derivative of neuronal activity? (7) Does internally perceived awareness reflect the physical order and reality of nature more accurately than consensual consciousness?

References

1. Sperry, R.W. An objective approach to subjective experiences: further explanation of a hypothesis. *Psychol. Rev.* 77:585-590, 1970.
2. Cook, S. & Harry, R.E. The verbal conditioning of the galvanic skin reflex. *J. Exp. Psychol.* 21:202-210, 1937.
3. Dixon, N.F. & Lear, T.E. Electroencephalograph correlates of threshold regulation. *Nature* 198:870-872, 1963.
4. Schwartz, G.E. Cardiac responses to self-induced thoughts. *Psychophysiology* 8:462-467, 1971.
5. Barber, T.X. Physiological effects of "hypnotic suggestions": a critical review of recent research (1960-1964). *Psychol. Bull.* 63:201, 1965.
6. DiCara, L.V. & Miller, N.E. Long term retention of instrumentally learned heart-rate changes in the curarized rat. *Comm. Behav. Biol.* 2:19-23, 1968.
7. DiCara, L.V. & Miller, N.E. Heart-rate learning in the noncurarized state, transfer to the curarized state, and subsequent retraining in the noncurarized state. *Psychol Behav.* 4:621-624, 1969.
8. Fetz, E.E. & Finocchio, D.V. Operant conditioning of specific patterns of neural and muscular activity. *Science* 174:431, 1971.
9. Brown, B.B. Recognition of aspects of consciousness through association with EEG alpha activity represented by a light signal. *Psychophysiology* 6:442-452, 1970.
10. Headrick, M.W., Feather, B.W. & Wells, D.T. Unidirectional and large magnitude heart rate changes with augmented sensory feedback. *Psychophysiology* 8:132-142, 1971.

11. Stephens, J.H., Harris, A.H. & Brady, J.V. Large magnitude heart rate changes in subjects instructed to change their heart rates and given interoceptive feedback. *Psychophysiology* 9:283-285, 1972.

12. Brener, J. & Hothersall, D. Heart rate control under conditions of augmented sensory feedback. *Psychophysiology* 3:23-28, 1966.

13. Booker, H.E., Rubow, R.T. & Coleman, P.J. Simplified feedback in neuromuscular retraining: An automated approach using electromyographic signals. *Arch. Phys. Med.* 50:621-625, 1969.

14. Brown, B.B. Awareness of EEG-subjective activity relationships detected within a closed feedback system. *Psychophysiology* 7:451-464, 1970.

15. Basmajian, J.V. Control and training of individual motor units. *Science* 141:440-441, 1963.

16. Basmajian, J.V. Electromyography comes of age. The conscious control of individual motor units in man may be used to improve his physical performance. *Science* 176:603-609, 1972.

17. Petajan, J.H. & Phillip, B.A. Frequency control of motor unit action potentials. *Electroenceph. Clin. Neurophysiol.* 27:66-72, 1969.

Quintessential Consciousness

Among the many ways fully functioning compartments of consciousness can separate themselves from the whole and come to dominate the sentient being, there are two that appear to display the essential, magical nature of mind. In their qualities they are as different from each other as sight and sound, yet both may be expressions of the way mind uses mind to know itself. One is the mysterious conversion of a workaday consciousness into an awareness of insights and understandings that transcends all ordinary knowledge, a state we describe as mystical experience. The other is the inescapable, psyche-sustaining state created by the scriptwriting inner self we call imagination or imagery. Both states reveal the extraordinary ability of mind to muster its inner intelligence and reorganize relationships between self and not-self, being and not-being, old and new, experience and concept, and use the information of the world, its logic and order, to create the psychic roots of human life. A completely interior faculty of mindbrain makes sweeping surveys of things and events not simply not present but never existing, and weaves them into visions, enlightenment, fantasies, allegories or journeys of self-discovery. Little is known about the operations of mind and consciousness that create the mind-state of images or the mind-state of mystical experience. The following may be a beginning.

Mystical States

Mystical states, such as samadhi or satori, are usually regarded by searchers for the meaning of life as the penultimate experience.

As it is usually described, the state of mind during mystical experience is one of awareness of the unity of all elements, natural and contrived, a "knowing" or understanding of the essence of life flooding the spaces that once were mind and feeling and thought. There are, we are told by some who try to explain, no physical sensations, no feelings, no interpretations from ordinary human experience. The observer and what is observed seem to be the same.

It is curious that no one has tried to puzzle out what happens in the mind itself that leads to mystical states. Mystics and gurus give us clues about what to do to achieve such states and can tell us what we may perceive is happening, but neither scientific nor philosophic experts are much interested in analyzing how mental processes interact to arrive at the mystical perspective. Perhaps the disinterest comes from an unconscious superstition that looking at the operations of mind in mystical experience might somehow contaminate our appreciations of supernatural experiences. But mystical states need not be studied in terms of mechanical processes of brain; we can instead, examine some operational features of mind characteristic of mystical experience that neither philosophers nor psychophysiologists have described. As a matter of fact, learning more about the nature of mystical experience, how it occurs and how it achieves its insights, might be one of the most productive exercises we can undertake.

Let me make it clear that my analysis has nothing to do with either the content or the objectives of mystical experience. It is concerned only with the nonmystical features: the operations of mind and thought and perceptions that can be inferred to underlie, or be associated with, the generation of insights; how the experiences are appreciated in consciousness; and how they can be recalled to be communicated.

There are, surprisingly, several previously unnoted but quite important and unusual mental activities leading to or accompanying mystical states. They follow from an analysis of commonly observed qualities of mystical states: their dissociation from ordinary states of consciousness, their insights that synthesize knowledge in a nonordinary way, their ineffability, and the curiously different nature of the way the experience is perceived, put into memory, and recalled.

Mystical states are so called because they are most often associated with religious pursuits, yet their occurrence is much more frequent in the more philosophic, nonreligious searches for an understanding of the nature of life, and perhaps should be called "quintessential consciousness" states. I feel, in fact, that mystical experience may be much more common than is generally believed, and that many people have such experiences but do not fully recognize them or appreciate or communicate them because their reservoirs of concepts or words are too limited to bring them into full flower.

The knowledge that the mystics and saints report from mystical experience is knowledge that the elements and events of the universe are all manifestations of a universal order and pattern. The idea that information about the relationships of material elements can be reordered (information being knowledge understood through the activity of the brain) becomes difficult only when no orderly process causing the reorganization can be detected. Virtually every human being since the beginning of time has learned about the world through teaching or by verifying observations of direct experience. Yet some of our most profound insights into the nature of the universe have come through altered states of consciousness, either of a mystical nature or closely related states.

What we can deduce is that during mystical experience the mind makes (or accepts) an extraordinary synthesis about the essence of life and about relationships among things and happenings within the natural universe—a synthesis that transcends expression except as it can be expressed by analogy and by behavior in the larger dimensions of time and space, yet a synthesis that contains recognized harmony and order.

Despite its mystical, supernatural nature, we must also admit that the phenomenon of reordering relationships among the essences of things or events in the universe that lies at the heart of mystical experience depends upon physical, orderly processes in the brain. When an individual comes into an awareness of the flow and pattern and oneness of all in the universe, that awareness would seem most logically to be related to a process of reorganizing information already within the memory banks of brain. *That* part of the process can validly be considered to be a natural physical operation. What may be supernatural is either the impetus to begin the process, or the unique ordering of information contained in the physical substance of the brain that causes it to flow into unifying coherence and the special way the information is then put into memory so that only the essence of the experience is available for recall.

One persistent enigma of mystical states is the ineffability of the experience. This, of course, represents a tantalizing contradiction. If, as it is universally agreed, the mystical experience defies accurate description, how is it that the memory of the experience is so completely appreciated that the memory impression seems to be permanently embedded in the consciousness-unconscious structure so that those experiencing the states do, nonetheless, try to and do communicate something about them? It would seem that the experience is not only put into memory (impressed on neural tissue), but can also be recaptured from memory in a way that, through analogy and relationships to sophisticated, evolved philosophic concepts, allows the conscious mind to approximate the experience abstractly.

Since we human beings are so constructed that the transmission of ideas and feelings occurs only with intact neural substance, we are almost compelled to deduce that the cohesive, organized information representing the experience becomes impressed on neural tissue, the only source and mechanism we possess that allows us to recapture experiences and communicate them.

The absoluteness of this law makes it difficult, if not impossible, to explain or accept mystical states as anything other than a reorganization of knowledge, learned and experiential, accomplished by the natural faculties of human minds. That it is a special state is clear, but it is not clear whether mystical states are accidental or are contrived by desire, teaching, or by other unknown activities of mind. Regardless, it is impossible to separate out the elements of mind and consciousness that initiate the process, knowing as little as we do about the realm of the unconscious and its push-pull relationship with conscious awareness. All desire to know the unknowable can reside in unconscious awareness equally as well as in conscious awareness.

Another observation about the altered state of mind we call mystical experience is that there is an apparently paradoxical impression of sensations. While it is agreed that during mystical states there are no ordinary sensations, the fact that the state is appreciated and can be recalled as an experience means that some sensory apparatus of the brain can sense (detect, appreciate) thought, and that some organizing mechanism is also available to detect the "ineffable" and understand it (organize it) even though the meaning and type of sensation does not translate into ordinary forms of communication. Nor are these the kinds of sensations scientists can measure and classify.

This brings us to the basic difficulty in our efforts to understand unusual mind states. We have no suitable words to describe our appreciations of "pure" thought, yet appreciate them we do. I believe this results not so much from the limitations of language, as from the restrictions of scientific notions of mind study, which are not appropriate in examinations of the higher-order processes of the mind. The term sensation is usually reserved by scientists for perceptions associated with stimulation of a sense organ or with a specific body condition, while "perception" is most often used to express awareness of the meaning of things or events.

But mystical states are not simply the source of a special awareness. The impression for the human being is also one of feeling—much as are sensations that are recognitions of other events impressed upon the body. The difficulty in the language is that "sensation" is used rigorously for responses to physical stimuli. But the fact that mystical experience impresses itself on the physical substance of the body (the brain) should be enough to qualify the response as a sensation, albeit one originating from an apparently intangible stimulus. For it does appear that we do have sensations about abstract thoughts and experiences.[1]

---

[1]It can be argued, of course, that the sensations about mystical experience arise as a result of emotional appreciations of the difference between depersonalized and physically identified states, but I doubt those who experience mystical states would agree.

It is not enough to discuss thoughts in terms of their *meanings* only; from reports of mystical experience and of other states of dissociation of consciousness come clear indications of a true *sensation* of thoughts and concepts, as if we possessed an ability for "mental auto-appreciation." Certainly this could qualify as a legitimate sensory process of man, for the brain's neural tissue is, in fact, the seat of all perceptual activity, where sensations are appreciated and felt. The existence of thought-sensations would explain the deep imprint in memory that such experiences have.

The same could apply to the mechanisms of self-awareness. In other sections of this book, I have discussed some of the "evolved" senses, such as a sense of biological awareness and a sense of order. Philosophers have long recognized the aesthetic sense, but there would seem to be others, such as the sense of self, of identity, the senses that recognize harmony and continuity. Hindu philosophy recognizes many levels of consciousness, some of which seem to be way stations to samadhi, and it also recognizes nine *nava rasas,* the basic aesthetic "emotions." Indian philosophy recognizes sensations of the mind's activity; Western science does not. Yet the mind-brain processes that evolve such sensations as compassion, a sense of justice, etc., from experiential information would seem to be not so different from those that could produce our appreciations of beauty or harmony or order. It seems to me that if we were to study these more sophisticated appreciations with the same fervor as we study the more primitive emotions of hate, anger, and fear, we could come much closer to fulfilling the human potential.

There are many experiences in daily life that approximate mystical experiences. We can, for example, intellectually, consciously come to an understanding of the Taoist concept that the flow of life *is* and that no human intervention can ever capture that is-ness, and later have moments of sensations of that is-ness. The same unconscious recognition is evident in the creative process—art, literature, music, landscaping, molding, inventing—when the artist-creator becomes lost, absorbed in the creative process and the flow and harmony and order of the creation. These states of mind bear a remarkable resemblance to mystical states.

Assuming that the insights of mystical experience do not appear fully developed (as in revelation), the remarkable synthesis and *experience* of complex, abstract, quintessential ideas reveals the capacity of mind to reorganize information to evolve higher-order concepts, concepts that are ordinarily beyond conceptualization. If the capacity for superior, creative, enlightening conceptualization exists, as obviously is indicated, then one of the more exciting questions for human potential is, Can we learn to use this capacity at will, rather than waiting a lifetime for one or another so-disposed individual to experience insightful altered states? We do know that more and more people are experiencing spiritual enlightenment, partly because we now know this is possible for ordinary human beings through mental discipline, and partly because there has been a growing systematization of appropriate mental exercises.

The third—or perhaps first in order of importance—observation is that mystical states are also dissociated, or altered, states of consciousness. The nature of the dissociation is quite different from that in other altered states, save perhaps the nonpathological state of depersonalization and special states induced by mescaline. The mystical state appears to be characterized by: (1) a dissociation of thought from both the emotions and sensations; (2) a total focus of attention and all mental operations on quite special kinds of thoughts; (3) insights and enlightenments that do not usually occur in most states of mind and consciousness activity; and (4) the subsequent usefulness of the insights, certainly to the individual, and often to much of society.

The phenomenon of nonpathological depersonalization (never studied to my knowledge) seems to share the most prominent characteristic of mystical states—that of divorce of thought from body sensations and from an awareness of sensory information from the environment. The feelings of mind being detached from the body and from the body's senses, and the simultaneous absence of all sensory input (or blockage of it from recognition) leave for recall the indelible impression of the *lack* of ordinary sensation. (These nonemotional depersonalization states are not to be confused with neuotic depersonalization, in which emotional anxiety about the mind-body separation is usually terrifying.)

For some individuals certain mescaline experiences can scarcely be distinguished from mystical states, a fact strongly suggesting that information about mystical states is information about some state approaching the desired Void, not the Void itself. Although there are some who deny the similarity between spiritual and mescaline mind states, there is always the question as to whether the critics have experienced both kinds of states, or even either. Or perhaps the denials reflect a spiritual prejudice that excludes the possibility of a drug-induced mystical vision. Aldous Huxley and John Blofeld are two who have described the similarities, and it was as a consequence of discussions with Huxley that my one and only mescaline experience came about. It was as close to the mystical state described by Blofeld in his books *Wheel of Life*[2] and *The Tantric Mysticism of Tibet*[3] as if it had been prepared according to his script, even though I read his books years afterwards. In a discussion I later had with Blofeld in Bangkok, he indicated few, possibly no, differences between his mescaline experience and the satori he achieved after years of training in the tantric Buddhist (Vajrayana) tradition.

Although the events leading into and out of my mescaline experience were typically drug-related (nausea, changes in perceptions), the bulk of the experience was, by clock time, a prolonged state of complete detachment from all sensations, and a state of total depersonalization. There were no sensations of any ordinary kind, only the "knowing" and the "sensation" of being a part of the essential nature of the universe. As the drug waxed and waned in its effect, there also came an awareness of the chaos and disorder of the familiar, "real" world, conceptually, in understanding and appreciation only, with no words or emotions or logical thinking, and between the detached state and this awareness of the real world there developed a conflict. It was short-lived at first, but, as I remember, as the awareness of the man-made and disharmonious elements of the world grew and the drug effect diminished, I was

[2]Berkeley, Calif.: Shambala Publications, 1972.
[3]New York: E.P. Dutton, 1970.

seized by the realization that I was not sure of wanting to return to the real world at all. When it became inevitable that I would, I became increasingly immersed in the swells of the mystical state. The enlightenment of the experience was so profound, so pervasive of being and all life, that, like Blofeld, I never felt even a twinge of desire to repeat the drug experience. There were more insights in those hours than I could ever hope to fully appreciate in the whole of my life.

I suspect that the unity and harmony that is perceived during such experiences touches and is absorbed into being in a way that is quite different from the way ordinary sensory stimuli are appreciated, although I'm sure most neurophysiologists would disagree with me. Certainly the curious access hypnotic suggestion or religious conversion or peak experiences have to impact on neural tissue for appreciation of the material communicated and to be put into and recovered from memory suggests a Gestalt, patterned impress of information, perhaps a set of triggering, conceptual stimuli that touch the "organizing button" of the mind-brain's highest-order abstracting and consciousness processes.

There has never been a satisfactory explanation for the sudden profound insights from mystical or related states, or from poetry, inspiration and revelation, which appear full blown and developed in consciousness with no connection to conscious thought or even to attention. While we can postulate about concept formation and the mind's ability to use learned abstractions and logic, we cannot yet understand revelatory concepts, especially those that defy known processes, such as Einstein's relativity theory.

The magic of posthypnotic suggestion, or the sudden intrusion of an irrelevant thought into daydreaming (Oh my God, I left the roast in the oven!), illustrates both the potency and complexity of the unconscious intellect, but more, it illustrates the existence of quite different "sets" of intellectual activity concealed from conscious awareness. If the unconscious operations can and do arrange the priorities of thoughts and respond intelligently to an irrelevant command, then surely these unconscious mechanisms, under the right conditions, can reorganize their stored information in many ways, some of which lead to appreciation of fundamental truths about the universe—the kinds of insights and understanding we believe derive from the "mystical" state.

I believe that these processes are aided and abetted by the innate intelligence of man, which has been evolving for a long time, just as his physical structure has evolved. But the intelligence of the individual human being has been repressed by the process of species adaptation for the survival of man as a group, the need for human beings to struggle at a social level for survival. Perhaps the new awarenesses about the capacities of mind augur a new stage of evolution, a stage in which individual innate abilities are emerging to evolve a harmonious state of understanding among all human beings.

Insights into the nature of the universe—those insights and our appreciations we call ineffable, beyond description—can, interestingly enough, leave quite different imprints on an individual's psyche and this too may be a part of the evolutionary process of the psyche. For the most part, we hear only of the heavenly or divine or universal appreciations that dispose man toward saintly paths. But there can be consequences dangerous to the individual as well. Gopi Krishna, for example, in his book on the dundalini[4] describes his sudden realization of samadhi and the fullness of the kundalini energy within the highest chakra. Even after seventeen years of preparation through disciplined meditation, the revelations he experienced at that moment were so pervasive of being and mind and spirit that he suffered several years of schizophrenia-like behavior and sensations before his mind-body-spirit became aligned with his enlightenment.

I have questioned many yoga masters about the incidence and degree of emotional problems among student practitioners of various kinds of yogic meditation, and have been regularly informed that such untoward reactions are frequent. The same is known to occur in Christian and Buddhist religious communities.

It is tempting for religionists to interpret such emotional disasters along the way to understanding the true nature of the spirit as

[4]*Kundalini: The Evolutionary Energy in Man* (Berkeley, Calif.: Shambala Publications, 1970).

resulting from a lack of proper preparation or lack of truly spiritual motivations. Psychologists also speculate on motivations, but they tend to emphasize more the conflict between material desires and ways of life and the spiritual ideal. And it is true that the intense anxiety that can often occur after moments of mystical experience for some people does suggest a deep conflict between desire for a nonmaterial and unknown spiritual reality and fear of the loss of the known material reality.

I favor the latter hypothesis because of a dramatic incident that occurred in my research laboratory. A prominent visiting internist, also involved in psychiatry, asked me if he could experience alpha brain wave biofeedback. (This was in the early days of biofeedback, when I had the most sophisticated laboratory conducting alpha brain wave research.)

As the session was proceeding, I suddenly noticed the appearance of giant alpha brain waves in the EEG recording I was, by habit, monitoring. I quickly checked the equipment for any faulty operation, and after some ten to fifteen seconds I realized with considerable fear that the giant waves were indeed from the physician's own brain. He had not given me any signal through either of two intercommunicating systems, and I dashed madly down the hall into the isolation room where he was. He was in a frozen attitude, and as I shook him he gasped violently, then gave an enormous sigh as his posture began to relax.

Later he explained that while concentrating his attention on the biofeedback signals of his own alpha activity, he had suddenly lost all sensation of his physical being. His mind or consciousness seemed filled with a "nothing." He had no body sensation with which he could identify his physical self. The state terrified him. He became powerless to move, and could not even press his fingers on the switch beneath them or speak into the microphone by his head to signal us in the recording rooms. He thanked me profusely for saving him.

Still later I learned that he had been a serious student of Buddhist meditation but had given it up after six years of practice because he could never achieve any sign of a mystical state.

I can only surmise that his meditation practice habits returned during the alpha biofeedback experience, and that his single-focus attention to a signal of mind state let his consciousness slip past the barrier that had for so long resisted his spiritual search. Perhaps, also, the greater weight of his unconscious mind during his meditation practice was occupied by the meanings of his material universe and material security, the attachments to material things he needed to maintain a sense of well-being. Whatever unconscious struggle occurred, the victor was fear, fear perhaps of loss of identity, fear of the unknown, fear of losing what his being believed to be life itself. This experience, incidentally, was not unique. Two of my colleagues in biofeedback have reported similar ones, and they are, in a way, similar also to certain LSD experiences where the fear of losing touch with the customary reality sometimes touches off irreversibly distorted perceptions.

There seems to be a common theme in mystical states and depersonalization in that both have the potential to be either unsurpassedly enlightening or to cause mental turmoil. The difference in consequences would seem to be caused by the ability of the unconscious-conscious interactions to accept loss of identity and socially accepted values; this in turn suggests considerable differences in the ways in which conscious perceptions structure unconscious mechanisms and affect their operation. The same effect may be the reason for the differences between hypnotizable and nonhypnotizable people. What this does seem to tell us is that the unconscious mechanisms for reordering information about the universe do exist within the human psyche, and that spiritual or meditative exercises are a way of relieving the weight of a social, consensual consciousness dependent upon agreeing about what is safe or not safe for survival of the human species. The increasing incidence of mystical states may, after all, be evidence of the evolution of a new "creative flash," a new system of life in which understanding replaces competition and possessiveness as the reward and purpose of life.

Imagery, Imagination, and Mental Images

Imagination is by far the most neglected and underdeveloped of the normal abilities of the human mind. The ability of mind to create and re-create mental pictures of things and events not present (which we call imagination and the professionals call imagery), is little understood as a mind resource. Psychotherapists use imagery to dig for psychologic problems and to conjure up better ways of coping with and understanding life, but most people rarely, and scientists virtually never, consider the creative potential of imagination for improving the condition of man. Certainly they rarely try to understand the process of imagining and how to cultivate it to make it more productive or more efficient. More often than not, imagination is seen as the tool of fancy or illusion and only regretfully admitted to be of occasional use. Yet imagination is the forgotten and rusting key to many treasures of the mind. Imagination is the marvelous uniquely human ability of mind to create and re-create life's experiences and life's thoughts and hopes and dreams in infinite variations both pragmatic and chimeric. Imagination can re-create the past with the highest fidelity or transmute it to fit the whims of emotion. It can project its fabrications into any future it chooses. Images are used to solve problems or to gain relief from mind pressures by fantasy, or just to amuse one's self.

Imagery may not generally be considered to be an altered state of consciousness, but perhaps it should be. There are times when imagery clearly represents an altered state, as in dreams, drug states, psychoses, or hypnosis. But there is also the imagery of daydreaming and worry and active imagination, when images intrude upon conscious awareness. The line between imagery directed by conscious intention and imagery arising uncalled for from unconscious activity is uncertain at best. When we engage in imagery and try to construct images intentionally, more often than not the images from the unconscious crowd out the ones we intended. For the most part imagery is the handiwork of the unconscious.

Far more important than its talents for work or play is the power of imagination to determine human behavior. It is called upon to interpret sensations, to analyze experience, and the images of desire hover over thoughts and behavior irresistibly, beckoning toward fulfillment. Images, moreover, don't merely guide behavior, they exert a very real action on the physiology of the body. Any kind of mental image—visual, auditory, tactile, muscular, emotional or intellectual—all determine the physiologic activity of both body and brain.

Imagination is recalling from memory bits of information obtained from all kinds of experience, then shaping them into some kind of meaningful train of thought or reverie. There are as many ways to imagine things as there are ways to perceive things. So little is known about imagination and how it is accomplished in the brain and where it comes from the general public is, by and large, totally unaware that there are great varieties of imaginative processes.

Imagination—the making of mental images—is nearly always assumed to be a process of conjuring up *visual* images. "Picture that in your mind's eye," or "Can't you just visualize him doing that?" are phrases we learn in childhood. Our early learning is saturated with the teacher's urging us to "Close your eyes. Now, do you have a good picture of that?" A large part of intelligence testing is based on the assumption that everyone can visualize, that they can imagine by using visual images. Yet the real fact is that perhaps only 25 percent of human beings are capable of making reasonably good visual images.

For many people mental images are not visual, but are dominated by memories of sounds, or of touch, body feelings, muscle activity, emotion, or even abstract concepts. Relatively few people have "pure" images, confined to one sense or one emotion. People who have intense, real-as-life, vivid visual images are relatively rare, perhaps less than 10 percent of the population, and just as few possess the ability to make intense, vivid auditory images. Most of us create and re-create images that reflect the way we see, hear, feel and think about experience, with sensations of "seeing" or "hearing" mixed in with sensations or feeling and emotion.

Two remarkable effects of imagery, scientifically validated but woefully underexploited for their powerful effects on human minds and bodies are (1) that the more specific the image, the more specific the effect, i.e., the image excites exactly those physical mechanisms of the body to produce reaction to the image; and (2) the effect of the mental image is to cause *an expenditure of physical energy.*

The imagination makes the body work. Imagine lifting a heavy weight; you can feel the muscles tense. The body is working, it is expending real physical energy. Mental images direct and activate the nerves to make the body work, and work in exactly the way the imagination dictates.

The athlete who concentrates, projecting performance in mental images, uses imagination for something even more remarkable and subtle. He is not just projecting and imagining, he is *preparing* the nerves, the muscles, the heart, and the mind to unify their physical action toward a single-minded, determined objective.

The mind focuses and the nerves respond. Some mechanism somewhere in the profound complexity of dynamic, moving thought pushes aside all interfering and distracting mind and body activities, and this too reflects the power of mind to select its own physical implements for action. The nerves are fed by the electrical impulses from the brain, yet the brain is also the handmaiden of the mind.

The best-known trick of imagination is the unpleasantness of neurosis. The mind and emotions are tricked by imagination into believing the self has insoluble problems. Disturbing images can become so global as to occupy or freeze the logic of the mind. The critical role imagination plays in neurosis and other stress-related disorders is described elsewhere. Mental images can make the body miserable, if the images are miserable. A fleeting mini-neurosis might be the numbing fear of failure in one's first public talk, or the breathless agony of waiting to be asked to the prom. Uncertainty begets anxiety and anxiety begets a rapid pulse, spastic breathing, dry mouth, sluggish gut, and muscles so tense they become tender. Fullblown neuroses are runaway imagination, an imagination so detached from reality that consciousness can no longer make the connection between the worry and the images that the worry has excited.

Images can be exuberant and stimulating, healthful and therapeutic. Just today I read a report on using sexual fantasy exercises by senior citizen groups who had been misled into believing they had seen the end of their sexual lives. If your sexual partner of thirty years is no longer the ravishing beauty or macho strong man of yore, then use the imagination. Re-create the excitement, the physical delights in the mind. A well-oiled imagination is what made the excitement happen in the first place. If you don't think so, try it without images and the feelings those images excite.

Sexual fantasies are the old reliable of psychotherapists and psychiatrists. Nearly everyone has them. But the role of the imagination in sex is far broader than psychology has realized. First experiences are often built up from images built up from hearsay or suspicion; subsequent experiences are generated from memories, fantasies, need for testing, and other emotional-mental triggers. Whatever qualities the experiences give, they are incorporated into new fantasies. And while we know little about all of the mind activities that are not communicated, and lie unexpressed in the subconscious, we do know that the emotions, thoughts, feelings, and actual physical sexual activity become tied together in great complexes. What is not recognized in plain language is that a great share of the *sex drive is in the imagination.* It is a clear example of a feedback system. The drive for sex comes from the images of excitement and pleasure projected by the mind, and the images are fed and strengthened by the sensations produced by the sexual activity. It is the mind that gets it all going.

Images, unformed or repressed or magnified by conscious awareness, are the driving energy of all normal appetites and behavior, but they are, as well, the culprits when human appetites and behavior become disturbed. (The central importance of images in all varieties of reactions to the stresses of life is covered in chapter 6.) It is images that churn the emotions, images that make the body feel and express turmoil, images that set attitudes and behavior. Images are the germ substance of supermind.

The bottom line is that mind controls its creator brain and the product of the brain's activities we call mind, directing them to make decisions, to create images, to conceive desires. These intangibles of mind initiate the flow of nerve impulses and direct their passage throughout the nervous system, including the complex neural networks of the brain itself, with extraordinary precision.

This is supermind at work, a superior mind unrecognized and unrealized.

On the Nature of the Human Mind

The producers of this unusual event requested the speakers to talk about how they view the nature of man. For a moment I exulted in having an opportunity to indulge any arrogance life might have left me—for it does seem arrogant to declare you have found *any* truth about your fellow man—but my reflections finally persuaded me that we do live in a conventional world, and so I should behave in a conventionally scholarly way. Chafing considerably under this restraint, I instructed my mind to do its professorial, scientific best, and produce a substantial, erudite, and enlightened essay on the nature of man. What my mind produced surprised me as much as it may surprise you.

I am going to describe my views on the nature of man by listing the articles for what might be called *A Proclamation for the Emancipation of Mind*. I have evolved a series of fundamental principles about the mind of man which, to tickle my ego, I call Brown's Laws, but which perhaps might better be called Laws of Supermind. I don't mean to equate Brown with supermind, but then again, why not. No one else will.

I use the word laws in one of its basic meanings, meaning that laws are statements about natural phenomena which, so far as is known, are invariable.

The laws describe what I have deduced from considerable scientific evidence to be some of the fundamental features of the human mind, and from the evidence and laws, I have made two major conclusions: one, that the intellectual apparatus of man is a totally new creation in the evolution of life forms, and two, that mind is an energy of brain capable of functioning independently of brain although born of it and sustained by the physical activity of the brain.

I believe that, as modern civilizations evolve, so also simultaneously evolves supermind. Here and there in the recorded history of man we see evidence for these kinds of mind that appear to maximize the mind's abilities for thought, for insights, for intuition, analysis, snythesis, and creativity. I believe, moreover, that a similar potential to maximize and expand the functions of mind exists in every human mind as either latent and unrealized or active but frustrated capabilities. Any future of supermind to emerge as the dominant characteristic of the human species may well be the result of man's own fear that the most potent force of the universe may lie within his own mind. Certainly science has paradoxically both renounced the notion of a mind that can function independently of its own physical substrate, and as a consequence, science has failed utterly to investigate the qualities of mind that make the species homo, sapiens.

The laws of the human potential I have drawn up describe properties of mind that much of the expert knowledge of science has been blind to for much too long. If any scientists disagree with me, they do so *not* on the basis of fact, but from a prejudice that comes from experience limited to too specialized areas of study rather than from comprehensive study of the multiple facets of human life.

Law One

Human beings possess an innate awareness of the state of their biological being from the total physical body image down to a single cell.

I call this biological awareness, and classify it as a specific component of the consciousness spectrum, but a consciousness that is subjectively, privately appreciated only and an awareness that is not ordinarily accessible for objective description.

Nearly every human being has proof for this kind of awareness.

Think about your sensations when you try to change the part in your hair. Most people have either a natural part or one they have become used to, and when they try to part the hair in a different place, there is distinct discomfort. It is an awareness that something in the head area doesn't feel quite right, but the exact sensation is almost impossible to describe.

One of the most extraordinary examples of biological awareness was related to me by a friend who is a neurologist and electroencephalographer and who does brain wave biofeedback. A small, seven year old girl, believed to be a mental retardate, was referred to him for diagnosis of her seizures. My friend wired the whole head for recording the EEG, and then, just because his biofeedback equipment was there, the child could watch the complex EEG being written out on a TV monitor in front of her. For the first ten minutes of the recording the brain waves were normal, then, almost buried in the complicated EEG scribbles, there appeared a small, abnormal brain wave. The child put her hand to her mouth and whispered, "Oh, excuse me." She had felt her body make a mistake.

This exquisite sensitivity to the hidden functions of one's body is almost too bewildering for us to appreciate fully. Yet other biofeedback studies have repeatedly demonstrated that people can readily become aware of the activity even of single cells once they learn something about how those cells behave.

Law Two

Human beings possess an innate ability to form complex, abstract concepts from primal sensory data.

The story of Helen Keller, the famous blind, deaf mute who attained extraordinary intellectual heights, is the only real example we need to verify this law. When the child Helen Keller was seven, after the turmoil and distress of an intellectually deprived childhood, she was given a tutor. The tutor began by tapping the child's hand, spelling out the letters of words standing for objects she gave the child to feel and touch. In less than two weeks the child had not just learned the word-object associations, but most remarkably, she had also formed several complicated concepts about the structure and organization of language.

Suppose you touch something squishy in the dark. Immediately you call up from memory the information you need to identify the squishy thing, and mainly from touch you form a concept about what the thing most likely is.

A friend of mine had a cousin who, as a child, was judged to be mentally retarded. The parents refused to believe it, and after some effort, they discovered the child could learn quite well through the tactile and kinesthetic senses. The child ultimately became a chemist and won one of the country's most valued prizes for scientific achievement.

Such observations suggest that there is a generally unused mechanism of the intellect capable of forming valid conclusions about the nature of the universe from raw sensory information. This capacity may explain why we begin to understand more about our world when we take the time to contemplate nature itself.

Law Three

Human beings possess an innate ability to exert control over the direction and flow of nerve impulses in any nerve of the body of their choosing.

The proof of this law is obvious. Take intentional relaxation and its opposite, purposeful physical activity. In the first case, when you intentionally relax, you voluntarily *decrease* the rate of flow of nerve impulses to the muscles and viscera, while in the second case, physical activity, you intentionally *increase* the rate of flow and specific direction of impulses in the nerves of your choosing.

Scientific proof comes from biofeedback, the process of learning control over body functions. In stress disorders, such as emotional or psychosomatic problems, there is a generalized neural hyperactivity causing the muscles and viscera to be uptight. Using biofeedback learning or any relaxation technique, you learn to voluntarily slow the rate of nerve impulses and direct them toward a specific physiologic function. The opposite activity, increasing the rate of flow of nerve impulses, is easily learned as in rehabilitating muscles paralyzed following a stroke. Here the patient learns how to speed up the flow of nerve impulses to the muscles.

The implications of this law are so great they are almost beyond comprehension. The nervous system, and that includes the brain, implements every action, every function, and every thought of human beings. The inborn ability to control all nerve activity means that man has the potential to prevent the malfunction of body activities, the potential to nourish and enhance mental capacities, and the potential to correct disordered body functions, in effect, to improve the human condition. This, in fact, is the meaning of law four.

Law Four

The human mind has the innate ability to supervene in and direct the physical activities of every physiologic function of the body, within the limits of physical nature.

The scientific evidence comes from the success of all the new awareness techniques being used today, all the body awareness techniques, biofeedback, and also many psychologic procedures such as imagery. We now know, contrary to previous biomedical beliefs, that human beings can learn, within physical limits, to regulate virtually any body function, from gastric acid secretion to skin electrical activity to the size of blood vessels. And we have finally verified what yogis have known for 5000 years, their ability to control nearly any body function they choose.

The ability of the mind for absolute control of body functions can occur also without any conscious awareness. This phenomenon has been demonstrated endlessly under hypnosis. When the hypnotist instructs the subject not to bleed when a needle is thrust into the hand, the subject intentionally but unconsciously prevents bleeding.

Now that we have widespread proof for this law (that mind can control physiologic functions), there should be no further excuse for the therapeutic communities not to implement it. Unfortunately we also have politics in science.

Law Five

The mind of human beings can control the physical activities of the brain.

One of the clearest examples of this ability is the learning to control brain wave activity, such as learning to control alpha waves. Alpha activity is a complex activity of the brain neurons, and a physiologic activity for which it is completely impossible to have any prior sensory experience whatsoever. You can't see, hear, feel, touch, or smell brain waves. Yet people easily learn how to control alpha brain wave activity by using instruments in which alpha waves are represented by lights or tones. When one uses light or tone signals to learn how to control alpha waves, it is the mind controlling the activity of the brain.

The ultimate control of brain by mind is, of course, thinking. During thinking, the mind must direct a search of memory for both relevant information and for the appropriate logic to process the information, as well as rejecting inappropriate, nonrelevant information and shunting it away from thought activity. Thinking is voluntary control of the brain.

Law Six

All diseases of society originate in the intellectual processes of man.

Diseases of society are the emotional and physical disorders of man produced by the stress of life. These are the disorders such as neuroses, hypertension, headache, ulcers, asthma, insomnia, drug abuse, and some fifty other disturbances of functions that comprise some 75% of all human illness. Biomedical theory has a weak explanation, believing stress causes arousal of the primitive physical defense mechanisms of man, particularly muscles and viscera. The implication is that human beings react to stress as instinctively as animals to threats to their physical well being and survival.

I contend that reactions to the stresses of life begin with absolutely normal intellectual activity, that when a person feels stressed, it is because he detects, consciously or unconsciously, a problem somewhere in his social environment. And when one detects a problem in social activities and social relationships, one begins to worry, and with good reason. Worry is a normal problem-solving activity. Emotional problems and physical problems of an emotional origin occur only when the intellectual problem solving processes are frustrated for any of many reasons. *Not* being able to solve one's social difficulties is a threat to well being.

We worry when we cannot seem to resolve problems in social relationships or in our social environments, and when problem solving fails or is frustrated, we can develop all of the well known behaviors we call emotional: apprehension, anxiety, feelings of inadequacy, of insecurity, uncertainty, frustration, irritation, hostility, loss of self-esteem, and related emotions.

All of these emotions are rooted in an intellectual concern, concern about social activities, about adequate social performance, intellectual concern about meeting social criteria, and concern about ensuring one's social well-being and social survival. The subjective sensations we call emotions are all expressions of a disturbed intellect, a disturbance of the intellect about the way in which social relationships are perceived and appreciated and interpreted. Stress, in a word, is manufactured by the intellectual systems of man. What he needs to relieve the stress is information to solve the problems.

There is a corollary to this law that stress disorders are a matter of the intellect. The corollary is that the universal disease of society is the distress of being sick from any cause, and what I call "the second illness."

The second illness is the stress of being ill. The stress of being ill comes from the intellectual appreciation of the loss of capacity to perform, to participate in life's activities, the loss of capacity to behave as a normal human being. When we are sick, emotionally or physically, from any cause, we are socially disadvantaged. Being even the slightest out of the mainstream of life is stressful.

It is my hope that when we recognize the universal prevalence of the second illness, we will begin to treat this as the real illness it is, and in doing so we can relieve this distress and speed recovery from the primary illness.

Law Seven

> *Man has evolved new sophisticated senses within the unconscious mind. One of these is the sense of order.*

That is, man possesses a sense that can anticipate (project) the order of events and sequences of all natural events to move from chaos and disorder to a naturally ordered, unified result.

A sense of order can be deduced from the evidence that disorder occurs in the unconscious mind in different states of consciousness, such as the disorder of dream logic, the unconscious conflicts and disorder that are manifest as neuroses, or the disordered perceptions under hallucinogens. If the unconscious mind can become disordered, then it must be capable of maintaining order in its normal functioning.

The most dramatic illustration of the sense of order is when people learn to control single cells in the spinal cord. Called motoneurons, these cells control the activity of small groups of muscle cells, even as few as three. Using an instrument to detect and to display the activity of a single motoneuron, virtually anyone can learn to control the activity of that cell in a few minutes. From watching a light on an instrument to intentionally controlling a single cell is a mind feat of consummate orderliness. Exactly those nerve cells and their connections to accomplish a projected result are selected out of trillions of cell connections, and are activated in precise order.

If we accept that human beings do possess such a sense of order, we can better understand how individuals can come to sense and to understand the unifying order of the universe and may become aware of the universal consciousness.

Law Eight

> *The will of human beings is an independent function of mind, an independently operating energy of mind that decides upon the ordering of biological activity to produce an ordered alteration of the body's functions.*

There is no more scientific evidence for the scientific theory that intention, the will, is merely the outcome of mechanical decision-making processes of the brain than there is for concluding that the will is an independently operating function of the mind. The will is the process of mind that makes decisions to act or not to act based on an evaluation of the ways to reach the goals and the merits of the goals. Two bits of evidence show the will to be an independent function: first, the fact that the will can be exerted on any body system, muscles, viscera or the central nervous system itself, each of which differ remarkably in chemical and cellular composition as well as in structure and cell organization. The second bit of evidence is:

Law Nine

In order for the will to act, another independently operating function of mind, a coordinating director or will executor is required to turn volition into action.

The will executor anticipates the goals and selects the correct channels of neural networks to put into effect the intended action and to produce the change in body activity.

My favorite example of the need of the will for an executor is the time when, in a hurry for a cup of coffee, I found the sugar bowl empty. Grabbing the sack of sugar, I promptly poured it into my coffee. The intention was present, but the executor of the will was out to lunch.

Law Ten

Man has evolved elaborate, as yet unrecognized, intellectual mechanisms to ensure his survival in an evolving nonphysical environment.

The biomedical, psychological, anthropological and related sciences tend to view man as surviving largely because of various innate, instinctual, inherited physical mechanisms organisms use to defend against threats to physical well-being. One of the major mechanisms is held by science to be the fight-or-flight response to danger.

I argue that man has his physical environment rather well under control and the need for physical defense mechanisms is rare.

What threatens modern man's well being and survival are primarily the result of the mental activity of other men (here's where I defend male chauvinism; let them take the blame, not women).

It is utterly inappropriate and incongruous for intelligent man to depend upon body mechanisms useful only to defend against threats to physical well-being when it is the malfunctioning of the society of man that threatens man's existence.

The two major sources of danger for modern man are psychological and social. Either ordinary human beings cause psychological problems for other human beings, or dominating hierarchies of human beings in all manner of organized human activities from the local PTA to the government cause both psychological and social problems for man.

If we look closely at the direction of many human activities today, we can see the rapidly accelerating evolution of mechanisms of the intellect directed toward ensuring social well being. One has only to look to the new techniques in psychology and counseling to see that it is the mind that is being evoked as man's primary survival tool. And we in California have Proposition 13 to remind us of ways to deal with social problems we once believed almost beyond our control.

Law Eleven

The highest order intellectual capacities of man reside in, and may always reside in, what we call the unconscious. That is, unconscious mental processes are elegant, sophisticated, and of superior intellect, but they are also unrecognized by society and are untapped human potential.

The most dramatic example of this comes from emotional pathology: hysterical blindness. I personally witnessed such a case in a college friend. The girl was popular on campus, very pretty, and quite a good student. One day, about two weeks before finals for the year, she suddenly became blind. In hospital, the diagnosis finally came down: hysterical blindness.

It doesn't take much more than common sense to reconstruct what must have happened in the mind of this girl, and what similar kinds of mental operations likely happen in all cases of neurosis or psychosomatic illness. Briefly, the girl came to believe that she might not be able to continue her high achievement level in the upcoming final exams, and her solution was to create, quite unconsciously, an apparently foolproof defense: physical blindness, a disability guaranteed to prevent what she thought might be imminent failure.

The question science has neglected to confront is: What are the fundamental operations of intellectual function that produce such reactions, and how indeed can thought processes, which are obviously involved, cause such selective change in the physical activity of the body?

Another marvelous example of quite elegant intellectual capacities in the absence of conscious awareness occurs in the sleep walker. The sleep walker formulates a very specific intention and recruits all his body activities to carry out the intention, usually not stopping until the act is completed or frustrated.

One of my favorite examples of the unconscious intellect is the prank some psychology students played on their professor. Learning that people could be unconsciously "conditioned," one day the students all conspired to assume postures of great interest and eagerness and attention when their professor lectured from a certain spot at the side of the classroom. When he moved from the spot, the students would slouch, whisper, and otherwise look bored. Within minutes the professor became glued to the spot where the students paid attention. To me this is not a mechanical "conditioning" as the psychologists are wont to explain, but an instance of the remarkable abilities of the unconscious intellect.

Law Twelve

We cannot directly know or experience or have any conscious awareness of the nature of our own mental processes. That is, we cannot be aware of how we are thinking when we are thinking.

Take trying to learn anything. All you know is that when you have certain bits of information and make some mental effort, you learn something. You have no idea how you accomplish the learning, i.e., you have no awareness of *how* you were learning *when* you were learning. Thinking about this puzzle, I developed a principle to explain this paradox modelled after the Heisenberg principle.

In quantum mechanics, the Heisenberg principle states that if you know the momentum of a particle, you can't know its exact location in space, and if you know the energy of a particle, you can't know its exact location in time.

Because I often find science very amusing, I devised the Brownenberg principle which says that if you are busy processing information in your brain, you can't know you are processing information because the information being processed is occupying the same neuronal space that is needed to become aware of what is being processed.

And of course, conversely, if you are aware of information that *has been* processed, you can't be processing new information at that moment of awareness because the mechanisms for awareness occupy the same neuronal space needed to process new information.

In summary, it is on the basis of these laws that I conclude human beings possess capacities of mind that are literally beyond genius.

Until this present decade there have been many prohibitions, both scientific and philosophic, against exploring the reality of the nonphysical mind. But today, at last, there are a multitude of signs that at least part of the extraordinary and untapped human potential is emerging to be recognized and used. We cannot project the future for the coming Age of Mind, for, as I wrote elsewhere, "the new horizons of mind revealed to an expanded awareness will be known only when awareness takes us there."

The Group Mind: Consensual Consciousness and the Group Subconscious

The Terms and the Logic

In the essay *Biological Awareness as a State of Consciousness* I posited two aspects of the subconscious: one concerned with private, exclusively subjectively appreciated information which is communicated to conscious "consensual" awareness only through analogy to external events, and a "biological subconscious" that is concerned with awareness of biologic events and is communicated either by biological expression or through the "integrative subconscious."

Rather than the imprecisely defined consciousness and the even more nebulous concept of the subconscious, individual consciousness may be considered as a dynamically associative organization of at least three levels of integrated mental activity: conscious awareness, the integrative subconscious, and the biological subconscious.

I would now like to propose that human beings *as groups* possess analogous forms of consciousness and conceptual activity.

The group mind is generally interpreted to be the result of cooperation among *objectively* appreciated conscious activities, i.e., consensual consciousness. Since, however, the group mind results from interaction among individuals, the probabilities are that subjectively appreciated consciousness, as both an integrated subconscious *and* a biological subconscious are projected into the mental processes of the group. It is the limitations of concepts of communication that have limited extrapolation of the role of the individual in the group and the interactions between individuals as individuals and individuals as members of groups.

When applied to groups, the role of the biological subconscious can be inferred since evidence exists for quite striking differences in physiologic reactions among different ethnic groups. Because influences of the group biological subconscious are less easily recognized, the following discussion is concerned chiefly with the concept of a "group subjectively appreciated consciousness" which is that portion of perceptual-cognitive integration not directly communicable to the conscious group mind.

If one postulates both a biological subconscious and a consensual consciousness, then the integrative subconscious can be viewed as the function of a set of mental processes that associates subjectively appreciated perceptual data on the one hand and consensual data on the other. Since the Jungian notion of a problem-creating conscious awareness seems experientially consistent, the role of an integrative subconscious in group activities could provide an important element for the understanding of society.

Historically and until the present, it has been largely consideration of social forces that has shaped concepts and changed behavior of both individuals and groups. It should, therefore, be as productive to examine consciousness within the frame of social energy systems as it is to examine it within the frame of physical energy systems, although not necessarily implying the same qualities of energy involved.

Neither animal nor human societies can be characterized completely by documenting behavior of their individuals and their social structure. It is also necessary to document interactions between the group and the individual functioning both as an individual and as a member of a group. Another link in this chain of interactions is the difference in response of the group to the individual acting as an individual and to the individual acting as a member of the group. These complex interactions are not generally acknowledged, but may exert great influences on the activities of both the group and the individual. One group activity that illustrates the complexity of individual-group interaction is that which is directed toward actual physical survival of the group with loss or death of the individual: war.

Does the Group Mind Always Sacrifice the Individual?

By and large, group mind action is often illogical for the survival or security of the individual. Although actions taken by the group mind claim to be justified by representing a conscious, deliberate, higher intellectual consensus, in essence, the result of group mind action tends to reflect more instinctual, unconscious, primitive qualities than it does conscious, deliberate, higher intellectual qualities. Much of group behavior and actions taken by the group mind occurs in circumstances requiring action for protection and survival of the group. Since physical survival is of lesser general consequence today, group mechanisms tend to concentrate more on the survival of group thought and mental activity. Nonetheless, the result of conscious group mind action rarely displays evidence of higher intellectual activity. Consensus is required chiefly for group security and defense (e.g., Congress), and only exceptionally approaches the intellectualized, philosophic ideals conceived by individuals.

If a fundamental drive is to survive, meaning to control or become dominant, then a perspective of the environment must be constructed for the purpose of manipulating the environment, and elements not apparently necessary to survival may be omitted. The ordering process continues partly to sustain control over the environment and partly to sustain the social order which subserves it, resulting in a group consciousness whose objective is group survival (e.g., Congress). The survival of the individual is, however, not essential to the survival of the group and, in effect, a perspective on individual life and consciousness is evolved which is skewed by the group mind. While science and society have acknowledged these as social effects and have emphasized their positive values in the evolution of man, what science has *not* done is to examine their negative effects on both the group and the individual. The inhibitory effect of the group mind on the individual needs only the one example of war.

One interesting way of looking at the group-individual interaction is Robert Ardrey's proposition that there are three primary needs of all higher species which motivate their behavior; i.e., identity, stimulation, and security which are antithetical to anonymity, boredom, and anxiety, respectively. To date these needs have been answered more effectively through group interaction. The definition of these particular needs have not been responded to by many scientists, presumably because it is difficult to mechanize and quantify their potency within existing physically oriented theoretical frames of mind and behavior. Nonetheless, there is an intuitive appeal in the definition and they are well supported by Ardrey. The enormous power of these needs is obvious when viewed by the extraordinary effort expended in ritualizing the answers to the needs, such as in war, religion and politics. *The more successful the ritual, the greater the sacrifice of the individual. Particularly in war.*

Groups may be viewed as coalescing and amplifying the individual needs. It is not difficult to identify identity, stimulation, and security as group needs as well as individual needs. They retain, however, a primary and primitive nature.

If the needs are, as Ardrey believes, immanent to living organisms, the needs are instinctual in quality and depend more upon subjectively appreciated mental activity than upon an objectively appreciated conscious awareness. It seems reasonable to postulate that if social order and action evolves from cooperation among individual consciousnesses, it is likely that both components of individual consciousness (objectively and subjectively appreciated) are mirrored in the group consciousness. If individual consciousness involves the interplay between subjectively perceived and objectively perceived mental activity, then the group mind may be examined on the same basis. It is relatively simple to reconstruct influences of conscious cooperation upon group activities and the definition of the group's goals. It is much more difficult to ascribe to social evolution the effect of an internally derived, exclusively subjectively appreciated consciousness or a biological consciousness, yet both may exert discernible influences on the stability of social order.

Interactive Social Evolution

A major shift is apparent today in the "balance" between individual and group and between subjective and objective sets of consciousness. Many of today's generations are concerned with subjectively appreciated consciousness on both an individual and on a group level. Not only is there an extensive and intense effort to experience altered (currently difficultly or non-communicable) states of consciousness, but there is evolving a variety of new modes for communication—something like a double translation. New symbols of experience have been created to "stand for" bodies of experiential data. Today we speak of "where my head is," not of "where my mind is" as in the past. A "trip" now means a head trip. The reference to internally appreciated consciousness as "head" signals changing concepts of *consciousness as shaped by interior experience*. The current changes may be viewed as emergence of the subjectively appreciated group consciousness and the emergence of new modes of communication for it.

These various observations suggest that consciousness and "higher mental activity" may be the result of interactions among individual subjectively and objectively appreciated aspects and group subjectively and objectively appreciated aspects of consciousness. The objectively appreciated aspects of both individual and group consciousness are accepted entities. The concept of individual subjectively appreciated consciousness is newer but has considerable support. The concept of a group subjectively appreciated consciousness is an extrapolation, which includes in it a group biological subconscious derived from the impact of social interaction of groups on biological systems.

The essential question is whether identification, manipulation, and communication of subjectively appreciated aspects of brain activity represent an evolving consciousness and whether this process may have a unifying consequence between both individual and group subjectively and objectively appreciated aspects. This might occur when the group is a faithful extension of the self. Is it, for example, that Eastern concepts of consciousness tend to represent subjectively appreciated group consciousness while Western concepts tend to represent objectively appreciated group consciousness? If the analogy is pursued, perhaps the "universal" consciousness will be achieved.

Conflicts between the group mind and the individual subconscious, reflecting in part conflicts between subjectively and objectively perceivable aspects of consciousness, can be observed in neurophysiologic processes. There are many examples. One is based upon the fact that when two similar shapes or forms are shown stereoscopically, there is a fusion into a composite form. For example, if two rather similar faces are perceived steroscopically, consciousness appreciates the two as a fusion into a composite face. When one face is white and the other is Negro, the average American sees the resultant as a brown face. If, however, the subject is a South African, the images do not fuse; there is, instead, an alteration between the white and brown faces. The gating influence of the subconscious becomes clearly demonstrable. A similar phenomenon occurs in Kahn's experiments with tachistoscopically presented pairs of pictures controlled by the firing of pairs of individual muscle units. The possible different modes of neuronal transfer of information, linear and network, can extend to an explanation of different central mechanisms for conscious and subconscious mental activity.

An Example from Modern Scientific Society

The operation of the group mind is readily apparent in any group activity today. Take, for example, scientific societies. The organization of science into disciplines, societies, conferences, department and other group activities, satisfies the individual needs for identity, stimulation and security, as well as for facilitating the efficiency and effectiveness of individual effort. As an extension of the individual, the groups also manifest needs for group identity, stimulation, and security. In one view, the scientific organization provides for amplification of consciousness (mental activity). At the same time it also may develop a self-inhibitory effect: expansion of its own consensus which suppresses its individual subjective perceptions. In the current hierarchy of these needs, security is outstanding. The effect of grouping that has not been considered, is the relationship between the group mind and the individual mind. As a society, science provides one of the better vehicles for examination of the 4-way group-individual, subjective-objective interactions.

To retain identity with scientific organizations, or any society organized for more intellectual pursuits, requires objective communication, hence the group mind tends to exclude subjectively perceived information. What the *group* may have subjectively appreciated, representing a separate entity, has so far had little relationship to individually subjectively perceived information. There is, moreover, evident an interaction between the general group mind and the scientific group mind.

The history of the biofeedback phenomenon is an example. While the process may be viewed as the evolution of new concepts by the conventional group process of conscious application of the Scientific Method, the process can also be viewed as the influence of both the objectively and subjectively appreciated aspects of the group mind on the performance of individual minds. The biofeedback phenomenon was recognized in part through the application of conditioned learning techniques by individuals behaving as members of a group, and descriptions of the phenomenon and further considerations of it were thus conceptualized in that framework. At the time, however, sufficient numbers of individual minds behaving as individuals recognized the same phenomenon in the absence of the conditioning theory constraints. In the absence of these constraints, it was necessary for individual identity, security and stimulation to formulate the process in terms of group acceptable communications. The formulation was a priori "disinhibited," (from the group's consensual consciousness) and the result was a realistic expression of the phenomenon as a private process, *in terms of a private process,* (i.e., *I* handle information), utilizing more fundamental concepts of life processes. The point of interest here is that the formulation, unrestrained by group mind processes, although apparently more exact, both intuitively and in its mechanistic parsimony, eroded the structure of the established conceptual consensus and thus temporarily threatened the basic security mechanisms of a group.

The dis-inhibition provided by individual concepts uncovered an error in the mental activity of a large group of individual minds (i.e., failure to observe the significance of information-bearing environmental signals). Moreover, development of the group's consensus had simultaneously affected a basic element of individual consciousness; that is, subjectively appreciated mental activity was suppressed (e.g., individuals did not ask the question, "How do *I* subjectively perceive conditioning?").

The process can readily be dissected for interactions among individual and group subjectively and objectively appreciated mental activities. Among the events which may have occurred were, for example, (1) events in private consciousness directing non-group objectives, (2) private mental processes which were multidimensional and poorly communicable through ordinary channels, (3) need for individual security, (4) "intuition" by individuals and groups recognizing individual, subjectively appreciated observations, (5) breaching of defenses of one group by another, (6) shaping of individually subjectively appreciated mental activity by the restraints imposed by the (scientific) group, (7) group defense posture, (8) dispersion of the individual (effort) to strengthen group need for identity.*

Summary

A fuller consideration of the group mind and its interactions with both its own states of subjectively and objectively perceivable consciousness as well as with the two sets of individual consciousness (mental activity) could allow interesting conjectures, such as:

---

*The resulting rearrangement of group activities was interesting. None of the groups expended significant effort to examine the mechanisms of the phenomenon, perhaps since the contrasting of individual with group behavior threatened the security of both the individual and the group. Instead there the effort was directed toward extracting the most immediately useful survival habits or techniques of each other's concepts.

1. Consensual consciousness may be as independent an entity as individual consciousness may be an entity behaving independently of biologic processes. Each may have characteristics in common.
2. The influence of the group mind may be greater than the influence of the individual mind, as the influence of the objectively appreciated consciousness may be greater than that of the subjectively appreciated consciousness.
3. Changes in group consciousness may occur when it is transcended by commonality of individual consciousness.
4. If individual consciousness directs brain-body processes independently of group mind direction, and vice versa, then these may reflect the two neuronal processes of linear vs. network information transfer.
5. Individually appreciated consciousness may be able to deal with more dimensions of mental activity than can consensually appreciated consciousness.
6. The group mind may be more inhibitory to individual consciousness than it may be excitatory.
7. The group mind may contain a subset of consciousness: group subjectively appreciated mental activity.
8. If individually appreciated consciousness is now being expanded, it may have the potential to utilize new modes of communication and evolve commonalities of internal consciousness and lead to a "universal" consciousness.